D0969145

The Angry Marriage

OVERCOMING THE RAGE,
RECLAIMING THE LOVE

BONNIE MASLIN, PH.D.

MJF BOOKS
NEW YORK

Published by MJF Books
Fine Communications
Two Lincoln Square
60 West 66th Street
New York, NY 10023

The Angry Marriage
Library of Congress Control No. 00-130536
ISBN 1-56731-386-8

Manufactured in the United States of America on acid-free paper

MJF Books and the MJF colophon are trademarks of Fine Creative Media, Inc.

10   9   8   7   6   5   4   3   2   1

Acknowledgments

From conception to completion, *The Angry Marriage* has been a collaborative effort, and I am most grateful for the goodwill and assistance given to me by all those involved in the creation of this book: Meg Schneider and Lynn Sonberg are advisers and friends, who offered great skill and imagination in shaping this work. Guy Kettlehack masterfully assisted both in crafting the proposal and in editing the ongoing manuscript. Judith Riven of Hyperion contributed her editorial expertise and Vicki Di Stasio, also of Hyperion, ably shepherded *The Angry Marriage* all along the way. I am grateful, as well, to many at Hyperion, whose editorial, art, public relations, and sales skills were mobilized on behalf of *The Angry Marriage*.

I found the work of Winnicott to be eminently useful in the enterprise of writing *The Angry Marriage*. Lear's excellent book, *Love and Its Place in Nature*, also had a great impact on me, and I respectfully acknowledge the infuence of these two remarkable men on my own thinking.

On a personal note, I am most grateful to Sarah and David for doing without their mom while she was trying to make a deadline and to my dear husband, Yehuda, who has the remarkable talent to be a most wonderful father and mother. My own mother still does not have the word "No" in her vocabulary and I am, as always, indebted to her for her generosity of spirit. Bev Maitland gets my thanks for keeping my household moving, no matter what. Paula Butscher gets my thanks for always being there, even in dead of winter! And to my dearest friend and, as usual, first reader, Themis Dimon, I offer my gratitude and appreciation.

"If I can stop one Heart from breaking
I shall not live in vain
If I can ease one Life the Aching
Or cool one Pain
Or help one fainting Robin
Unto his Nest again
I shall not live in Vain."

—Emily Dickinson

Contents

THE ANGRY MARRIAGE

One

THE GIFT OF ANGER

No one needs to learn how to get angry. From the very first day of our lives each of us knows, instinctively, just how to do it.[1] Anger is built into our nervous system: It's part of the way we're wired. As infants, it was one of our most essential tools. In fact, the life of every human being depends on anger for survival. Our first angry wails were insistent distress signals beckoning our caretakers: feed me, hold me, warm me, soothe me. Born unfinished, unable to fend for ourselves, we weren't equipped to let our needs be known in any other way.

Our original or "primal" anger successfully communicated "this is what I need from you," and our good enough caregivers lovingly, responsively heeded our call. Ironically, our first loving attachments were safeguarded by these angry protests.

In the beginning, anger is a remarkably effective tool. It not only ensures our very survival, it ensures that human beings become attached to one another. In this way anger is nature's first gift, bringing the possibility of protection and love.

So, why is it that by the time we reach adulthood and marry, things change so radically? How is it that in our marriages anger invariably erodes rather than nurtures bonds? Why is anger more likely to be love's executioner than its guardian? And most important, how can we learn to restore anger to its original purpose—nature's offering meant to help us bond, not drive us apart?

Regrettably, anger as a force corrosive to love is what we know best. And, more often than not, as marital anger drives us apart, it leaves us with an unhappy feeling—we don't always like the person we love. No doubt we have all seen anger operate destructively in the marriages of others, if not our own. You might, for example, have witnessed something like the angry couple—I'll call them Mr. and Mrs. Roberts—I bumped into on a recent weekend shopping trip.

At first they seem an amiable pair. Mrs. Roberts tries on coats while Mr. Roberts nods in approval or disapproval. Agreeing that the navy blue coat looks smart and flatters Mrs. Roberts, the shopping trip seems pleasantly at an end. So Mr. Roberts mills aimlessly through the aisles while Mrs. Roberts stands near the register paying for her new coat. As the clerk walks away from the desk to call in Mrs. Roberts's credit card number, Mr. Roberts ambles up to the counter. Suddenly he spies his wife's open wallet. Rolling his eyes, he mutters in exasperation:

"How many times have I told you not to use that card for personal expenses—it's only for business."

Though taken aback, Mrs. Roberts is not at a loss for words. Without a moment's pause she shoots back:

"Damn it, don't tell me what to do. It's no big deal. When the bill comes, I'll just separate it."

Exasperation quickly turns to anger. With little effort to hide his feelings, Mr. Roberts hurls back his response:

"Sure. It's no big deal because you have no concept of what we spend. When the bills come, you won't do it—I will."

His wife parries with a bitter ring to her voice:

"Of course you will because you *always* take over." Then it gets ugly:

" 'Father knows best.' Father always knows best. But if Father knows best, why did he just lose his best account at work?"

"Witch," he snaps back. "I'm leaving. Find your own way home."

"Loser," his wife counters. "Don't worry. I can find my own way without you."

Anger in this marriage is no champion of love. Hardly. Mr. and Mrs. Roberts feel more like enemies than lovers. Theirs is certainly an *angry marriage*. Ill-will, not affection, fills the void between them. Anger resolves nothing, accomplishes little, and serves only to bruise and wound. Anger has gone wrong—very wrong. But such obviously ineffective and destructive fury is not the only way anger goes awry in a marriage. There are other very different types of angry unions.

Some people in angry marriages have a very different sort of problem. Here anger is mute. Anger cannot work as nature intended because . . . we dare not get angry at all! Unwittingly, people bury their wrath. Ironically, you can be in an angry marriage and not even know it. *Frequently, in an angry marriage, anger is hidden.* But, regrettably, quiet, hidden anger is as destructive to a marriage as its noisy and more obvious counterpart. Unhappily, couples may be driven apart by anger's silence as surely as they may be driven apart by open hostility toward each other.

We all know couples whose anger is quietly destructive to their partnership. The difficulty is that we (and they) don't realize anger is the culprit because, in fact, many angry marriages don't look the least bit angry. Imagine, with me, another couple on this same checkout line in "Ladies Outerwear"—Mr. and Mrs. Smith. You've seen them. You know them. They stand silently; they neither touch nor talk. They are there, with each other, and nothing more. They are the couple that seem to have run out of things to say to each other. The couple you see and think nervously to yourself—"I hope we never come to this." You wonder, "What do they still see in each other?" You can't imagine there is much going on in their bedroom.

Are they bored? Indifferent? Sad? No; like the Robertses, they are in an angry marriage. They may not look or feel like a couple whose anger is driving them apart, but hidden anger can be just as corrosive to marriage as anger that is openly hostile. It can rob a marriage of its vitality and joy just as surely as open enmity. And even if our anger is hidden, it can leave us with that same nagging feeling—we

THE ANGRY MARRIAGE

don't always like the person we love. Whether anger is apparent or hidden, enabling couples to resolve this unhappy predicament, to like as well as to love each other, is the very heart of this book.

Anger: The Odd Emotion

Anger is a strange emotion. Some of us will do anything—actually anything and everything—in order not to feel angry. The ends to which we can (and do) go in order *not* to feel angry are quite remarkable.

These efforts are often quite unintentional. It isn't that we set out not to be angry. Most of the time it is quite unwitting. An angry person who doesn't acknowledge his or her own anger is *not* being dishonest. Rather, they are in the predicament of being in the dark when it comes to their own emotional life.

This doesn't mean that anger ceases to exist. Absolutely not! It isn't that it disappears. Rather, anger gets buried; it goes underground. When that happens, the usual signposts and signals of anger cease to exist. The anger is there, but all the usual hallmarks of this emotion are lacking.

Later in these pages we will attempt to explore the numerous complicated and fascinating reasons why anger is taboo and why so many of us end up "in the dark" about our own feelings. But whatever the reasons, the extraordinary consequence is that anger can become a well-guarded secret—even from ourselves. When some of us say, "I do," we may unwittingly also take another secret vow: "I won't . . . feel angry."

While overt anger gives us our share of marital woes, buried anger destroys love also. It is *always* insidious and damaging to a marriage.

This is the reason for the plight of Mr. and Mrs. Smith, a "low-energy" relationship. Their angry marriage is *covert*. Anger has gone underground; and with it all the usual, recognizable expressions of anger. The only thing left in its wake is a low-level discontent. Their sort of marriage doesn't feel angry, it feels dull.

Throughout the years, in my office, I have encountered couples like the Smiths, couples whose anger assumes this same guise; the

6

marriage looks more dull and lackluster than it ever looks angry. What we can come to discover is that a boring marriage may actually be an angry marriage in disguise. Anger that is suppressed under a facade of calm often results in a marriage that feels unenergetic and depressive.

Angry Marriages: More Disguises

More than anything else, the purpose of this book is to let you, the reader, identify whether yours is an angry union. This is a particularly challenging task since, as I have just suggested, buried anger may undergo a striking and altogether unrecognizable transformation. Indeed, when hidden anger resurfaces, it manifests itself in a variety of different forms. The dull marriage is not the only guise an angry marriage may take:

· Audrey and Orin can't remember the last time they had an argument, but they spend their time in the opposite ends of their rambling Victorian house—Audrey suffering from yet another migraine, Orin puttering about with tools in the garage.
· Suzy and Dwayne never raise their voices to one another, but Dwayne's been known to explode at his employees. On her job, Suzy can't stand it when her supervisor blows off steam in her direction. (Over dinner they swap stories of "just how bad it is out there.")
· Pearl and Dwight are perfectly civil to each other, but they respectively lose themselves in food (Pearl's obesity has gotten worse with every anniversary) and affairs (Dwight can't seem to help getting sexually involved outside the marriage: "It doesn't mean anything," he insists, "it's just like a game of tennis").
· Marianne and Scott are a calm couple, but both can work themselves into a lather over Scott's mother—she's the proverbial battle-ax of a mother-in-law.

These couples are all stuck in angry marriages. They are burdened by anger but don't really know it. They, along with the Smiths, share the common attribute of hidden anger, but they differ in the way in which anger then reemerges and finds its expression. For each of these couples, as it might for any of us, anger wears a different disguise. And regrettably, no matter the particular cloak anger comes to wear, silently and insidiously it affects our work life, home life, and most assuredly our sex life.

Angry Marriages: Overt/Covert

So, anger may do its damage quietly for some couples, while others suffer because they cannot use anger constructively. Whether overt or covert, the net effect of *both* styles is to keep us from having what we want and need from our intimate connections. Both put a strain on intimate relations. Both make us suffer. Both make our marriages emotional compromises.

And oddly enough, while these two "management styles" seem so different, they are actually quite similar. They serve the same master—they perpetuate the status quo. They keep us locked in our frustrations and disappointments with one another. They keep people trapped in predictable, self-defeating, and self-perpetuating patterns—the very hallmark of an angry marriage. And the consequence of both styles is regrettably the same: They leave us with marriages that are less than we might wish them to be.

Flexibility, adaptability, spontaneity, creativity, joy, enthusiasm, exuberance, sexuality, passion—all the qualities that bring pleasure to a marriage—fall victim to the rigidity that is inherent in an angry cycle.

Angry Lovestyles: The Types

While the most obvious difference in such marital styles is whether couples display their anger or conceal it, if we look closely we can actually discern six fairly distinctive types of angry lovestyles in which couples can become ensnared: the angry-and-know-it crowd—I call them *venters* and *provokers;* and the angry-and-don't-have-a-clue contingent—*enactors, displacers, symbolizers,* and *suppressers.*

These are among the most typical patterns with which couples struggle, and if you are in an angry marriage, you will very likely be in one of them.

THE ANGRY-AND-KNOW-IT STYLES

The two most common styles of overtly angry marriages are venters and provokers. While differing in their intensity and display of wrath in responding to the question, "Are you in an angry marriage?," both would readily and similarly answer, "Yes!"

Venters are couples whose marriage is a tinderbox. They fight, quarrel, argue, bicker, shout, and stamp. Anger is retaliatory; tempers flare. The anger escalates and the goodwill evaporates. (The Robertses with their parry of insults, blame, accusations, and recriminations are indeed venters par excellence.)

Provokers are couples whose anger is not reciprocal; rather, one drives the other to distraction. A good guy/bad guy marriage in which one partner grumbles in exasperation while the other feels "blameless" or innocent of the accusations is characteristic of this one-sided angry marriage.

THE ANGRY-AND-DON'T-KNOW-IT STYLES

The four most typical covert styles of anger comprise enactors, displacers, symbolizers, and suppressers. While they share the common bond of hidden anger, they are remarkably distinctive for the ways in which anger is transformed and disguised.

Enactors are couples who substitute action for anger. Gambling, drinking, affairs, work, or even food may be the facade behind which anger hides itself. (Pearl and Dwight, who respectively lose themselves in the "love" of food and extramarital "love" affairs, are enactors.)

Displacers are couples who know what it's like to be angry but never direct such anger at each other; outside enemies are their whipping posts. Always finding themselves in the right, employees, siblings, and above all in-laws are the external targets onto whom they direct their "justifiable" ire. This couple banishes anger from their own union only to displace it onto others outside their partnership. (Suzy and Dwayne, never angry with each other but always swapping irate horror stories over work, are a displacer duo.)

Symbolizers are couples who symbolically express their rage—often using their bodies to signal their ire. Ailments, maladies, aches and pains appear in anger's stead. Anger is nowhere to be seen and is instead transformed, typically, into symptoms that one of them actually has and the other nurses. Symbolizers "divide" the work of hiding anger: One becomes infirm while the other runs the infirmary. (Audrey with her migraine headaches is in a symbolizer marriage with her husband, Orin.)

Suppressers are couples who truly bury anger, avoiding conflict at all costs, or swallowing their anger if it ever comes near the surface. Anger is unwittingly banned from home and hearth, leaving a relationship apparently anger-free but without zest, passion, and liveliness as well. (The Smiths, whose marriage seems so lifeless and lackluster, are locked in a suppresser union.)

Toxic Anger

It is important to reiterate here that covert anger in the last four angry lovestyles is *not deliberately or consciously expelled from the relationship*. These are no emotional charades. People don't knowingly wish or will their anger to go away and hide. Our efforts are neither premeditated nor calculated. Never! Rather, these are the things we do *unconsciously* in order to banish anger from a marriage.

Thus the significant question remains, Why on earth do we need to engage in such self-deception? Why must we be so estranged from such a seemingly ordinary, everyday emotion—anger?

Surprisingly, many of us grow up feeling that anger is dangerous, even toxic. We have an unconscious set of frightening assumptions about anger and they may read like this:

If I am angry . . . I will be abandoned.
If I am angry . . . I will be foolish.
If I am angry . . . I will be unlovable.
If I am angry . . . I will be unfeminine.
If I am angry . . . I will be too powerful.
If I am angry . . . I will be ugly.
If I am angry . . . I will be irrational.
If I am angry . . . I will fall apart.
If I am angry . . . I will be destructive.

If I am angry . . . I will lose control.

If I am angry . . . I will die.

If I am angry . . . I will go crazy.

If I am angry . . . I will do something shameful.

If I am angry . . . I will find my hateful wishes coming true.

If any of these are our hidden premises about anger, it is not hard to understand why we need to avoid it at all costs. If we believe that anger is potentially so harmful, threatening, and destructive, it makes sense that we would go to any and every length to avoid it.

How do we unwittingly engineer this avoidance? In a way, our unconscious helps us make a bargain with this "devil" called anger. We can think of this pact as *the big trade-off*—we "trade in" our overt anger and get, in its stead, an unhappy marriage. It's as if our unconscious says, "Let's make a deal. I'll protect you from feeling angry, but you'll pay with your happiness." And regrettably, many of us take the offer.

As odd as the big trade-off might sound, we have to remember that in a curious way it makes sense—we "save" ourselves from what we believe is the deadly and devastating force of our anger, though we pay so dearly.

While there is a strange sort of logic to the big trade-off, there is something almost tragic about our behavior: We never challenge our hidden assumptions. We never confront our fears!

Our "logic" rests on our emotional mythology about the "devil" anger and its enormous power. And as long as we never express our anger, we never offer ourselves the opportunity to discover that anger is *not* the potent weapon we unconsciously imagine it to be. As long as we keep enacting, suppressing, symbolizing, or displacing, we never have a shot at discovering that our assumptions about anger are wrong. Anger is the monster in the closet called our unconscious, and we never manage to open the door to see that it isn't real and can't hurt us.

For those of us battling anger in this way, moving on from here will take courage. To relinquish these frightening assumptions is no easy task. As strange as they may sound to our adult mind, they are the tenacious holdover of our childlike feelings. And on some level, even though we are mature adults, we really, really do believe them.

In this book you will be offered by example after example the reassurance that anger may be something other than an untamed beast. Above all, we will see how angry feelings can be put into words. We will get the monster anger to speak rather than wreak its imagined havoc. Language has a great power to civilize. And words, when they give expression to our angry feelings, are our way to banish what truly needs to be exiled—our *fear*.

THE CYCLE OF ANGER

Whether we are trapped in an angry lovestyle because of openly destructive anger or unexpressed hidden anger, the net effect is the same: We are stuck in a self-defeating cycle of anger. Whether we are venters who scream or suppressers who stifle, this is the hallmark of an angry marriage.

Why is it that angry marriages, whether overtly or covertly so, deteriorate into these predictable patterns? Why is it that an angry marriage degenerates into a predictable style—a dance of anger?[2]

Couples become locked into a cycle of anger because they cannot get what they need from each other. Needing and not getting, they are left in a perpetual state of unrelenting frustration. And this futility lies at the core of every angry marriage. Unmet needs—and the repeated frustrations created by them—are the central problem of every angry union.

The essential predicament of an angry marriage is each person's constant struggle with the frustration of having an unbearable gap: the great discrepancy between what they *get* from their partner and what they *need* from their partner. In an angry marriage, whether covertly or overtly so, there is always this "missing piece."[3]

But here is the irony. While unmet needs cause so much misery in partnerships, most people don't have a clue as to just what these needs are all about. In short, angry couples certainly feel the consequences of the "missing piece," but regrettably they don't know how to fill it.

Why is this the case? The needs of individuals in an angry marriage are submerged in their unconscious. So, the paradox is that while unmet needs drive the engine of an angry marriage, people are in the dark as to what those needs really are.

The key to breaking the deadlock of an angry union is to uncover these unconscious needs, to fill in this missing piece, to close the "frustration gap" so that the very things we need from a lover are the very things we get. Accomplishing this requires insight. The development of insight is no small task. A good deal of what follows in this book is designed to put you, the reader, on this helpful path, the pursuit of insight.

Insight: Our Way Out

Couples can break the impasse of an angry marriage, but it does not happen through pep talks, lessons, advice, directions, rules, reprimands, slogans, or admonitions. While well intended, such approaches don't prompt people to give up bad emotional habits or relinquish self-defeating patterns of behavior. Our minds and hearts are not quite as simple as that.[4] Unfortunately, knowing better is just not enough; we need a lot more.

We need to develop insight. We need to become self-aware. We need to know *why* we are caught in the self-defeating grip of an angry marriage. We need to know what unknown forces compel us into a particular angry lovestyle. Breaking an unproductive cycle of anger cannot occur until we fully understand why it has such a grip on us in the first place (and remarkably, as you will see repeatedly in this book, most of us simply don't know why it does). In a sense, we can't say no to an angry marriage until we have gained the insight into why we have said yes.

Such self-awareness is the necessary ingredient to change an angry marriage into a more productive and pleasurable partnership. And it is critical that we do so. Insight is the route through which we discover what is really the "missing piece." Gaining insight makes a difference. Insight makes us different.

Insight: A First Step

It's not all that difficult to activate your capacity for insight. In fact, this mechanism is already set in motion by suggesting that in partnerships people may fall, broadly speaking, into one of two types of angry marriages: those in which couples express anger that is overtly destructive, and those in which they don't express anger at all. The possibility that you are venters, provokers, enactors, displacers, symbolizers, or suppressers is another refinement of this new idea. Making the assessment as to which you might be, speculating on the possibility as to whether your angry marriage is of the noisy or mute variety, musing over the question, "Am I this, am I that?," is the spadework of insight.

If your reflections help you to zero in on your angry style, you will have certainly achieved a great deal. (Bear in mind that we don't expect this kind of recognition to happen here right off the bat. Hardly. More time and thought will be devoted to these six profiles in the pages to come.) Assuming as you proceed that you do figure out the nature of your own angry style, the question is, where do you go from here? What's the rest of this book all about? To a great extent, uncovering the mystery of your own mind and your own marriage is the task at hand.

LEARNING ABOUT YOUR NEEDS:
THE ANATOMY OF A MARRIAGE

It's already been suggested that people in angry marriages don't know their own needs. So here's the rub: We may desperately wish that our needs be met, but ironically that's impossible since most of us don't even know what they are.

This is so central to the problem of an angry marriage it bears repeating: *Each and every angry marital style is driven by unconscious forces.* We live out an angry marriage because the real, psychological reasons for our entrapment are unknown to us. Actually, hidden and buried feelings are the driving force beneath our marital styles. Yet we don't have a clue as to what they are and how they motivate our behavior.

This is the trap. Real needs are buried in the subconscious, unavailable and inaccessible. As a result, we cannot communicate them, and must live instead in helpless angry frustration—always needing but never getting.

It is possible, however, to understand this problem of the unconscious needs that drive unhappy unions by exploring the Anatomy of a Marriage. You can actually dissect a marriage psychologically in order to analyze the way in which your angry lovestyle and the unconscious needs that propel it works its damaging way into your own partnership. A good deal of this book will be devoted to exploring this "Anatomy of a Marriage." An angry marriage is actually split into three distinct tiers:

- *The Actual Marriage*—the everyday relationship you "think" you are in. The one in which your particular angry lovestyle (venter, provoker, enactor, displacer, symbolizer, suppresser) manifests itself.
- *The Invisible Marriage*—the marriage beneath the surface—the marriage in which your *unconscious needs* reside;
- *The Primal Marriage*—the "source marriage," unwittingly dragged like excess baggage from the pain and disappointment of your childhood from which your hidden, unconscious needs spring to life.

You will learn how breaking out of an angry marital style hinges on discovering and understanding these different levels and unearthing real yet unconscious needs. This concept, that an angry marriage is fractured into three distinct warring levels, is something to which you will be asked to pay close attention. In fact, much of the work of reclaiming your marriage will center on recognizing these three tiers in your own union.

This book is structured in such a fashion that each of the six different marital styles to be explored will lead you through this process. Initially, as each angry lovestyle is profiled, you will have the opportunity to work on identifying the particular style of your day-to-day life together—your actual marriage. In turn you will learn how to unearth the unconscious needs that drive your invisible marriage. And finally, by guided exploration of your past, you'll discover the origins of your needs as they developed in your child-hood, primal marriage.

Since it's clear that much of this information about yourself is unknown, even to you, this book will help you develop a route to this otherwise inaccessible information through a self-reflective technique I have developed—*Decoding Your Complaints.* Remarkably, embedded in every complaint is a psychological clue to the uncon-scious. Therefore, it is possible to look at the ordinary, everyday gripes and grievances of an actual marriage and decipher the hidden emotional truths they reveal. Through analysis of your complaints you will discover that you can actually illuminate and reveal uncon-scious needs.

You will learn how to relinquish an angry union and in its place forge an adult marriage. You will discover that the possibility of finally breaking the deadlock of marital frustrations comes when a couple can leave their discordant three-tiered marriage behind and live in one unified adult marriage, unfettered and unencumbered by hidden needs.

Living and loving in a truly mature way—in an adult marriage—means letting insights transform the ways in which you relate to one another. To do this, partners must learn to communicate their needs effectively. It requires a new language of love, a form of communi-cation based on insight and emotional understanding. The practical matter of learning this "art" of emotional and psychological conver-sation—which is very much at the heart of the *new language of love*—is a subject you will read about in great detail. In fact, much of this book will be devoted to translating newfound insights into this different and thoughtful form of communication. Finding the words, the right words, that truly express formerly hidden feelings can have a powerfully transforming impact on a marriage—forever!

Now that you have the general scope of the ideas on the angry marriage, just what can you expect?

*You Can Expect Questions That Will
Help You Find Your Own Solutions

Each of the six angry lovestyles briefly mentioned so far will be explored in depth. You will find a good deal of information, but also many questions. In fact, in many ways *The Angry Marriage* is a book of questions. Expect them. Inquiry, investigation, exploration are the means by which people arrive at self-understanding. Questions bring this about. So, a good question is eminently more useful than a pat answer. A good question may make you consider yourselves differently; a good question may alter your perspective or change your vision of yourself and your partner, and that is the route to renewing your marriage.

*You Can Expect to Find Yourself and
Your Angry Lovestyle

The idea of setting forth these six most common types of angry marriage is simple: expect that you will find yourself in these pages. It will happen. If you are in an angry marriage, you are very likely to be a variation on the theme of venting, provoking, enacting, displacing, symbolizing, or suppressing (or maybe a combination of more than one).

You can expect, therefore, to use this book as a primer or jumping-off point for developing a psychological perspective on your own relationship. But don't skip a style just because it doesn't seem to ring a familiar note. The exploration of every pattern, whether it fits you to a tee or not, is part of the process that will move you toward understanding your own pattern.

*You Can Expect Things to Get Better

This book *can* make a difference. This isn't a glib promise that you will live happily ever after simply by thumbing through these pages. Rather, it is a statement about optimism and the belief, grounded in years of experience, that with the right stimulus we can all be galvanized into changing and growing. Human beings are remarkably resilient and resourceful. When we know what it takes to make a difference, we can make it happen. Time and time again, even with those marriages that seem entirely depleted of pleasure, joy, and goodwill, things can and do get better. Passion, sex, laughter, communication, joy, respect, friendship—all can return and flourish in a marriage where couples have found the "missing piece."

And in the end, when your marriage has no hidden angry agendas, when you truly know your deepest and often most painful emotional truths and how to talk about them with one another, you will be able to say no to your angry marriage and yes to your love.

Can You Expect Anger to Go Away?

In the beginning, anger is a signal. It calls out to the world, announcing, "I am here, please respond to me." Anger asks the world to pay heed. In this way, anger establishes who and what we are. Through our anger we shape our world and are in turn shaped by it. Through anger we gain self-definition—we come into being. Through anger we come to love and be loved.

Along the way anger loses this value and meaning. It loses this crucial purpose. Our aim is to restore anger to its original design. And so the end of an angry marriage does *not* mean an end to anger in marriage. Instead, it means learning to use anger as it was first given—a gift through which we define ourselves, through which we ask the world to take heed, through which we shape our world and in turn are shaped by it, through which we come to love and be loved. Anger has its rightful place in the nature of love. Our task is to restore it to that rightful place. This is the subject and the heart of this book.

First things first. Before you go any further, there is an important assessment to be made: Are you in an angry marriage? Do you know whether yours is, indeed, an angry union or on the way to becoming one? How can you tell early on? What do you look for? Our next endeavor is to help you answer these questions—of course, as you might expect, by posing many more!

ARE YOU IN AN ANGRY MARRIAGE?

66 **M**y wife and I have a rule—never let the sun set on an argument. It's a second marriage for both of us and we learned the hard way what happens to love if ill-will is allowed to linger. We make a point of going to sleep feeling kindly disposed toward one another. I think this is why we managed to get it right this go round."

The distinguished Australian gentleman of eightysomething who managed to "get it right" the second time around—his current marriage was edging amiably into its fourth decade—has gained wisdom from which every married couple, especially angry couples, may benefit.

Love isn't enough. It is love and goodwill that we all require to make our marriages work and flourish.[1] The ballast that keeps a partnership steady, stable, firm is the kindly, sympathetic sentiment a man and woman bear for each other. Passionate attachments also need to be friendly attachments. We need to know and to feel that the people we care about have generous, kind, and loving feelings toward us. We need to know that we are wanted and cared about, that we matter. We need to know we make a difference. We need to feel valued and appreciated. These feelings must exist and they must be reciprocal.

Where there is contact, there is friction, and in marriage goodwill is always being put to the test. Always! An angry marriage, in particular, erodes the spirit of goodwill spouses feel toward one another. If goodwill is the glue that keeps people together, there's nothing like angry frustration to make couples feel as if they are becoming unstuck.

Goodwill is not an inexhaustible commodity in a marriage; it can be used up. Most often it goes little by little. Certainly, there may be marriages in which a dramatic event robs a couple immediately and completely of any good feelings they might have for each other (if we are betrayed in some extreme fashion, for example, our feeling of goodwill may leave us quickly and entirely). But for most people, this is not the case; it is far less dramatic.

In an angry marriage, the erosion of goodwill takes time. When we love someone, we don't just wake up one morning and discover it has disappeared overnight. Rather, in an angry marriage, it is a slow and often imperceptible process. Because of this, couples may fail to tune in and see it happening. They miss the signs and signals. The very things that could alert them to the possibility that anger is starting to weaken the fabric of their marriage may happen so gradually that they fail to gain their attention—until it is too late.

Alyson and Steve are an angry pair who missed the signs and signals—until it was too late. Even a therapist could offer no help. When Alyson came to my office with her husband, Steve, she was contrite with remorse:

"I'm sorry, Steve. I know we should have come to a therapist earlier. I know what's wrong with me, what I have to change. I know you can't stand my screaming, the way I can get so furious and nasty with you when I'm upset.

"I'm sorry. I'm so sorry," Alyson sobbed desperately.

Despite Alyson's candid admissions and her distress, Steve remained impassive. He made no gesture of comfort. It was not that he seemed either cold or unloving. Rather, he seemed worn out—as if he was without the energy to offer Alyson anything any longer. I suspected that for Steve it was too late.

Most of this first encounter consisted of Alyson's emotional litany of her inability to control her temper. By the end of the session, she had made an appointment for herself—"to work on my stuff." They agreed to meet again jointly. We would work toward evaluating the course treatment might take.

I never saw them again.

Regrettably, what I had suspected seemed as if it might well be true. Perhaps Steve had ceased to care. Perhaps the light of goodwill had been extinguished in him. If that was the case, Alyson's impassioned insistence could bring him to a single session. But without the goodwill of both partners, there was no work to be done. An angry marriage rasping with its last breath of goodwill can be resuscitated. An angry marriage where goodwill is dead can never be resurrected.

The problem of Alyson and Steve, as it can be for many people, is that they paid attention to their angry marriage only when it was in the most obvious state of distress; when it was, in fact, beyond the point of no return. When it wasn't simply an angry marriage but a dead one. *This can be averted!* There are many opportunities, long before the terminal stage of an angry marriage, to do something. The key is to pay attention when goodwill first begins to evaporate.

And remember, goodwill erodes in *all* angry marriages, whether they are overt (venter or provoker) or covert (enactor, displacer, symbolizer, or suppresser). Sometimes marriages go out with a bang of ill-will (venters, for instance), or with a whimper (suppressers, for example). But such dead ends can be avoided if we pay attention at the very start.

What follows is an exploration of the ten most common early indicators, warnings that goodwill may be vacating the premises and an angry marriage is taking up residence. Look them over carefully to see if you are ignoring any important "signals."

1. *He Doesn't Bring Me Flowers Anymore: Have Loving Gestures Begun to Fade?*

Mary, a young writer, describes the "gift" she frequently receives from her husband, Tony:

"When I am working late at my computer, just before Tony goes to bed, he might go to the kitchen, put some cold chicken on a thick slice of bread, smother it with mayonnaise, and appear with my midnight snack up in my attic office.

"I could easily do it myself. But it seems to taste better when it comes from him!"

We all relish and look forward to special gestures in our marriages. If you feel disinclined to do them, if they are becoming fewer and increasingly far between, this may be symptomatic. When you begin a cycle of anger, a willingness and interest in doing favors, extending yourself, treating each other in "special" ways falters. An early sign of anger's presence—the selfless gesture takes a powder.

If your spirit of generosity feels depleted or bankrupt, it may express itself in any sphere of your married life together. It may be seemingly unintentional:

"I know Seth loves that mocha coffee from the store near my office. It's just that I keep *forgetting* to run over there on my lunch hour."

It may feel as if you have a valid excuse to explain its absence:

"Yeah, I know I always used to pick up the paper for Kathy before work, but these days I just don't have time."

Or it may feel intentional and regrettable:

"Millie never used to mind my going to the Bulls game. In fact, she surprised me with a pair of tickets last year. These days, if I want to watch a game it's like she's doing me the biggest damn favor."

Whether it is intentional or seemingly unintentional, whether it is an act of omission ("I forgot it was our anniversary") or commission ("I passed the florist but I didn't feel like being nice"), when you stop indulging, pampering, and pleasing each other, when you cease treating each other carefully and gently, you may very well be feeling the erosion of goodwill.

2. What Does It Spell—Relief?: Does Time Apart Feel Necessary?

Happy lovers value privacy. Couples with a reservoir of goodwill don't mind spending time apart. Sometimes it's even refreshing. However, for a couple on the road to an angry marriage, "time off" is salvation, not just rejuvenation. The movie *City Slickers* explores the adventure of three men in midlife crisis embarking on their annual week of male bonding. Billy Crystal's wife urges him to go—she'll go to her parents in Florida with the kids and she'll be fine.

Crystal protests, insisting he'll give up the trip in order to be with his wife and their two children.

Again she proclaims emphatically that it will be fine if he goes his own way.

Crystal dutifully insists once more on accompanying her.

Finally and brutally the truth is revealed:

"No. You don't get it," his exasperated wife blurts out. "I don't *want* you to come with me."

Crystal is hurt to the quick.

This declaration is not from a woman who is trying to hurt her husband, nor is it completely benign, that she just wants and needs some private time on her own. These words are from a weary woman who desperately requires relief—from her spouse. These words are spoken by a woman quietly and desperately moving into an angry cycle.

Might your goodwill quotient be ebbing in the area of togetherness? Do you feel wiped out, exhausted, as if you want and must have a time out from being a spouse? It is not that you want to jettison your relationship; it is just that you feel burdened by your marriage and anxious to have some respite from the tensions.

Perhaps you feel more relaxed separated from each other; the thorn may feel temporarily removed from your side. Or you may breathe easier, feel more carefree and lighter, when you are alone, and wish it didn't have to end. Would you say, "I can be more like myself when he/she isn't around"? This frame of mind is indeed a telltale sign.

Where and when might you register these sentiments? Perhaps you find yourself welcoming a business trip—a night alone in a hotel room begins to feel more relaxing than lonely. Or might this be the scenario: Your husband announces that he's leaving for a business trip, and you feel as if you'll start a vacation once he steps out the door. Are long hours at the office more relief than grief (and do you pretend to be asleep when he finally does come home)? Have you stopped looking forward to your family vacations and wish they weren't so long, that he'd go back to work already? If your separateness feels far easier than your togetherness, you may be brushing up against your own angry marriage.

3. Reach Out and Touch Someone: Are You Less Physically Affectionate?

One summer, not long ago, I stood waiting outside a five-and-dime store in the small seaside town of Sag Harbor, Long Island. This busy Saturday afternoon I watched couples coming and going as they drove up to the village stores, parked, and alighted from their cars for an afternoon stroll. Within a few minutes two couples, both probably in their forties, drove up in their respective cars.

In the first car, while the wife took time turning off the engine, the husband got out immediately. And though looking as if he had no apparent destination other than window shopping, he went off at his own pace, leaving his wife to catch up.

In the second car, the wife also drove. Her husband also alighted first. But instead of sauntering off, he waited. And when his wife joined him on the sidewalk, he gave her an affectionate kiss, took her hand, and they strolled off together.

In these two couples I recognized the presence and absence of goodwill—happy couples touch more than angry ones. Taking the time to make contact, to allow that moment of unconstrained affection, is something that is easily lost to those couples on the road to an angry marriage. Though it may express itself differently within each of our partnerships, when a marriage gets angry, spontaneous, physical contact is *sure* to go. Gestures of touching or embracing your lover, just for the sake of it, are a mark of goodwill. They are a reminder of the intimacy you may share so pleasurably with each other. When people are angry, these kinds of gestures are a source of pleasure they are often incapable of providing one another.

Do you spend more time being touchy than touching? Perhaps you've stopped bussing one another at your morning departure from home. Or you may kiss, but it's more force of habit than depth of feeling behind the gesture. Is it mere formality, empty and perfunctory, rather than expressive of the warmth you used to feel for your partner? Or maybe this deficit appears at the end of your day: you read in bed while he's watching the Late Show in the den whereas you used to relish wrapping your warm bodies around one another as you fell asleep.

Do you find "things to do" to keep from being close and cozy under the covers together in the last moments of your day? (The big fib, "I'll come to bed in a minute, honey," is a certain marker of growing marital discontent.) Or do you pop out of bed quickly when your favorite time of day might once have been the early morning hours when you could enjoy the close physical presence of your spouse? Have you taken to early morning aerobics in place of early morning cuddling?

Do you no longer give your spouse "your famous back rub"? Or would it be hard to remember when you last hugged each other or took a walk down the block just as a way of being together?

Pay attention and you may see the stirrings of an angry marriage in your lack of physical stirrings for the person you presume to love.

4. Love Is Having the Decency, Generosity, and Intelligence to Say You're Sorry: Do You Find It Difficult to Apologize?

Erich Segal's *Love Story* was an enormous success in the sixties. Its motto—"Love is never having to say you're sorry"—became the marital credo for that decade. Yet anyone who has been married for more than ten minutes immediately recognizes how lame-brained and misguided a credo this is!

Being able to apologize, being able to forgive, are the most necessary capacities in our intimate connections. Regrettably, when we are trapped by our anger, it becomes increasingly difficult for us to say, "I'm sorry." In order to make such a declaration, or for that matter to receive one, ill-will has to be put to rest. Unfortunately, you may not be able to do this when the fires are beginning to burn within. If you can't say, "I'm sorry," your marriage may be moving to a sorry state.

5. Drink to Me Only with Thine Eyes: Have You Stopped Looking into Each Other's Eyes?

A lover's gaze has been immortalized in romantic literature through the ages—and with good reason. All of us who have been in love know that we connect emotionally with the person we love when we look into their eyes.

As is so often the case, science belatedly catches up with what is common knowledge. Scientific study has now demonstrated that when people feel romantic, their pupils get larger, and the resulting blackness is more inviting to gaze upon. Studies have also shown that angry people don't make eye contact!

Exchanging glances, gazing into one another's eyes, are the routes through which we make emotional contact with someone we love. If you are unable to have or are uninterested in having such an intimate exchange, it may be indicative of anger with your spouse.

Perhaps you've stopped trying because it feels silly or fake. Or is it that you can't find the time or the place? Or are you looking back to a time when all it would take to feel understood was a look ("We used to hardly need words . . .") and now things are so very different?

If this nonverbal form of communication has ceased to be part of your language of love, this could well be a sign of underlying anger and frustration in your partnership.

6. Only When I Laugh: Do You Laugh Less?

I know a couple, Bill and Helen. When you hear them laugh to-gether—which occurs very often in the course of their day—you have the feeling you are hearing two very good buddies having a great time. In fact, if you were to hear their peals of laughter and not see them, you would assume that they were young friends having a good time together.

Remarkably, Bill and Helen are in their seventies and have been married close to fifty years. In the fifteen years they have been my next-door neighbors I have heard their joyous sounds on a daily basis. Helen and Bill are *not* in an angry marriage.

In an angry marriage, laughter, gaiety, and mirth are often in short supply; a marriage can begin to feel gray and colorless, without vibrancy and vitality.

Lydia is a woman who became aware of just how low her reservoir of good humor was falling in her marriage. She noticed it and she didn't like what she saw. Being a woman of action, Lydia decided to enter group therapy for couples with her husband, Dick.

When group members asked why she and Dick had joined, commenting that the couple didn't appear to be very miserable, she offered this explanation:

"You know, Dick and I have had our share of bad times, but it never prevented us from having fun together. But recently I feel as if our marriage is a case of 'all work and no play.'

"I'm feeling cheated. I want us to be able to have fun again."

Lydia and Dick didn't seek marital counseling because they were in pain or very unhappy (they didn't wait until their anger became that pronounced); they came because their marriage lacked the joy they felt it deserved.

If you are bogged down by anger, the joy you are able to find within your marriage is sure to be affected. Perhaps you've noticed that the spiritedness has diminished and you no longer have much fun together. When you have ceased to smile at each other or there are no funny stories to recount and you look back nostalgically at the good times you used to share, you may be feeling the erosion of fondness that is part and parcel of an angry marriage.

7. The Silent Treatment:
Have You Stopped Talking?

A study on marital communication came up with a startling fact: "Happily married couples" spend very very few minutes of each day speaking with one another! If goodwill leaves so little time for communication, ill-will virtually wipes out the allotted time we talk to our spouse. The "meaningful" exchange in the life of an angry couple often deteriorates to little more than "It's your turn to take out the trash." When couples start to get angry, they start to talk less. They don't want to bother (a common ploy: We turn on the TV at dinnertime to avoid talking). They become more guarded in their exchanges ("He just won't open up to me").

The discussions in an angry marriage tend to be more informational and less personal. A husband and wife talk less about how they feel. They may stop sharing their secrets or their fears. They may have a growing sense that they have lost the confidant they once had. (If the feeling that "I can tell her/him everything" goes, anger has probably arrived.)

Perhaps you've become wistful for the days when it felt as though talking to your spouse was like talking to your best friend. When you lose the capacity for exchange that feels intimate and trusting, it is an important marker that goodwill may be ebbing between you.

Sometimes the lack of communication is more malevolent; a kind of barren silence befalls a marriage. In the movie *Two for the Road*, Albert Finney plays a man in love with Audrey Hepburn but disinterested in marriage. Finding lodging in a small, romantic hotel, they sit near a somber, lifeless couple who say not a word to each other during the entire evening.

On the way up to bed, Hepburn turns and looks at the couple.

"Who are those people?" she asks, evidently puzzled by their stony silence.

Finney replies cynically, "Oh. Those are married people."

Finney's cynicism no doubt served his character's desire to steer clear of marriage. But when we are in an angry marriage, the same stony silence of indifference may well be what we come to. This apathetic silence is a serious hallmark. So is the lonely silence where we have things we long to say but no longer feel our spouse is the one to be told.

These last examples are serious hallmarks of an angry cycle taking hold; the general rule of thumb is, the less talk the more anger.

8. Aboutface: Have You Become Critical of the Very Thing You Once Found Attractive?

Happy couples don't think of each other as perfect. But goodwill provides a cushion; shortcomings are perceived as limits, not faults. Goodwill allows partners to feel accepting, sympathetic about foibles, weaknesses, imperfections in a husband or wife. Happily married people may even turn a seeming liability into an asset ("I love your crooked smile"; "A bald man is really sexy"; "It's sweet the way you can get so emotional at a grade B movie"). Angry partners are considerably more judgmental—and invariably critical. They harp, nag, scold, find fault, correct, challenge, second-guess each other. They find a spouse's weakness or idiosyncracy annoying, never endearing ("Do you *always* have to bawl at every movie?").

What is enormously interesting is the particular and highly characteristic way in which couples do this if they are indeed in an angry marriage. Emotionally, husbands and wives seem to do an about-face. *Ironically, they become critical of the very thing that attracted them to their spouse in the first place!*

Lee Anne is a woman well into her angry marriage. In therapy, this irony did not escape her. "I grew up in the most boring middle-class family you could imagine. When I met Roberto, he was like a breath of fresh air. He was so exotic I couldn't believe it.

"Of course, now I'm always complaining that he won't make an effort to fit in with my family and friends. Can you believe it! I fought my mother tooth and nail to marry this man and now I'm complaining to him that he's too different."

Test yourself out on this one. Remember the very things you found most appealing? Now where do you stand? Have the virtues become the vexations, the attractions aggravations? If you liked your spouse for her drive, do you now complain of her pushiness? When his kind, gentle demeanor was his featured attraction, do you now hound him for being insipid and having no backbone? Where quietness was her appeal, are you currently criticizing her for having so little to say?

There is no more reliable indicator of anger than this reversal of feelings toward one's partner. Have you done this aboutface in your own marriage?

9. A One-Way Street: Do You Feel as If You Get Less from Your Marriage?

Happily married people are happy to be married. They feel as if marriage is a "deal" from which they derive a good deal of benefit. They put in but they get out as well. This feeling—it's really good to be married—sometimes hits home with a force; we are especially aware of this element of goodwill in a crisis.

My friend Carol went for a routine mammography. As she was

about to put on her clothes, the technician returned to her examining room and asked her to hold off dressing—the doctor needed more photos.

"It was a terrifying moment. I had the most morbid and frightening thoughts—the doctor must have seen something ominous and that's why they needed to check on it further. I was about to get frantic.

"I excused myself from the technician and asked if there was a phone I could use. A moment later I heard my husband's voice on the other end of the line. I was so grateful he hadn't left his answering machine on as he usually does when he's working: I badly needed him on the other end of the line.

"The next half hour of waiting to speak with the doctor was the worst. Until she told me that I was okay—she had seen something but it was the result of a technical problem with the mammography—I saw my life closing in on me.

"I called my husband immediately to tell him I was all right.

"When I got home that night, I was completely drained. While I was allowing my sense of relief to sink in, I wondered what I would have felt like if I hadn't had my husband in my life. The overriding feeling I had was this sense of great good fortune to be married."

In Carol's extreme state of potential crisis she was well aware of how important her marriage and her husband were to her. She was reminded, as we often are in the darkest moments of our life, of the benefits we derive from our intimate partnerships.

For the most part, the notion that we benefit from being married is a sentiment that goes unacknowledged in the routine of daily life together. In all likelihood, when a marriage hums along with a reasonable degree of happiness, joy, and goodwill, this sense that the marriage is worthwhile is something couples feel but generally take for granted.

When people are angry, they often feel quite different: They begin to doubt the value of their partnership. A bad day, an aggravating encounter with a spouse, and an angry partner finds herself silently posing the question, "What am I getting out of this marriage?" Only angry men and women begin to tally the worth of their marriage. (We don't ask ourself this sort of question *unless and until* we are beginning to feel angry with our spouses. And when we are very angry, it ceases to be a question; we catch ourselves muttering under our breath, "God! I don't get anything out of this marriage," or, "I think I'd be better off on my own.")

Perhaps you feel undervalued and overused. Or you find yourself wondering, What has he done for me lately? With mounting exasperation you might hear yourself griping that marriage is a give and take—"I give and my spouse takes." Your marriage may feel like a one-way street.

When this imbalance happens, partners may not feel better; just worn out, done in, exhausted. ("I just can't do this anymore. I don't know if I can go on like this.") More than anything else, it is anger that throws a marriage out of kilter, sapping the energy right out of a partnership.

If you find yourself in this situation, tallying up your marriage as if there is an emotional balance sheet and your spouse has a deficit, these may well be sentiments indicative of mounting anger and ill-will.

10. Allied Forces/Safe Havens: Do You Undermine Your Spouse/Do You Fail to Protect Your Spouse?

None of us expects consensus of opinion when we are in a marriage; differences, disagreements, diverging points of view are an anticipated and important aspect of our shared life. In our marriages we don't need each other to act as rubber stamps.

But we do need to feel that our spouse is our friend and ally, that we are on the same side. Even when we don't see eye to eye, we want to be assured that we are watching out for each other's welfare and well-being.

The sense of a marriage as a well-forged alliance starts to evaporate when couples begin to engage in angry struggles. You may notice this shift if you stop feeling protective of your spouse. If his trials and tribulations leave you feeling that "he got what he deserved," for example, this is a bad sign about your goodwill.

Perhaps you regularly find yourself on the side of his detractors or adversaries and don't feel like taking his side, defending him. Or you know your spouse's Achilles' heel and take some satisfaction in his vulnerabilities, instead of feeling as if you want to offer your lover safe haven where these things can be shown without fear of ridicule. You might feel little compassion for your spouse in his disappointments and, for example, point out that his problems are really "his own fault."

Even in its mildest forms, when you feel like undermining your spouse, when he can't come to you to lick his wounds (and you're more inclined to rub salt in them), this is a warning sign.

If your marriage stops being a safe haven, a place to refuel and restore yourself before you go out into the world again, you are most surely and regrettably in an angry marriage.

CONSTRUCTIVE VS. DESTRUCTIVE ANGER

The loss of goodwill in all its various forms is the subtle sign of an angry marriage. Whether yours is a covert or an overt angry cycle, you may very well recognize these indicators and now know something is wrong. But the erosion of goodwill is not the only marker of an angry marriage. The presence of destructive anger is the sine qua non of an angry partnership. How does destructive anger differ from constructive anger? Constructive anger doesn't threaten goodwill; it allows people to express negative feelings without attacking. Constructive anger communicates, informs, notifies. As a result, couples not only survive constructive anger, they even benefit from it because its aim is to open up channels between a husband and wife, not close them.

Destructive anger attacks. It is a weapon, not a tool; it has the effect of tearing down a partner and a partnership rather than creating a means of communication. Destructive anger wounds. Its aftermath is hurt, harm, and even hate, rather than greater understanding and empathy. Regrettably, far too many couples see destructive anger as normal and acceptable, without realizing it is ripping apart the very foundation of their love. Are you one of them? You may be if your anger ceases to be a signal and instead takes on any of the following characteristics.

*There She Blows!:
Do You Simply Let Off Steam?

Letting off steam is overrated as a device for handling anger. In fact, recent research suggests that the more we get angry, the more we feel angry and the longer we stay angry. If we let it all hang out, we may often be grappling with anger that is actually quite out of control. If our anger feels Vesuvian, it is a symptom of a cycle of anger.

(It may be obvious, but nonetheless it always bears repeating: If our anger is so volcanic and uncontrollable that it becomes abusive and/or dangerous, it is more than a sign that we are in an angry marriage. It is a sign that we must get professional help. No marriage can or should be worked on until violent, dangerous, or abusive behavior is no longer part of the picture. A violent marriage is not the same as an angry marriage and we cannot treat it as if it is.)

*The War of the Roses:
Does Your Antagonism Escalate?

In the film *The War of the Roses*, Michael Douglas and Kathleen Turner play a couple who are waging an ever-escalating battle in their attempt to divorce one another. Refusing to move out of their shared home, they get to a point where they inhabit their own house—a line down the middle to separate their respective territories—as two warring enemy camps. Things go from bad to worse to downright monstrous.

This is a number-one example of destructive anger (in fact, the final ante up is that the "Roses" pay with their lives, since they manage not just to drive each other crazy but by movie's end have actually succeeded in killing each other off!).

When couples are in distress, anger becomes negative and punitive. They may get nasty; they may fight "dirty." They often abandon the high ground for the low blow. Perhaps they insult, embarrass, or humiliate. And when one begins to use these guerrilla tactics, the other partner inevitably responds in kind.

Hillary and Ian, whose upper-crust British accents might seem to belie the very notion of "guerrilla tactics," actually became masters at this sort of angry one-upmanship during a particularly stormy part of their marriage. Ian recounted a moment when their antagonism escalated to new heights:

"I was bloody angry at Hillary and retreated to a bath before dinner. 'Retreated' isn't exactly correct. I told her that her culinary creation could just wait. That we'd be good and ready to eat when I felt like it.

"We exchanged some pretty devilish words through the closed bathroom door. Then after a moment of respite in our duel Hillary burst through the door to the bath carrying our dinner, which she proceeded to dump into my tub!"

Some couples might just get as colorful as Ian and Hillary. (In marked contrast to the distinctive ways our angry antagonism can accelerate, social scientists have labeled this sort of marital interaction with the most colorless term—"reciprocal aversiveness.")[2] Others might simply hear their words getting harsher, their voices getting louder, their silences getting longer.

For those husbands and wives without the venom of Mr. and Mrs. Rose or the imagination of Ian and Hillary, there is still something of which you can take note: When your anger, your disputes, your fights escalate, you are showing the telltale signs of an angry marriage.

*J'Accuse!: Do You Angrily Blame Your Spouse (and Excuse Yourself)?

When we are in a pattern of anger, we often engage in blaming. We accuse. We find fault and see the responsibility for our marital malaise in our spouse ("You're so damn demanding"; "You're so bossy it's unbearable"; "You . . ."). If we were to stop and listen to our language, we would notice rather easily how often we begin our angry interludes with the words "You're so . . ."

When you feel angry, you are more likely to feel dissatisfied with a spouse and see the reasons for conflicts as the result of your spouse's shortcomings: It is *his* personality or *her* attitude that makes for your marital difficulties. By contrast, you see your own negative behaviors as externally caused. The net effect is that when we are angry we become accusatory—but only of our spouse!

Anne, a young newlywed, unwittingly illustrated this contrast but completely missed the signals of her anger.

Jack, her husband of nine months, had forgotten to pay the electric bill before they left on their summer vacation. Receiving a disconnect notice forwarded to their summer cottage, Anne spent a whole day fuming at Jack—"You're so irresponsible. You're so careless. You're so forgetful."

A few weeks later the tables turned. Arriving home after a month, Anne and Jack pulled into their driveway to find a month's worth of their daily paper piled on the gravel; Anne had forgotten to stop the delivery service. But Anne did not "accuse" herself. Unlike Jack, she was neither irresponsible, careless, or forgetful—just over-worked:

"Jack, don't be unreasonable about this. It's no big deal. And anyway, you know how busy I was with my new account. It just slipped my mind in the rush to get away."

When you find yourself hurling "Yous" at your spouse for his or her foibles while letting yourself gently off the hook, you might well consider that anger is percolating.

The Not So Merry-Go-Round: Do Your Battles Always Take the Same Form?

My friend Themis once offered me her "take" on marital discord:

"You know around Christmas time every year Johnny Carson always used to say that there is one and only one fruitcake and it gets passed around in a new box from person to person around holiday time.

"I think," she went on philosophically, "that marriage and this fruitcake have something in common.

"In my marriage, Ted and I really have one and only one fight. It may not always look it but it's always the same argument. It just comes rewrapped in a different package every time we have it. And you know I think it's about as stale as Carson's fruitcake!"

Another indicator of the cycle of anger is the sameness of a couple's fights and accusations. Do your arguments always center on the same issues? Do they begin and end the same way? Do you assume the same role in your dissension (victim, not victimizer, for example)? Once your arguments feel like a broken record and today's fight seems like an instant replay of yesterday's battle, you would be well served to suspect that destructive anger plays a significant role in your marital discord.

*Everything and the Kitchen Sink:
Do You Drag Old Grievances into a Current Fight?*

Something else often occurs in our arguments when we are beginning that downward spiral into an angry marriage: We blame in a fashion that professionals have dubbed "kitchen sinking"—any and every grievance we have, past and present, gets tossed into our quarrels. We may start with one issue or gripe, but it enlarges itself. In a short time we may be throwing into this basin of accusations any old dirty problem that readily comes to mind. If you get messy when you argue, if you air all the dirty linen all the time, if you recall every past injustice in the face of the current one, you're in a cycle of frustration.

Sweet Revenge: Do You Hang on to Your Anger?

How long we hang on to our anger and what we dream of doing or actually try to do with it are certain indications of our pattern of anger. If we find that after an argument we cannot calm down, forget ill-will, and get back good feelings toward a spouse, we may well be on the road to trouble.

When you feel retaliatory ("She's gonna pay for that!") or vengeful ("I feel like calling his boss and telling him where he really was the day he called in sick!"), when you can't let go or unhook from your anger, it most certainly suggests you are in the grip of a cycle. Bear in mind that the scale of your vengeful wishes and actions doesn't have to be grand to be significant. If the morning after a fight you think, "Let him get up and make his own coffee," it is as significant as that "If I had a sledgehammer, I know where I'd like to put it" fantasy you concoct lying in bed after an aggravating day with your spouse. Both spell trouble.

Remember: Not looking angry, not feeling angry, not acting angry doesn't get you off the hook. You may not have overtly destructive anger, but in spite of this, anger may still be doing its destructive work.

Where's the Beef?: What About Angry Sex?

We haven't mentioned sex—*angry sex!* Invariably, if we are angry, our anger finds its way into our lovemaking. Our bed may indeed become our battlefield. It may be obvious; we may feel as if we are sleeping with the enemy. But the effects of anger on sexuality and lovemaking can be more varied and infinitely more subtle. In fact, the effects of anger on sexual drives are not always as we might predict them to be. For some the danger of anger can fuel passion, while for others it can douse the fires completely. The wide variety of ways anger can derail our ardor means there's a lot to think about, and that is the subject of our next chapter—angry sex. You may discover that the first resting place for your anger may be your conjugal bed. That is the next place for us to explore.

Three

ANGRY SEX?

S
ex still worries most of us. Am I normal? Do we do it enough? Why do I feel this way? Why do I think this way? Most people are not immune when it comes to sex and self-doubt. Even in the safe haven of a therapist's office, husbands and wives are remarkably shy about broaching the topic.

It would be easy because of these common and normal misgivings about sexuality to overgeneralize, to see everything and anything that disturbs people about marital sex as a problem with anger. Not all sexual problems are, as a matter of course, anger problems. Every sexual glitch between a couple doesn't need to get explained away by pointing the finger at anger. In fact, if every misgiving men and women had about their marital sexlife got chalked up to "Hey, this is really anger at work," we would end up concluding that every one of us is in an angry marriage. And it just ain't so!

In order to avoid this as we explore the notion of angry sex, there will be a continual effort to distinguish it, whenever it seems appropriate, from more ordinary sexual misgivings. The focus will be on what's *right* with our lovelife in order to zero in more precisely on the ways in which anger can and does make it go wrong.

But before going any further, let's give a nod to a nearly universal anxiety—that a change in the level of lust for a lover is a marker of a troubled marriage. If you lose sexual hunger, or more correctly, if you go from feeling sexually insatiable to taking a pass on what's available to you on a daily basis, are you in an angry marriage? Does a change in your sexual appetites mean you've "filled up" on anger? Not necessarily.

Ah Yes, I Remember It Well!
Does Less Sex Mean More Anger?

Sigmund Freud once remarked that a woman loses her lover when she takes him for her husband.[1] The randier version of this epigram is captured in a raunchy joke that made its rounds some years ago: How do you cure a nymphomaniac? Marry her!

Whether these words were uttered by the sage of psychoanalysis or the street comic, both are probably referring to the same phenomenon: Sexual encounters eventually lose the glow of romantic excitement they had when couples first meet. Burning love doesn't continue to burn indefinitely.

Instead, ardor undergoes a transformation. Irving Singer, who has written three books on the nature of love, describes this shift as one in which couples move from "romantic passion" to "marital passion."[2] It is not likely, he suggests, that as married people we are going to be wildly and tumultuously absorbed in one another. The day-to-day necessities of living change our sexual responses to one another. Taking out the garbage, driving the kids to school, and staying late at the office all have their impact on the way people make love.

Sexual humor may indeed reveal this very natural evolution. When it comes to sex drive, there may be more truth than poetry in the quip, "What are the three stages of a man's sex life?"

"TRI-WEEKLY

TRY, WEEKLY

TRY, WEAKLY"

We may laugh ruefully because we recognize the kernel of truth in the jest. When we're married, things do change—considerably!

When couples marry, sex gains legitimacy but it undoubtedly loses its sense of urgency. The more we "can," the less we "do." But marrying someone doesn't necessarily make people roll over and play dead in bed, either. Hardly. An erotic lovelife, intense physical arousal, tenderness, sexuality, even without the fervor we once knew in our courtship, is part of most good marriages (in spite of what the jokes suggest).

Nonetheless, when people are in a committed, monogamous partnership, sexual appetite undergoes a metamorphosis; they do lose their ravenous hunger for sex. By appreciating this natural transformation, you may be less likely to confuse this process with the impact of anger on lovemaking. The absence of mad, passionate, head-spinning sex is not the sine qua non of an angry marriage. If anything, it is simply the sine qua non that you are indeed married!

Trying to detect whether couples are angry through a change in their romantic ardor for one another will tend to be misleading. The before and after comparison test of sexuality—"How was sex before, when we were an 'item,' vs. after, when we became a 'couple'?"—is far too glib and sweeping. We'd all, too easily and too quickly, arrive at the same answer—"Different!" And different doesn't equal angry. So, if cooling passion for one another is not the marker of angry sex, what is? Actually, there is more than one marker, and none of them is obvious.

*Take That . . . and That!: Do You Turn Your Lover into an Object?

When anger makes its way into the bedroom, it does so in subtle and complex ways. Sometimes it may affect erotic life in a manner you might not ordinarily expect; anger may heighten, not diminish, the arousal we feel. Jason was a man who experienced this in his angry marriage.

"I would begin to have an erection and I would enter my wife and my jaw would tighten. I would push myself into her like I was giving her a pummeling. It was almost as if she wasn't a person but a kind of sexual punching bag, and I was saying to myself (like you do when you're swinging at a punching bag), 'Take this and take that.'

"It was never violent. That wasn't the feeling at all. But it was unbelievably intense, and I'd have an orgasm like I was exploding."

Jason's anger created in him a growing resentment toward his wife. He unwittingly felt as if he needed to vent his anger on her as though she were a sexual object. His anger made him dehumanize the woman he loved. His anger made him forget her humanity.

We needn't assume, however, that all "rough and tumble" sex is angry sex. Often during intercourse couples use this "turning our lover into an object" in order to create excitement. Many of a couple's most pleasurable and exciting fantasies may come from sexual play acting, where they pretend to treat each other badly, as if they don't feel tenderness toward a partner, as if they are just the object of lust. Perhaps husband and wife play act as "love slaves," or tease one another, or act sexually aggressive in other ways in order to foster eroticism.

Getting "down and dirty" when making love can be a turn-on. In the privacy of a bedroom, this may be a way men and women get their sexual adrenaline running. In fact, Dr. Robert Stoller, writing about sexual excitement, theorizes that these aggressive feelings are crucial to the maintenance of sexual arousal.[3]

But this does not describe Jason's dehumanization. He was not pretending or playing; this was not some exercise of his imagination over which he had control. His behavior was not a melodrama from his fantasy life that played itself out in his marriage bed. No. It was simply the agitated way he felt when he began to make love to his wife. His was sexual aggression untempered by any concern other than his need to discharge his pent-up tensions.

Perhaps the clearest marker that this was Jason's anger in action was that this was not an experience he shared with his wife. They had no mutual understanding, no agreement, no communication that would suggest it was a way they might both choose to arouse their joint passions.

When couples are angry, this lack of mutuality is likely to enter lovemaking. If your sex is action rather than interaction with your partner, you might want to be suspicious of why this is so. When sex seems to bear more resemblance to animosity than love, anger has surely arrived on the scene.

Good Sex/Bad Feelings: Do You Turn Off After Sex?

Sometimes anger shows up in bed *after*, not during, intercourse: You don't mind having sex but you do mind being in bed with each other—after the fact. If after lovemaking you are indifferent to and detached from your spouse, even if it is without rancor, this response may be the harbinger of anger. In their fifth year of marriage, Nick and Tammy encountered this problem. As Nick recalls:

"I would have these amazing orgasms. This was the best sex of our marriage, from a purely physical point of view. I always came, no matter what. But afterward I wouldn't really want to have anything to do with my wife, and I think Tammy felt the same way."

Even after "good sex," Nick and Tammy had bad feelings about each other. Nick said:

"Tammy used to call this our come and go sex: We'd come and then we wished we were gone!"

Tammy and Nick had no obvious bitterness, no intense aversion to each other; just postcoital indifference—a quiet yet powerful indicator of anger.

Sexual intercourse is quite literally about union. It is about approaching someone we love to be as close as is humanly possible. If you lose that sense of affiliation with your lover, if you don't want the closeness, if sexual apathy supplants affinity or, in the extreme, antipathy replaces sexual yearning, anger is invariably the culprit.

But let's put these reactions in perspective. Not all sexual inattentiveness implies anger; attitudes, rather than just actions, are what we need to consider to discern the presence of animosity. Sometimes avoidance has little to do with marital malice. When you are happily married, you might be too exhausted at the end of the day to do much else but have intercourse. You might just have an orgasm, roll over, and conk out, anxious for some sleep.

This behavior does not necessarily mean anger is percolating. Sometimes tired is just tired! After all, in contemporary marriages most of us find two people have to work in order to make *one* living. Indeed, with the demands of work and family, both partners may legitimately feel fatigue's fallout on passion.

Couples need to be wary of their actions in bed only if they reflect disinterest, distaste, or, in the extreme, disgust for one another.

Sexual encounters that leave you feeling more detached than attached to the person you love may well be markers of your growing resentment.

*"Grin and Bear It" Sex:
Are You Sexually Submissive?

We can't always be in sexual sync with our partners. Women, because of physiology, can always say yes even if they're feeling no.[4] (For men, nature doesn't make this possible; you'll see how this factor relates to anger a bit later.) Saying yes when you feel no is not an anger problem—unless it feels oppressive to submit. It did to Julia, and it was indeed a marker of her angry marriage.

"I would have sex with Ben even though I wasn't up for it. I'd sometimes pretend to have an orgasm, but a lot of times I'd close my eyes and just wait for it to be over."

When we are angry, some of us engage, like Julia, in "grin and bear it" sex. We may not feel antagonistic or experience dread about "just doing it." Instead, we just go along without feeling much of anything. The pejorative expression—invariably used to describe women—"She has sex like she's a dead fish," may actually be a sign of this fury.

When a woman is "just doing it," it is quite likely that she doesn't reach orgasm. So, if you are a women who is "going along with it," "taking it," "putting up with it," and feeling rather anesthetized during what seems to be your spouse's moment of sexual ecstasy, anger has probably entered your sex life.

But, remember, being out of sexual sync is not always about anger. "I'm in the mood for love, simply because you're near me," is a romantic impossibility. The idyllic refrain of a song and the reality of our disposition toward sex don't always match up. There's many a time when your sexual thermostat and your spouse's don't have the same reading—he wants to but you don't. In spite of "not being up to it," there are moments in marriage where a wife accommodates to her husband. Giving in to your husband's desires even when they don't match your own is not, in and of itself, an omen of anger. It may be an act of generosity toward someone you love—giving rather than giving in.

When a woman is sexually accommodating—"out of the goodness of her heart"—she often ends up having an orgasm even if she didn't expect to. This sort of compliant sex is not about anger. Sexual martyrdom, feeling as if you are in bed only so your spouse may relieve himself, is the more problematic sentiment. When you find yourself, like Julia, mentally muttering how little you are getting from sex, suffering in silence, or sniping sarcastically about a husband's sexual insensitivity, you are certainly struggling with anger.

Dead on Arrival: Are You Disinterested in Sex?

"Grin and bear it" sex is *not* a characteristic way in which you express anger if you are a man. A man's physiology doesn't easily allow for this emotional/physiological splitting of which women are capable. As a man, whether you are "into sex" or "not into sex" is far more noticeable. When you aren't—you "can't get it up." (Perhaps this slang and pejorative phrase is the equivalent male slur to the "dead fish" insult used to describe women. In both cases they are insensitive and belittling swipes we make at each other when we are not attuned to our struggle with anger.)

If anger is brewing, a man who unconsciously feels like resisting his wife's sexual advances may become (with increasing frequency) impotent and unable to perform—and there's no hiding it. And what's more, an angry husband often just rolls over and goes to sleep, not making the effort to do anything about it.

Impotence that is the result of passive and submissive anger is probably accompanied by a general disinterest in having intercourse. It is not as if a man becomes aroused, tries, fails, and feels frustrated. Rather, he suffers from sexual indifference.

These angry husbands make few overtures to their wives or perhaps stop trying altogether. Typically, they don't try to have sex if they are unable to have intercourse. A sense of erotic possibilities gives way to a "why bother" mentality. Knowing his lovemaking won't go anywhere before he even begins, the angry man experiences a feeling of futility, a growing sentiment that sexual intercourse is a useless undertaking.

These attitudes that accompany impotence are markers—an unwilling body and an unwilling heart and mind reveal whether anger plays a role in a couple's erotic life together.

Anger may make it impossible for a man to become sexually aroused and to stay sexually interested and interesting. But every performance problem is not necessarily an anger problem; sometimes a man may be struggling with an uncooperative body rather than colluding with his anger. Fatigue, alcohol consumption, medication (i.e., some antidepressants; some blood pressure medications), illness (i.e., advanced diabetes; stress) are agents that can get in the way of arousal, erection, and/or ejaculation.

Anger is not always the culprit. And there are ways to tell the difference. An uncooperative body needn't mean an uncooperative mind. A man who isn't in the mood and isn't angry typically remains interested in giving pleasure even if he can't receive it. Sexual generosity doesn't have to end because of an unwilling body. And when people are in a good marriage, it doesn't.

If a wife wants sex and a husband doesn't (and they still like each other), there are all sorts of pleasure-giving alternatives to intercourse—sex play, oral sex, manual stimulation. A husband who has goodwill can create pleasurable options even when he can't achieve an erection. In good marriages if our body isn't cooperative, our sex life doesn't necessarily come to a dead end. In an angry marriage such generosity goes by the boards and we are altogether different—it comes to a halt.

*I've Seen Better:
Do You Engage in Sexual "Putdowns"?

Good sex doesn't always lead to a good climax. When we make love, whether each of us or both of us reaches orgasm is more a matter of percentages. Often the familiarity of marriage, the fact that through a marriage bed you may become knowing and knowledgeable about your own and your partner's body, helps raise those percentages.

Nonetheless, there are still those days when lovemaking doesn't conclude as planned. But this "failure" doesn't make an angry couple. What does is how a man and woman react to each other when they don't hit the home run every time they step up to the plate.

If people are descending into an angry marriage, they see these moments as failings and attribute these shortcomings to their spouse. A wife might declare: "He doesn't know what he's doing"; a husband may complain: "I'd have an erection if she'd only be more relaxed and look like she enjoyed touching me"; or, "She just doesn't turn me on."

Then again, a partner may offer comparisons that suggest greater sexual know-how or prowess in someone other than their spouse ("My first lover really knew how to get me excited"; "I never had a problem with dryness with my first husband"). Things can even get harsher; in a very angry marriage, one partner may even resort to sarcasm or mockery of the other's sexual prowess ("Some performance tonight, Mr. Hot Shot"). Such "putdowns" are your anger in motion.

But bear this in mind: The frequency of intercourse and the regularity of its ending in mutual orgasmic satisfaction are not, per se, barometers of anger (this is not to be confused with the impotence just described, which is persistent, repeated, and is also very much tied to a feeling of defeat). Occasional impotence, erections that don't lead to ejaculation, clitoral excitement that doesn't peak to an orgasm are not, in themselves, significant indicators of angry sex. Every good marriage has its sexual mishaps.

Unlike angry couples, when people are happy with one another they let these things go. They are the tiny blips on life's radar screen. We go on. They don't matter much or we view them in a matter-of-fact way. Often couples find humor that unites them even if their bodies can't. Sometimes partners offer one another apologies ("I hope you're not disappointed") and respond with reassurance ("Look, it happens").

Anger doesn't allow for kindness, sympathy, or laughter in the wake of sexual mistakes or orgasmic dead ends. Instead, we defame our spouse's sexual power and vitality, sending the message: "You are sexually disappointing." When anger is brewing, partners feel victimized by sexual disillusionment and typically don't keep it a secret.

*You've Got to Give a Little: Do You Want to Change the Rules of Your Sex Life?

Sexual comfort zones vary. Some people feel entirely uninhibited sexually—anything goes—while others feel better in bed with the lights out. Sometimes what one adores the other abhors. Generally, when couples are happy with one another, they reach an accommodation over differences in sexual style or taste; both partners tend to bend a little. It's when you don't feel so inclined to oblige a spouse in bed that trouble may be brewing.

Arrangements that once seemed just fine may begin to feel onerous, burdensome, or taxing. You may feel you are now doing things in your lovemaking that are against your will and your desires. Where once you felt comfortable with sexual limits set by a partner, you may now experience your spouse as withholding.

Perhaps you make noises about how you want to renegotiate your sexual contract, how you believe you aren't getting what you want and need erotically, how you want your partner to change sexually—now! If you begin to feel as if you want to dump your "old" sex life in favor of new rules ("I know you don't like oral sex but I've had enough of doing things your way"), it may be anger that is behind this sense of upheaval you are starting to feel.

Probably the element in this situation that speaks most about anger is the emerging sense of a lover as a source of sexual deprivation rather than gratification. When a person begins to regard a spouse as an obstacle, an impediment to pleasure and passion, anger may be the real barrier.

If couples are happily married, they don't feel put off by having to "put out"; they make sexual accommodations to and for each other—willingly. For instance, you might appreciate that your spouse kisses your genitals but not insist they bring you to climax this way if it doesn't turn them on as it does you. Or perhaps you feel embarrassed when it comes to talking about sexual fantasies but overcome your reluctance and "talk dirty" because it clearly is a way to give your lover pleasure.

In good marriages, we willingly accede to a lover's reasonable erotic desires because this sort of sexual giving is part of the generosity we extend to each other in bed. If we're happy, our lovemaking is about giving pleasure as well as taking pleasure. If we're angry, it's not!

*The Meaning of the Fling That Didn't Mean a Thing:
Are You Having an Affair?*

I may not win any popularity contests among wayward spouses having their "meaningless" fling, but there is no question in my professional mind that an affair *always* means something, and it often means you are in an angry marriage.

But it doesn't always represent the same thing in every angry marriage. In fact, couples can use an affair in two very different ways, both of which reveal an angry marriage in their own fashion: We can use an affair to defuse mounting marital anger, or we can use an affair as a weapon to wield angrily at a spouse. These are two very different types of liaisons that share a common root—marital discord.

An extramarital affair does bring something "extra" to a marriage: It brings a third person. Invariably, this "other woman" or "other man" is a source of increased sexual gratification. Along with other emotional gratifiers like attentiveness ("She really listens," or, "He really understands me"), this erotic fulfillment is often a main attraction in an affair. And we may need this extra helping of good feeling because we are angry. Ironically, couples use an affair to save a marriage from becoming too angry (since this "symptom" is so tied in to the angry lovestyle of enactor, we will detail it at length later in these pages).

When you are loath to feel a sense of frustration within a partnership, you may deflate your mounting anger by getting good feelings on the side. The inclusion of a "good" lover in your life may help you tolerate the sentiment that you have a "bad" spouse. Vlasta let this happen:

"I had great sex and lots of understanding from my lover, Peter. It made it possible for me to go home to my husband, Andrew, and not care that he never found the time to listen to my problems. As long as Peter was in my life, I didn't have to feel resentment toward Andrew. I just felt resigned, never angry, because I was getting everything I thought I wanted—only it took two men in my life to make it happen."

An affair may make a lackluster marriage tolerable by obscuring the angry frustration over what is lacking in a marriage. That is the paradox—an affair may be the way both partners ensure that anger will not come home to roost.

But some people use affairs quite differently. Sometimes when couples are entering into an angry phase, an affair becomes a weapon aimed at the heart of the basic trust they have established with their life partner. Regrettably, anger may make us want to hurt a spouse, and an affair is frequently the way to do it. The revelation of the affair, often by "accident" (a number jotted on a back of a letter, a bill for a hotel room left on a bureau), is the way people unconsciously show their hand and their ire. A "clandestine" affair may really be about the treachery of disloyalty and the breach of trust. Unfortunately, when men and women grow angry, they may wish to strike a blow at the foundation of a marriage, trying to injure a spouse where it hurts most.

Leslie, reflecting on her husband's "office romance," which happened in the eighth year of their marriage, expressed this sentiment:

"I did not ever feel jealous of Tom's affair. I never felt threatened in any sort of sexually competitive way, but God, I felt like he was a traitor to our relationship.

"It's so strange. If it had been a one-night stand with a prostitute, my fantasy is that I wouldn't be nearly as angry or hurt. But for him to have had an affair with someone I know kills me. Maybe I'm fooling myself, but I feel as if I could forgive the sex but I'm not sure I can forgive the disloyalty."

If an affair makes you disloyal and breaches your shared trust, anger is at the heart of it. Happy lovers become custodians of each other's hearts; angry lovers may, regrettably, have the urge to see them broken.

*Not Tonight, Honey:
Do You Make Excuses to Avoid Sex?

The anecdote goes like this. A man sued his wife for divorce.

"On what grounds?" the judge inquired of the man.

"On the grounds that we live in a two-story house."

"What are you talking about?" asked the confused judge.

"The first story is, 'I have a headache.' The second story is, 'I'm not in the mood.' "

Excuses are the stuff of bad jokes. But the question remains, even if they are the fodder of stand-up comics, are they also the stuff of our angry marriages? Should we take the presence of sexual excuses as a marker of our anger, or should we ignore them, laugh them off, because they seem so commonplace in our married lives?

When people are angry, they may well find this most stereotypical route to express it. Finding excuses, distractions, diversions, better or more pressing things to do then being physical with a partner are behaviors that may seem ordinary. But these actions do indeed tell us something—if you know how to listen.

When excuses are routine, commonplace, and predictable—when we take aspirins more often than birth control pills—these are ways we reject a partner, make a spouse feel unimportant, or just generally put them off. Seemingly small and incidental actions repeated often enough ("Oh, I really wanted to watch the late movie tonight"; "The kids might hear us"; "I'm so tired, maybe tomorrow") send the larger message—"I don't want you, I don't desire you."

Angry people use excuses for sexual avoidance that convey aversion, disinterest, antagonism. Invariably, a spouse feels spurned, reacting with anything from hurt to exasperation to outrage. A legitimate excuse doesn't garner that sort of negative reaction because it doesn't carry the sting of rejection. If you are increasingly finding reasons not to have sex and your spouse seems dejected, sullen, or angry, it may be your own anger that is the real source of your myriad justifications.

But bear one thing in mind—occasional excuses can of course reflect legitimate problems, not anger. It's only when you live in a house where there is always another "story" being added—and it hurts a partner's feelings—that anger may truly lie at its foundation.

*I've Gotta Be Me and You've Gotta Take It: Do You Resist Being Sexy?

A friend and colleague of mine had a nasty encounter on *Phil Donahue*. As the psychological "expert" of the day, she was confronted with a couple on stage who were in a tiff about the wife's obesity and the husband's dismay at how she was no longer very appealing to him. The wife complained of the husband's constant harassment, and the TV audience, chiefly women, were clearly on her side.

My friend the psychologist intervened:

"Why are you fighting him? Why don't you do what he asks and lose some weight?"

The audience so clearly identified with this "beleaguered" woman that they were ready to go for my friend's throat as well as the husband's.

While it may not make you an audience favorite on the talk show circuit, my colleague was indeed responding to a point that we completely overlook when it comes to our sexual attractiveness.

When lovers are angry, they may unconsciously try *not* to be alluring. Fighting sexiness may well be a way to unconsciously and angrily fight a spouse. The husband or wife who has stopped caring about "looks," grooming, weight, fashion is certainly doing something to him- or herself, but they are also doing something to their spouse. Personal neglect may be a way to convey that we don't care, we are uninterested in sex. Letting yourself "go to hell" can be tantamount to telling a partner the very same thing. "I don't care about me" has another angry component—"I don't care about you!" Angry partners can be emotional kamikazes—destroying their own sexual attractiveness as a means of angry retaliation.

Letting yourself go to physical ruin is not the only way to turn off a partner when you turn on your anger. Everyone has sexual idiosyncracies—things that come under the category of "my biggest sexual turn-off." Anger is brewing if you persist in doing things that are high on a partner's "turn-off" list. For example, you consistently eat in bed though you know he's revolted. Or he gets in the habit of not showering at night when he knows you love to be squeaky clean under the sheets. By managing to become the embodiment of a partner's sexual pet peeves, you are actually launching your angry battles even before you begin to make love.

Of course, happy marriages are based on mutual respect. And that would include loving us for and in spite of our idiosyncrasies or our bad habits. But, in a marriage, being "ourselves" needs to be tempered by a sense that we don't impose on the person we love. In a marriage we need to be ourselves—in moderation. Respect needs to be reciprocal.

In angry marriages, that isn't what happens. Instead, the need to be "ourself" takes on an insistent, even strident, quality. If in your own self-assertion you trample on your partner's feelings, then anger, not respect, is at the bottom of things.

Don't Wake Me Up, I'm Having a Good Dream: Do You Require Sexual Fantasies to Become Aroused?

The place of sexual fantasies in a marriage is complicated. It makes ferreting out an anger problem from a more general and universal problem (sexual inhibition) a tall order. To discern anger, we first need to know something about the way most people feel about their fantasy life. Only then can we know the way anger affects our sexual imaginings.

Human beings possess the gift of imagination. This capacity allows for discovery and invention. It makes the new, the different possible. It makes life interesting. It can make sex a lot of fun—if only we would let it.

Shared sexual fantasies are often the greatest source of sexual arousal. This sort of playfulness, especially when couples have been married for years and have developed long-standing sexual habits ("We always have sex on Saturday night"; "I'm always on top") is especially important. They are ways in which the sexual vitality of a liaison is revived: Fantasies are a wake-up call to our sleeping hormones! The problem is that most people are loathe to unloose their sexual imagination in this or any other way. Most couples can't easily share the fantasy.

Couples may shun their sexual fantasy life for a variety of reasons, both personal and cultural; perhaps they are still laboring under the notion that sexual fantasies are tantamount to impure or unclean thoughts. It may make them feel guilty.

Perhaps you feel worried when you have a sexual thought that you regard as "peculiar" or "unnatural"; many people, for example, may feel quite frightened if they have sadistic sexual or homoerotic fantasies. Yet studies have shown time and time again that these kinds of fantasies are extremely common, if not ubiquitous and universal.

So, for a variety of reasons, some people put a lid on their deep, dark sexual imaginings and protest, "I *never* have sexual fantasies," while others get skittish and uncomfortable whenever thoughts of one cross their mind. Both have little to do with anger. Instead, the most telling aspect of sexual fantasies is not whether they do or don't exist or whether they do or don't disturb us, but *how they're used.*

For instance, if you find yourself immersed in fantasies that you don't care to share, this portends anger. If fantasies are yours alone and they keep you from being involved in sex with a spouse, this is problematic. Fantasies that serve to foster emotional removal may be a symptom of angry isolation.

This does not mean that during sex lovers are unentitled to private thoughts. Rather, it is the level of self-absorption that's telling. A preoccupation with yourself, a sexual detachment, a sense of isolation are the warning signs of fantasies suggestive of angry sex.

Fantasies are also problematic when they serve as an indispensable diversion designed to overcome an absence of passion or arousal: We feel little excitement or attraction to our lover, and erotic daydreams are the only way to make sex palatable. Simply stated, anger is suspect if in order to make passionate love with our mate, we need to create a secret fantasy lover.

Barbara, who had been in an angry marriage for a good many years, found this to be true about herself. Her sexual inventions were not a mental aphrodisiac she willingly added to "spice up" her lovemaking. Instead, they were an antidote to the sexual aversion she felt toward her husband:

"There was a point in my relationship with Bob that the only way I could bring myself to have sex with him was to dream up some fantasy. Sometimes I was a whore who was forced to do it; other times I was myself but I imagined Bob was Mel Gibson or some other actor.

"What I dreamed up really didn't matter. It just had to be something to block Bob out in my mind. In fact, if something broke my mood, I just felt myself turn to stone."

If your mental sex life is used to erase the reality of your partner, if it is the necessary counter agent to offset ill-will, it may be anger that you are really trying to eradicate.

*Thank You, I'd Rather Do It Myself: Does
Masturbation Replace Sexual Intercourse?*

If the place of sexual fantasies in a marriage is complicated, the place of masturbation is even more so. Masturbation has a complex cultural and social legacy. It makes distinguishing the problem of anger from the general and ubiquitous problem—guilt—quite a challenge. And it becomes imperative to know something of the role of guilt if we are to know the part anger plays in masturbation.

David Cole Gordon, writing on masturbation, entitled his work *Self Love.*[5] The history of our attitudes on sexual self-stimulation might suggest a more apt title—*Self-Loathing.* Traditionally, urges for autoerotic stimulation have been regarded as signs of aberration. In the early part of the century, psychiatrists meeting at the Vienna Psychoanalytic Society debated the "toxic effects" of masturbation.

The level of apprehension is perhaps best illustrated by a finding cited by the psychologist Dr. Louise Kaplan. In 1895, one sexual "reformer" had acquired three million letters from men and boys fighting a "losing battle" with masturbation; one told of carrying a strong cord in his pocket, "awaiting the blessed day when he might muster the courage to hang himself."[6]

These attitudes provide us with a not surprising legacy: Many people still feel a tremendous conflict about autoerotic urges. And marriage doesn't make these reservations disappear; even when it's "okay" to caress our partner, it still may not feel "okay" to caress ourselves. So, while there are partnerships where masturbation is part of a shared erotic life ("I get so excited watching my wife/ husband masturbate"; "When my husband manually stimulates my clitoris, I have my best orgasms"), many people are dogged by quite different feelings.

They may be worried that the interest and urge to masturbate is a bad sign. They may jump to the conclusion—especially if they masturbate alone—"I must be in an unhappy marriage." (This anxiety may be more pronounced for women since there is still, to date, a greater reluctance to address female masturbation; for example, even though studies suggest that many women masturbate, the research literature is dominated almost entirely by information on the male experience.) It's an unwarranted conclusion. Studies indicate that about 70 percent of *all* married people masturbate (though the literature suggests men do it probably twice as often as women). Masturbation isn't just "normal"; it's the norm. Everybody's doing it! Clearly, engaging in solo sex is not a sign of an angry marriage.[7]

So, if masturbating even when a partner is available is not a marker of anger, what is? When masturbation spells *RELIEF*, it may also spell trouble. If masturbation is tied to an urgent need to discharge tension, anger may be at work. Perhaps you "just have to masturbate" in order to wind down, to make yourself feel relaxed. When masturbation becomes an indispensable habit at the "end of a hard day," your level of tension may actually be related to the presence of unbearable frustration in your marriage. This is especially likely to be the case if you find greater solace in masturbation than in making love.

Anger is afoot if masturbation becomes a way of fostering isolation. An angry spouse may use masturbation not only as a way to withdraw from a partner but as a gesture that indicates to a partner, You don't have what it takes to keep me sexually satisfied.

In her psychotherapy group, Julie explained the way in which she dismissed her husband, Howard, through masturbation:

"I got addicted to my vibrator. Using it made me reach orgasm in a way I never could with my husband. He would try, but I couldn't get involved because I knew I could satisfy myself more pleasurably on my own.

"It really hit home how bad things had gotten when I made this sick joke to my best friend that in a divorce Howard could get the house and car as long as I got the vibrator. I shocked myself at my callousness.

"Once I understood how rejecting I was, I could start to talk about it. But, believe me, I had to wean myself off the vibrator. At some point I wondered if I could do it."

You may never suffer Julie's "addiction" to masturbation. However, in your own, more modified ways, you may use masturbation as a substitute for your spouse. If you do, and likewise convey the sense that you have found a better sexual alternative on your own, you might actually be transmitting your animosity and your anger.

There are other ways to discover if masturbation is something other than an erotic alternative. Lovers can unwittingly use masturbation in an angry battle against surrender: Sexual self-arousal becomes a way of declaring, "My body is under my control." Self-gratification then notifies a spouse that it is we, not they, who are in charge of how, where, and when we will take our pleasure. If stridency accompanies self-love, consider the hidden agenda—masturbation may be an expression of angry defiance.

In good marriages, masturbation takes on an entirely different quality. Self-stimulation may be the way partners excite themselves and each other, thereby intensifying rather than diluting their sexual union. Masturbation becomes foreplay rather than an end in itself. For happily married couples, masturbation may well be a part of a reciprocal process of mutual arousal, or it may be as neutral as an opportunity to partake of a private sexual act that provides intense pleasure. Both do not suggest anger. Rather, the presence of anger is implicated when masturbation ceases to leave room, in our sexual lives, for mutual, requited love. When masturbation cuts a partner out of your life, anger is factored into the picture.

*Ho-hum: Are You Sexually Bored?

Martha recalled her sex life during her seven-year marriage to Aaron. It wasn't simply that they had sex less often in their seventh year of marriage than their first (that, as we've suggested earlier, is par for the course and doesn't implicate anger); it was that lovemaking became so routine:

"We just got *bored*. We still had sex. But it was just so-so."

The root of sexual boredom is invariably anger—anger that is very much part of a marriage but that needs to remain unexpressed (this condition is something we will deal with in detail when we explore covertly angry marriages). A couple who are angry but have the need to suppress their anger invariably find that all intense emotions are stifled. Passion is blunted and eroticism numbed whenever couples have anger that they must quell. Angry couples who need to turn down their angry fires turn down their sexual heat as well. Therefore, if sex has become ho-hum, dull, lackluster, and unimaginative, anger is surely the culprit. And sometimes, the boredom that hides a couple's anger can become so great they stop having sex altogether.

This problem has even caught the attention of the media. In an effort to secure ratings, a well-known national TV talk show went for an unexpected twist. They bet their Nielsens on a show called "The New Celibacy." Not premarital but marital celibacy! These were "happy" couples who had "wonderful" marriages—but no sex. Sexless marriage may do well in the ratings; however, under most circumstances it's not a recipe for marital bliss.

In fact, abstinence is more likely to be a sign of a listless marriage—a marriage lacking in vitality, energy, spirit—than an amiable one. The most common cause for an emotionally and sexually barren marriage is all too often anger. It may not seem to follow that a complete absence of sexual energy equals the presence of anger, but psychologically it does. (We will be exploring this phenomenon in greater detail later.) Even if at this moment it isn't entirely clear how this is so, the fact is that if you are a celibate married person you are also very likely an angry one.

*But We Had Great Sex Last Night: Is Sex the Only Good Thing About Your Marriage?

"You know for a long time I didn't know I was in an angry marriage, until one day I realized the only place we got along was in bed."

These are the words of Ruth, a fifty-year-old woman who was in an angry marriage for more years than she'd like to remember. Her sense of disbelief that she could have missed the obvious signs still bewilders her.

Sometimes sex is the glue that holds an angry marriage in place. Sometimes we use it to repair the damage anger creates in our daily lives together. Good sex may ironically keep us from feeling we are in a bad marriage. It may provide a needed rationale—"I can't really be angry at my lover; look how good our sex life is."

How can you break through this need to deny? How can you catch on to the fact that your seemingly "good" sex life is really "bad" news when it comes to anger? There are many clues: If bed is the only place you touch; if your only contact is sexual contact; if the only time you have time for one another is in bed—and that's it—you may be in the throes of angry sex. If you make love after you argue—but don't apologize, resolve the problem, or act kinder to one another as a result of your lovemaking—it indicates a problem.

Sex can be a wonderful way to reunite after an emotional rift. It can be restorative to a partnership. But when we are angry, sex doesn't have that power to regenerate goodwill.

If bed is the only place where you are *not* dissatisfied with each other, you may be using this as a last resistance to letting the full force of your angry feelings become known. In this way sex becomes a protective device, shielding you from realizations about anger you might be loathe to confront. When bed is the only place in which you don't feel frustration, sex may indeed be working in the service of anger.

What You Know and Where You Go from Here

Are you in an angry marriage? At this point you must have a fairly good idea as to whether you can indeed call yours an angry union. By this time you have answers to many questions—questions about your marital goodwill: Does he bring me flowers anymore? Do I look into her eyes? Do we talk—really talk? Questions about your sexual relationship: Do we share sexual fantasies? Are we faithful? Is my body a gift I happily and generously give to my lover? These are just a few of the many queries for which you now have your own private and personal responses and understandings. And what you know—what you must know, if you have been honest and candid with yourself—is whether yours is indeed an angry marriage.

Where can we go from here? Now that you have answered the most general question, "Am I in an angry marriage?," we can begin to get considerably more specific. Why are you in an angry marriage? Why and how does it intrude on your love? Are you overtly or covertly angry? Venter, provoker, enactor, symbolizer, displacer, suppresser—which angry lovestyle is yours? In order to begin to answer these questions, and to understand what the answers are telling you about anger in your marriage, we need to investigate the structure of marriage itself, the anatomy of a marriage. That's what we'll do right now.

THE ANATOMY OF A MARRIAGE

C ouples stay victims of their anger because they do not know their own needs. This is why angry lovestyles have such a seemingly intractable hold over people. They can't break out of their self-defeating and self-perpetuating patterns because they don't have insight into just what their struggles are really all about. Why? As you will discover, in every angry marriage, no matter the particular style, *needs are hidden.*

Buried in the subconscious, emotional needs are a continual source of frustration and disappointment. Obviously, the task is to bring these hidden needs of an angry marriage to light. How can this be done? By investigating and unraveling the *structure* of marriage through the use of insight.

The Anatomy of a Marriage

Buried needs create a marriage splintered into three distinct, separate, and, in a sense, warring levels:

- *The actual marriage:* This is the marriage as it appears to you consciously—the marriage we "think" we're in. The one in which all the characteristics of a particular angry lovestyle are manifested and expressed. Your actual marriage is your everyday life together—the one about which you gripe!
- *The invisible marriage:* This is the marriage beneath the surface— the marriage involving unconscious and therefore hidden needs. The marriage where your conflicts over these hidden needs invisibly reside, trapping you in an angry cycle.
- *The primal marriage:* This is the "source marriage"—the childhood relationships that you unwittingly bring into your current marriage, giving rise to your unconscious needs, and setting in place the self-defeating patterns in your current relationship. This is the emotional legacy of your very first love relationship intruding unconsciously, yet powerfully, on your present union.

This concept of the three tiers of an angry marriage—actual, invisible, primal—is so central, it bears repeating: Unconscious (and therefore, hidden and unmet) needs fracture a marriage into three different and conflicting divisions. We think we are in one marriage, but unwittingly we are living out three at once.

This split, this division, within a lovelife is the core problem of an angry marriage. The way out is to heal this rupture and to have one and only one union—an *adult marriage*. Insight, as you will see, makes this possible. Insight, through which unconscious thoughts and motives become visible, lucid, and comprehensible, is the force that eventually unifies a three-tiered marriage into one truly adult union. Through insight, buried needs are uncovered, and by uncovering them an extraordinary opportunity is created—unmet needs once unearthed can be fulfilled. *And if needs are met, the cycle of angry frustration ceases to exist.*

Through this remarkable transformation, a primal, source marriage ceases to dominate a current union. In effect, the past loses its power to govern the present, and the division between actual and invisible marriage comes to an end. By this process of self-discovery all three tiers are melded peacefully into one. There is no missing piece! Insight makes this unification possible. Insight becomes the way out of an angry marriage into a happier and more joyful adult union.

The Actual Marriage: What's Your Style?

Actually, each person in an angry marriage is well acquainted with his or her actual marriage. This is the marriage that you see, that you live through with each other. This is the marriage you know, the one you can describe. This is the one where all the characteristics of an angry lovestyle are expressed—no matter the style. While every style will be detailed later, we can take a brief look at each of these angry lovestyles as they typically look in day-to-day life together. First are the actual marriages of those couples falling prey to obvious but ineffective anger—venters and provokers.

AN ACTUAL MARRIAGE: VENTER-STYLE

Venters are couples who fit the stereotypical image—"God, those two are an angry couple!" Venters may feel angry, look angry, think angry, and/or act angry. They harp on each other's weaknesses, shortcomings, foibles, and failings, and are driven to distraction by them. Open hostility, enmity, antagonism, animosity, belligerence are part of the picture. They battle; some declare all-out war, others skirmish intermittently. Conflict abounds—often over nothing or with little apparent provocation. Lashing out is a venter's modus operandi. Arguments accelerate and intensify: slamming doors is within the well-worn repertoire. Fights accomplish nothing except to fuel mutual ire. Nothing is resolved or worked out. Instead, they get worked up—over and over and over again.

AN ACTUAL MARRIAGE: PROVOKER-STYLE

Provokers are couples where anger is *not* reciprocal; only one spouse is fuming, while the other may be anything from perplexed ("What's all the fuss about?") to defensive ("Why are you so pissed? I didn't do anything") to detached ("Oh . . . you were angry with me? I did something wrong?"). While a venter might explode, the angry provoker is probably doing a slow burn. In this provoker partnership, the angry spouse feels in turn exasperated, annoyed, bothered, harassed, nervous, tired, vexed, peeved, and aggravated. The angry spouse may not yell and scream but she (or he) probably mutters, grinds her teeth, and feels her blood pressure rising. She feels provoked to anger by her spouse and it wears her out. For example, one partner procrastinates while the other feels slowly driven crazy. Like a venter, a provoker's ire is futile and fruitless, never making things change or get any better.

Enactors to Displacers: More Actual Marriages

In their actual marriages, venters and provokers are obviously angry—albeit ineffectively and even destructively. But as you've already learned, not every angry marriage has the look and feel of an angry liaison. Some angry couples dare not get angry at all! The mechanisms that accomplish this feat may vary. Sometimes anger is transformed or disguised, obscured or concealed; sometimes it is denied, ignored, or forgotten. No matter the unconscious psychological tactic employed, the net effect is the same—anger is hidden, and destructive. Enactors, displacers, symbolizers, and suppressers are the four angry lovestyles that keep anger well camouflaged in four very different ways. Their actual marriages won't look angry, but they may typically look like this.

AN ACTUAL MARRIAGE: ENACTOR-STYLE

Enactors don't look mad. They may appear drunk, high, financially unreliable, obese, unfaithful, overworked, or busy, but they don't look angry. Enactors substitute action for anger in their marriage. Rather than letting themselves feel their mounting frustration, they seek release. Enactors dissipate the buildup of angry tension by "doing." Alcohol, drugs, gambling, food, affairs, and even work may be the activity that spells relief.

As long as enactors find ways of gratifying and supplying themselves outside marriage, angry frustration on the homefront is kept at bay. Enactors are expert at finding ways to feel "good" outside marriage so the "bad" feelings—read frustration—don't come home to roost.

AN ACTUAL MARRIAGE: DISPLACER-STYLE

Displacers are no strangers to anger. They get irate, indignant, and feel animus on a regular basis—but not toward each other. Displacers always find a target for their wrath, but it's never either of them. They displace their anger onto someone or something else. A mother-in-law is a classic displacer target. But a "rotten" boss, a "disloyal" friend, a "good-for-nothing" sibling, a "mean" parent are also scapegoats of choice. Sometimes an inanimate object, like a cause, may also do the trick of redirecting anger.

For displacers, it's as if a common enemy keeps them from having to risk a faceoff with each other. Displacers bury anger under a heavy mantle—"It's us against the world." Locked in combat against outsiders, displacers lock out anger from their union.

AN ACTUAL MARRIAGE: SYMBOLIZER-STYLE

Symbolizers don't get mad, they get maladies. Symbolizers are couples who unwittingly find ways of expressing their anger symbolically rather than directly. Anger gets disguised; it appears in other forms. Often physical ailments become representations of anger (typically, one partner actually gets ill and the other becomes the "nurse"). Migraine headache, vertigo and a bad back, rashes and runs, fatigue and fainting, aches and unidentified ailments are some of the symptoms commonly (albeit unconsciously) chosen by this couple. Symbolizers often become so wrapped up in the struggles against these afflictions and ailments—one partner is so "busy" being infirm while the other is so "busy" running the infirmary—

that there is no time or attention focused on much else, especially anger.

AN ACTUAL MARRIAGE: SUPPRESSER-STYLE

Suppressers are the very last people on earth you'd think of as angry—and they'd share this view of themselves as well—because suppressers don't have the slightest clue that they're mad! A suppresser doesn't argue or fight and may find little in a marriage to cause outward dissension. If things get rough, a suppresser confronts situations that might realistically provoke anger by swallowing—hard.

Suppressers are silent sufferers. They may clam up, cry, become self-critical, or even depressed, but they don't become overtly angry. If ever anger is aroused, suppressers keep it under wraps in order to avoid confrontation. Suppressers have an unwritten motto: "Avoid conflict. Peace at any price." Suppressers give up their anger and pay the ultimate price—they lose their sense of self.

Actual Marriage Continued: What's Your Complaint?

On a day-to-day basis these actual marriages are diverse, but they do have something in common: discontent. Whether overt or hidden, anger does its damage. Every one of these actual marriages, from venter to suppresser, has its fair share of complaints (and these are as varied as the styles they reflect). Therefore, there is another way to think about an actual marriage, no matter the particular style: Our actual marriage is the one about which we can and do often complain (though in several of the covert styles our complaints may not always be about each other). Perhaps your complaints include some of the following:

> "All our married life we've both had the worst run of luck with lousy bosses."
>
> "He never finishes anything he begins; it drives me to distraction."

"I can't stand the fact that she never pays the bills."

"He never talks to me."

"Gosh, we do miss a lot of things since his headaches have flared up."

"We don't get a chance to make love because we're so busy."

"We both agree—the biggest problem in our marriage is his mother."

"His jealousy is driving me crazy."

"We don't go out much. I guess we're just the stay-at-home type."

"She's always pitting me against the kids."

"Wherever we've moved since we've gotten married, the neighbors are always impossible."

"She doesn't listen to a thing I say."

"He drinks too much."

Actually, angry couples (whether venter, provoker, enactor, symbolizer, displacer, or suppresser) can describe their actual marriage by listing the grievances they harbor about each other and their relationship. In a sense your actual marriage is the detailed response to the question: What's wrong with my marriage and my partner?[1]

The Invisible Marriage: Decoding Complaints

When couples are caught in an angry cycle, relationships stay on this level—mired in discontent. They engage over and over again in their litany of mutual complaints, but they never get anywhere close to making things better. It's only when couples can move deeper, beyond this surface level of their actual marriage to discover their invisible marriage—the level at which hidden needs (the real yet invisible source of angry marital conflict) reside—that they stand a chance of making things change.

And the way to do this is to *decode complaints;* that is, to look at grievances and analyze them in order to interpret what they reveal about a person's inner, unconscious emotional life. Remarkably, *in every complaint lies a clue to unconscious feelings!* Every complaint, once analyzed, sheds light on hidden needs and makes them visible. Specifically, every complaint issued by a wife can shed light on a husband's unrevealed inner life (his hidden need), and likewise every complaint voiced by a husband can illuminate a wife's unconscious thoughts and feelings (her hidden need). And with assistance every person in an angry marriage can become an expert at this psychological decoding system.[2] In fact, throughout this book, as each of the six styles is profiled, you'll have repeated opportunities to hone your own decoding skills.

To introduce this novel method, we can first look at the actual and tumultuous marriage of two venters, Abby and Brian. Initially, Abby (joined later by Brian) began this process of decoding their respective complaints and in turn making their invisible marriage come clearly into view.

LITTLE THINGS MEAN A LOT: THE MAKING OF A DECODING EXPERT

Some years ago, Abby had been in treatment for about six months when she came into my office completely furious with her husband.[3]

"It's been another one of those wonderful summer weekends," she announced sarcastically.

"Brian just didn't let up. All weekend it was, 'Abigail, do this! Abigail, don't do that!' "

Her sense of indignation was palpable. It grew as she went on.

"Can you imagine? We're in bed Saturday night. It's ninety degrees outside. He gets up. Turns off the air conditioner—of course, he doesn't ask me how I feel about it (not that he ever does)—and gets back into bed.

"I start to say something, and the king himself announces, 'You know, Abigail, you're really impossible. How many times have I told you? You know I can't fall asleep with the racket this thing makes.'

"How do you like that? *I'm* impossible! I'm telling you, Dr. Maslin, I know it sounds like nothing, but it makes me so furious I could scream.

"I just don't think you understand how impossible Brian can be at times."

Could I understand such disputes as the "air-conditioning battle"? Perhaps the limits of imagination actually lay with Abby, not me. In our weekly summer excursions to our country home, my husband and I often battled it out over ambient temperature: Unlike Abby and Brian, our battleground was usually the car, not the bedroom.

Despite the change of venue, our grievances against one another were uncomfortably similar.[4] They were similar, but what were they really about? Was Abby in my office twice a week spending a fair share of her hard-earned income so that I could get the temperature in her bedroom adjusted to her liking? Obviously not. But this was her actual marriage that Abby was describing so heatedly. One in which fights about air-conditioning, favorite television programs, or guests for a dinner party could all become bones of contention.

Abby and I embarked on this process of making her and Brian—who eventually joined us in our sessions—into "experts" on themselves and their marriage.[5] Actually, by decoding their complaints around the air-conditioning battle, we were able to realize that for Abby it was indeed a dispute about climate control—with the emphasis on the word "control."

For Abby, this angry fight between two venters (over the months of working with Abby and Brian it became evident that this was the style of their actual marriage; they most often managed their anger by letting it "all hang out") was actually very much about feeling that Brian made the rules and thus, as far as she was concerned, ran the show. Abby was fighting Brian because she felt he was trying to dominate her, and *that,* not the ambient temperature of their bedroom, was what enraged her.

For Abby, Brian wasn't a man who found the noise of an air conditioner disturbing. Rather, he felt like a man who wanted to overpower her. How did we come to understand this? We decoded Brian's complaint about Abby (remember our model: his complaint = her need). For example, a chief complaint of Brian's was Abby's intense reaction to things he did impulsively:

"I'm not allowed to do anything without asking Abby's 'permission.' If I'm spontaneous, or if I don't—heaven forbid—consult my wife before I do something, I'm some inconsiderate brute. ("The Great Dictator" and "King Brian" are two of the kinder nicknames my wife has for me.) The AC is a perfect example of what I'm complaining about. Abby wants a written announcement before I can even turn off the blasted machine!"

Decoded, Brian's complaint enabled us to appreciate that to his wife, silence was not just silence. For Abby, action without consultation was nothing less than complete disregard. Abby read Brian's unannounced actions as, "I want what I want and to hell with you!" In the face of this, Abby felt as if Brian was saying, "Your feelings don't count." In turn, Abby could only react with angry hurt.

To arrive at this sort of understanding, we mined everything we could about Brian's complaints. We paid close attention to Abby's language and attitude, for example. Why did she sarcastically call Brian "King Brian" or "The Great Dictator"? We deduced what these terms might reveal about Abby's emotions: Abby felt very violated. The derision Brian heard in Abby's tone suggested his wife regarded Brian as a mean "ruler." And again it strongly offered a clue to Abby's unconscious emotional raw spot—a *hidden need* to fight domination and control.

Decoding Abby's complaints about Brian led us in a different direction (remember the system: analyze a wife's complaints to reveal her husband's need). For example, Abby griped about her husband's apparent resentment of her strong-willed character:

"I speak my mind and all I hear is how selfish I am: I only do what's good for me. The air conditioner is the perfect example of what I'm complaining about. Because I think it's better for the two of us to sleep coolly, even with a little noise—and I speak up about it—I'm a miserable witch."

What clue could we unearth about Brian's hidden need? For Brian, Abby was not simply voicing a decision about the best way to achieve a comfortable night's sleep. Rather, Brian felt that Abby ignored his feelings, that his requests always fell on deaf ears ("She knows I can't bear the noise!"). Brian's conclusion: Abby didn't listen to him. The fact that Abby asserted herself meant one and only one thing: "Abby's not concerned about my welfare." And that hurt and angered Brian.

In the end we came to understand that Brian had his own *hidden need*—a desperate need to count, to matter, to be important to the person he loved. It left him acutely sensitive to the possibility that his feelings weren't being taken into consideration. Remarkably, a fight over an air conditioner was actually an *invisible conflict* over Abby and Brian's deepest vulnerabilities, their respective hidden needs (Abbey's—to fight domination; and Brian's—to matter, to count). To their mutual surprise, Abby and Brian discovered that each of them was much, much more sensitive and vulnerable then they ever thought. After all, two venters in the heat of battle rarely appear fragile!

Through our decoding, Brian and Abby became increasingly aware of how they read and misread each other, and how the things over which they seemed to argue masked their real emotional natures. They discovered, poignantly, that sometimes an air conditioner is not just an air conditioner.

The process of decoding complaints made Brian and Abby aware of their hidden feelings—respectively, the need to fight control and the need to be listened to—which were part and parcel of their invisible marriage. Together they made their invisible marriage visible!

The effect of this discovery was not some immediate quick fix to their conflict; but there was an extraordinary transformation, one that enabled them to find a *lasting solution* to their angry marriage. They could begin to express their feelings and their needs rather than hurl accusations at one another. And this made for them, as it can make for all of us, an enormous difference. It enables us to establish a *new language of love* based on insight and empathy, and free of conflict and frustration. And best of all, it makes it possible to restore our sense of loving goodwill.

As you make your invisible marriage visible, you are in fact *combining* your actual and invisible marriage so that there is no division between them. You allow yourselves to see, for the first time, what underlies the day-to-day anger you feel in your relationship. Your marriage ceases to be fragmented by your ire.

You become better partners for and to each other—more empathetic, sensitive, and responsive. But a crucial question remains. If you have these hidden needs, how did they come to be, and why on earth do they exert such an enormous influence on your lives?

This is not an academic question. Insight can only achieve its full measure of power and meaning when couples learn where and how hidden needs took root. Hidden needs are not just another aspect of personality. Needs are part and parcel of a person's basic emotional fabric. They are not casual or incidental to well-being. They are at our core.

Every need and the self-defeating pattern it sets in motion has its roots in an individual's past. To be effective, insight must be informed by these truths about ourselves. For it is only these truths, often very painful truths, of and about the past that make change possible and enduring.

The Primal Marriage: Where It All Began

Why did Abby acquire a need not to be controlled and Brian a desperate need to count? Why were these their particular, albeit hidden, sensitivities?

Brian may be Abby's one and only husband, and likewise Abby may be Brian's one and only one wife, but what they don't know is that this is *not* their first marriage. And here, they are not alone— *we've all been married before!*

Our first partnership, our first union of love, "for better or for worse, in sickness or in health," was the one we shared with our parents. *Our parents are our first partners.* This first alliance upon which our very life depended was our *primal marriage.* This relationship is the "source marriage," the one out of which hidden needs arise. Hidden needs are rooted in the primal marriage.

Hidden needs are the excess baggage which individuals unwittingly carry into marriage. They are the imprint of the past that intrudes on a couple's current life together. They are the residue of the disappointments and frustrations of a person's first, original "marriage." *It is here in this primal marriage that self-defeating anger originates.*

In Abby's case, a look at her primal marriage helps us understand where her original (primal) anger came from. Abby had an extremely intrusive mother. Unsuccessful and disappointed in her own life, Abby's mother threw herself into the lives of her children, especially her eldest daughter—Abby. Always conveying that her intervention was only for Abby's "own good," her mother continually ignored the possibility that Abby was a person in her own right. Abby's need not to be controlled and her anger over this are the legacy of this overbearing relationship.

And Brian's "first" marriage, what was it all about? Brian's parents were a self-involved couple. They had Brian in much the same way they acquired everything else they had, the good job, the right address, because it elevated their status.

From the beginning, Brian as a person held little interest for them. He was often left for extended periods of time, even when he was a very small child, in the care of nannies. School was a series of painful humiliations: Brian was often the only child whose parents couldn't make it to school events. In a word, Brian didn't count. And it is the residue of this angry pain he carries with him into his marriage with Abby.

What is remarkable about their respective needs is how these become tinder for their angry fire at one another. In fact, for all of us in this predicament it is the interplay of our needs that fuels an angry marriage. This is the most extraordinary legacy of a primal marriage and original unresolved anger—*we see our spouse through the prism of our primal need.* How so?

Our needs affect our personality and color the way we view our world and our marriage. Abby's need not to be controlled makes her wary, standoffish. After all, she's afraid to be close; she'll be under someone's thumb. And Brian unwittingly reads this behavior through *his* need: "Abby is not involved with me, therefore I mustn't count." And, of course, it makes him angry.

And how does Abby unwittingly "read" Brian? Brian's neediness makes him demand attention ("You should know a quiet room is important to me!"). But Abby's unconscious sensitivity lets her experience this *only* from the viewpoint of her need. "If someone is demanding, they *must* want to control me. And I'll have none of that!" And, of course, it makes her angry.

This is the trap set by hidden needs. They make us see new experiences through old pain. They make us replay old scenarios of a primal marriage with a new character—our spouse. They keep our anger spinning on and on.

A MATCH MADE IN NEUROTIC HEAVEN: YOU PUSH MY BUTTONS, I'LL PULL YOUR STRINGS

Abby and Brian, as with any couple in an angry alliance, unwittingly play out their past primal marriage in their present relationship, casting one another as the villain—and they don't even know it! How does this happen? Is it simply fate or bad luck that brings these two people or any two people into this predicament? No. Absolutely not. The startling thing about intimate relationships is that we manage always to find a person who fits squarely (and frustratingly) into our unconscious needs! (Of course, let's not forget to say that couples are also attracted for plenty of the right reasons, but these don't become grist for our angry marriages; they become the glue that keeps us together in spite of our ire.)[6]

In fact, unconsciously, Brian and Abby—as with all couples in an angry marriage—were attracted to each other precisely because of this "perfect," albeit painful, neurotic fit.

Think about it. Who did Abby marry? An easygoing or Milquetoast kind of guy ("Yes, dear, you want the AC on? Of course, your wish is my command") with whom the issue of control wouldn't come in to play? No. She married "King" Brian, a man more inclined to snap off the AC than follow Abby's lead or cater to her wishes and whims. And Brian? Did he marry a compliant woman who was, for example, so entirely devoted to him that he might never, for a moment, doubt just how much he counted? No. Strong-willed Abby was his choice. A woman who could make him feel as if he didn't matter. Abby is a woman who can push Brian's unconscious buttons, and Brian is a man adept at pulling Abby's unconscious strings. Brian and Abby may have fallen in love, but they also found each other because they fell within the range of personalities that would *remind them of significant people in their primal past.*

This is the paradox: We marry people who we undoubtedly cherish but who also serve to fuel the angry fires of our past. We seem to carry around an unwitting psychological sonar that leads us to the person who will make life emotionally difficult and trying in ways that remind us of the original frustrations of our primal marriage.

Why is this true? Adults who have experienced primal anger and pain try to relive the past as if each encounter in their marriage is an opportunity to correct old primal disappointments. Replaying the past in the present is a way in which people try to "do over" a primal experience in order to try to make it come out right. It is as if the child in them is secretly saying, "This time I'll get it right. I'll prove the past wrong. I'll show myself and the world that I was indeed loved the way I needed to be loved." The human compulsion (albeit unconsciously) is to rewrite personal emotional history in the hope that this time it will have a happy ending (for Brian, this time my parents/wife will treat me as if I mean the world to them; for Abby, this time my mother/husband will respect my autonomy).

Regrettably, while people have this compulsion to try and repeat the past in an improved version, they instead continue to relive earlier failures. For all their efforts to do it over and do it better, Abby and Brian find themselves mired in the same old frustrations over and over again. Things aren't better or different. The same disappointing pattern spins on. Sadly, this makes sense. After all, Brian and Abby don't have any alternative ways of responding to their frustrations except the same old ways that didn't work in their respective primal marriages. They have only the unsuccessful primal past on which to model their behavior.

And this is the problem that anyone in an angry marriage encounters: We are unwittingly compelled to do things over but, unfortunately, because of the grip of the past, we don't have the equipment to make things change. We only know and are best acquainted with the wrong and ineffectual ways to relate (for example, Abby and Brian, two venters, can only lash out at each other when they are disappointed and hurt). We want so much for things to be better and different, and yet, handicapped by our primal past, we find in our own marriages the same self-defeating cycle of anger that plagued us as children.

Though powerful and compelling, this repetition compulsion is not immutable. Things *can* change. We can be different; we can break the yoke of the primal past; we can heal our own wounds. As you will continue to see, insight makes this possible—that is very much the heart of this book.

An Adult Marriage: New Ways of Relating Through Words

The past, when we are unable to acknowledge it, can exert an extraordinary power over our present lives. It keeps us in the dark when it comes to understanding our true emotional nature. It keeps a marriage bogged down in archaic anger, fragmenting a partnership into these three distinct levels: *actual, invisible,* and *primal.*

People can truly change themselves and their relationship only when they can stop splitting their marriage into three discrete layers. What a husband and wife need is to be partners in an *adult marriage.* This is a marriage where insight has been used in the service of revealing true but hidden needs. And in this way a marriage can be transformed.

When Abby and Brian realized what their respective primal marriages were all about, and how they were affected by them, and more importantly, began to share their insights with one another, it was as if their marriage became a whole new relationship. The problems they thought they were battling turned out to be only the barest indications of something much deeper that needed to be addressed. They could mutually acknowledge that an air conditioner was not just an air conditioner!

As they continued to see how old patterns affected them today, they began to realize they had an option—as we all do—*not to give in to those old primal patterns.* They learned, as every man and woman in an angry union might learn, that we have the option to "civilize" the primal anger that once threatened to overwhelm us. We all have the capacity and power to develop new and mature ways of relating to someone we love.

How? By talking to each other and sharing insights, by continually working on a *new language of love* (something to which we will devote a good deal of time). Abby learned to give words to the anger and the pain. And *the words* are extraordinarily empowering; she can now control her destructive venting and instead tell Brian how she feels. She can let Brian know *with words* that she is afraid to get close, "scared that if I give you some of me, you will want more and more, like my mother did." Abby can tell Brian that she needs to assert "my boundaries," not because Brian doesn't matter but because Abby, given her primal marriage, needs that kind of breathing room.

And Brian? He has come to a point where he can find *the words* to express his vulnerabilities. If and when Brian feels disregarded, he can tell Abby that he feels overlooked and that he needs her assertiveness to be tempered by acknowledgment of his feelings.

And *the words* have made an extraordinary difference. For example, Brian doesn't get hurt so readily by Abby anymore. As she relates: "I'm not about to say we have all the kinks worked out, but because Brian asks me directly to be more responsive, I find that I'm actually more inclined to do it. And because he's more direct, Brian's less demanding and it's easier for me to let down my guard. And then it snowballs, in a good way. I'm warmer to him and he feels he matters, so he's not nearly so tense as he used to be.

"I don't want to sound like a Pollyanna, but we're calmer and much nicer to each other because of what we know about ourselves and the fact that we can actually communicate this to each other. After so many years of getting on badly, I find it hard to believe that we could be so different."

The truth is that I am, like Abby, often amazed at the extraordinary possibility for change in an angry marriage. But I do believe it because I have seen it work. I have seen couples gain new insights that in turn lead to new behaviors and a return of goodwill in a marriage. I have seen insight and the skills of communication that develop from such self-awareness heal even the deepest and most painful wounds. I have seen the three splintered tiers of an angry marriage become forged into one unified and happy adult marriage. And Abby is no Pollyanna. She is just a woman no longer trapped in an angry marriage.

Finding the "Missing Piece"

Brian and Abby have found the "missing piece." They now have the tools to get what they want and need from each other. As a result, they have found a way out of an anger trap. Able to relinquish their destructive fury, they can reclaim their love and goodwill. This transformation of a marriage is not easy to come by, for anyone. We must uncover the pain. We must uncover the failures of our first primal marriage. We must admit to our conscious mind what our heart and soul know—*we were not loved the way we needed to be loved. We were not cared for the way we needed to be cared for.*

Resistance to confronting pain is not our only impediment to change; angry lovestyles are habit-forming! Venting, provoking, enacting, displacing, symbolizing, and suppressing are stubborn and persistent self-defeating patterns. These styles of managing marital anger tend to be stable—and tenacious. Just think of your own angry marriage. Aren't you a predictable pair? Of course you are. This is the simple fact—the human tendency is toward consistency.[7]

From reluctance to touch the primal pain to feeling comfortable with old emotional habits, there are indeed many reasons to stay snared in the deadlock of an angry union. Yet once we have the courage to challenge ourselves, the differences can be dramatic. Warring couples like Abby and Brian can create marriages filled with tranquillity and peace. And, by contrast, couples who have spent a lifetime suppressing anger can see the sparks fly as a new vitality enlivens their relationship—all because of new understandings, new ideas. Nothing transforms lives as powerfully as new ideas. The power of self-awareness and self-knowledge is the greatest and most potent agent of change in our emotional universe. It is a power I hope to awaken in you.

The past few chapters have, hopefully, enabled you to find out a bit more about the nature of your own angry marriage. The brief descriptions of the six angry lovestyles have probably gotten your wheels turning about which one is most like yours. What's the best way to find out more about your angry lovestyle?

Read through *all* of the categories in the following chapters, even if at first they may not seem to apply to you. Venters, provokers, enactors, displacers, symbolizers, and suppressers all have fascinating ways of expressing and squelching their anger—ways that are a mystery even to them. You may find, for example, in reading about provokers or symbolizers that you or your spouse are more like one of them than you thought you were. Or you may discover that your marriage is a composite of styles or a combination of needs. You may see yourself entirely in one of these angry couples or you may see your marriage as a variation on one of these themes.[8]

Remember, above all, the stories to be offered here aren't just the stories of other people. They are our own stories—as long as we allow them to be. Throughout this book you will be asked to get involved. Actually, through the marriages presented here the goal is for you to become not just a participant but an observer of your own marriage. This book is structured in a way that will make this likely. Remember, there will be a lot of questions; knowing this will bring you to the solutions that really work.

So, don't skip over anything. At the very least, reading about every angry lovestyle will increase your psychological awareness, your capacity to investigate what might be creating the deadlock in your angry marriage so that you can break it. And, as I've suggested, it may acquaint you with a lovestyle that you didn't realize you were employing. Think of every couple you meet as an opportunity to become more psychologically sophisticated about yourself and your marriage. Stay open: You'll be amazed how much you can learn.

VENTERS

We have all encountered venters—couples who handle their anger by letting it "all hang out." A venting duo, like Barbara and Stephen (or the Robertses, whom we met in the coat department), can make us cringe with embarrassment because they can't put a lid on their rage, even in public places and spaces:

"Stephen and I can get so worked up that we just don't give a damn where we are. I'm telling you, we've battled it out in airports, movie theaters—even church! Last week it was at our favorite restaurant, Nick and Toni's: The way we carried on, I'm not sure if we'll ever get a reservation there again!"

Not all venters go at it whenever and wherever. Some check the urge to unleash until the car ride home or for the hour when the kids are finally asleep. Simply because venters are uncontrolled toward each other doesn't mean that they let others in on their battles. There are even secretive venters, privately furious couples like Jack and Mildred, whose friends "would be shocked to know the kind of rows we can have." Couples can be venters even when it isn't that obvious to those who know them best.

Whether anger is on public display or not, it is visible and audible: Venters raise their voices, not just their blood pressures. It is also mutual. Anger is reciprocal, so inevitably it intensifies and escalates.

From Bad to Worse: Low Blows to Threats

Disagreements go from bad to worse and maybe even to horrible. As hostility increases, respectfulness decreases. What starts out as "just plain angry" soon antes up to epithets and insults. Language, manners, decorum are whittled away by wrath.

Grace is not a venter's strong suit. Venters resort to the low blow and cheap shot:

"No wonder your first wife left you!"

"You're just like your impossible mother!"

"This is exactly why you have no friends!"

"It's no surprise that you always get passed by for a promotion!"

Venters don't refrain from hitting below the belt; threats come easily. In the heat of battle, a venter might vow to call a divorce lawyer, a mother-in-law, or the IRS. Monetary as well as sexual threats are in the bag of tricks ("See if I'll give you another penny!"; "Maybe I just *will* have that affair").

Venters are quite adept at fighting dirty, not sticking to the argument at hand and instead, "kitchen-sinking" it, throwing in every gripe and grievance in recent and not so recent memory.

Possessing an extensive repertoire, venters blame and reproach, accuse and threaten, belittle and berate, slam doors and stalk out of them, display hot tempers and give cold shoulders, hurl insults and sometimes even objects! Basically, venters develop a certain expertise at not being nice to each other at all.

It Doesn't Take Much:
Chain Reaction

This is an angry lovestyle that certainly includes fighting—some may declare all-out war, while others skirmish intermittently. Often very little is needed to set anger off. A venter's fury lies right below the surface.

Mary was able to see this in her marriage to Tony, as she recalled a typical flair-up between them:

"He asked me a question and I didn't look up from the magazine I was reading. And that was all it took. He got so teed off, so insulted. Then I got angry back because it drives me crazy that he's so unreasonable. And the next thing I know we're not talking for the whole night—over something that was really nothing. We can both be so 'touchy.' "

Mary and Tony are not alone in this. Venters are often thin-skinned and hypersensitive to their partner. Venters have Velcro insides—everything sticks. They miss nothing, ignore little, and find it hard to let things pass without comment. This mutual sensitivity means that venters tend to be *very reactive* to one another. Typically, venters don't have good boundaries or a well-developed sense of privacy or separateness, so they tend to be couples who interfere in each other's personal affairs, are critical, intrusive, and vigilant of each other.

Something, anything is always grist for a venter's angry mill. As with Mary and Tony, venters may fight over the little stuff, but the "big" stuff can be grist as well. Money is an especially "good" source of "bad" feelings:

"Why must you have a new set of golf clubs?"

"Look at these telephone bills; another month like this and I'm disconnecting our number."

"You're being a skinflint. I can't live on a hundred dollars a week for my own expenses."

Jealousy is another very big venter issue. It may be about competition for sexual attention ("Why did you flirt with him/her at the party?") or a more general rivalry with anyone perceived to be making an impact ("Why do you listen to your mother, friend, Oprah . . . more than me?"). Work, school, and even the kids are potential competitors ("Why do you have to spend so much time on the kids' Halloween costumes?").

Agitated venters can't and don't see themselves as allies. This is especially evident in child rearing. Often, parenting isn't a collaboration but a contest. Venters may think each other flawed or even "bad" parents ("You're so hard/easy on the kids"; "That attitude of yours is going to ruin the children, for sure"). Venters take sides— with the children—against each other. Parenting disagreements aren't saved for private pillow talk. Instead, venters challenge each other in front of the children, often humiliating one another and undermining their respective roles.

Generally some gender differences prevail in the way venters carry on, particularly in ending confrontations. Men are more likely to walk, balk, or stalk; that is, they try to end the fighting by taking flight, which may mean a retreat into silence, not just into another room, the car, or the local bar and grill.

Typically, women prefer to go on. Female venters might want to "talk" (read "argue") on into the night while their husbands are ready to leave the bed and sleep on the couch. Often these gender differences make couples even angrier with one another ("She won't get off my case!" vs. "He just walks out on me in the middle of what I'm saying!"). In a phrase, male venters like to finish fights; female venters like to fight to the finish!

What's So Bad About Getting Mad?

When venters enter a room, courtesy may fly out the window. And, once steamed, venters are adept at justifying their anger as the only possible and therefore excusable reaction ("Anybody in their right mind would be angry"; "Listen, if he/she did this to you, you'd be furious, too!").

Confirmed in the belief that it's quite all right to battle it out, venters can even rationalize that "letting it all hang out" is good, honest, healthy. Frankly, this is a misguided notion. *Venting does not dissipate anger.* If anything, it does quite the opposite; the more you let it out, the harder it is to contain yourself. Ill-will mounts. It becomes harder to realign with your partner, to restore emotional equilibrium. Common sense can confirm this; it's harder to stop being angry once we've let it gain momentum. Scientific studies have even demonstrated the ill-effects of venting: the more people rant and rave at each other, the *worse* they feel about themselves and their marriage.

Venting is the problem, not the solution, to anger. But it is a problem that can be solved. Though, when I met Frieda and David, who had been venters for most of their thirteen-year relationship, it was hard to imagine that their angry marriage had a chance.

The Actual Marriage of Two Venters: Frieda and David

When Frieda arrived at my office on a December Monday, she had barely closed the door before she launched into her diatribe against David.

"Saturday night was a perfect example of how impossible he is. We were getting ready to leave for his magazine's Christmas party. He walks out of the bathroom, sees what I'm wearing, and snaps, 'You can't wear that!'

"I was *burning*. This always happens whenever we're getting ready to go somewhere; he finds something wrong with me at the last minute. I couldn't keep quiet. Why should I? So I said, 'What do you mean, I can't wear that? It's a beautiful dress. Fran helped me pick it out. She has great taste. You know she's the boutique's fashion coordinator.'

"Then he comes back at me, 'I don't care what she does for a living. Anyway, your 'dear friend' just wants you to spend money in her store. She'll tell you anything to make a sale. And boy, does she have a cash cow in you! You spend it as fast as I bring it home.'

"This is so typical, Mr. Know It All! He knows I can't stand it when he attacks me. I was furious and I let him have it.

" 'Go to your first Christmas party as the big-shot publisher without your wife and see how that feels!'

"That threat made him nervous."

As Frieda went on, it was clear that the evening didn't get any better. They drove to the party in a stony silence and plastered social smiles on their faces when they entered the ballroom of the hotel where the dinner dance was being held.

"I don't like these big affairs—David knows that. I'm not like him; he likes the splash of the show. He loves to 'work the room.' I'm more low key. I don't like crowds and I especially hate to sit among complete strangers. Wouldn't you know that I arrive to find that we aren't even sitting together and I don't know a soul at my whole table.

"David was responsible for the seating arrangements. I'm sure he did it to spite me. To top it off, during the dinner he barely came over to me.

"Oh, I forgot to tell you. Adding insult to injury, the first dance of the evening he asks one of his assistants, not me, of course. And the way he carried on with her! She's half his age and he's whispering into her ear and swirling her around as if he's Fred Astaire. It was humiliating.

"If I had more nerve I would have gotten up and left. But I would never hear the end of it, and when David's angry he can be scary. I just couldn't face it.

"We had some row in the car on the way home. I told him just what I thought of his stupid antics at dinner. He topped it off by telling me that I'm a selfish witch, consumed with jealousy, especially around women who are successful and have careers.

"Even at home we went on and on at each other. Then David shouted, 'I've had it. Just shut up already.' And of course, as usual, that was that. We're still not talking. Some party!"

DAVID'S STORY: "SO I SAID, THEN SHE SAID . . ."

Several weeks after the Christmas party disaster, David agreed to come to my office. He offered his "take" on their actual venter marriage.

"I care about Frieda, how she looks is part of that, but my interest is always of no concern to her. Her friend Fran's opinion carries more weight than mine. In fact, if I do express my opinion, I'm some kind of pushy tyrant for doing it. That's what happened the night of the Christmas party.

"Anything I do or say makes me mean, nasty, or offensive. It drives me crazy!

"What's more, Frieda's forever scrutinizing my behavior and I'm forever coming up short: I'm too loud, I tell too many jokes, I'm flirting. She looks down her nose at me. After every party I get her critique.

"And her holier-than-thou attitude extends to bed as well. According to my wife, I'm clumsy, inept. Her favorite tactic is to make fun of the fact that I went to Catholic school ("Sister Mary Ignatius must have taught you everything she knew"). I know Frieda was really popular before we got married. Believe me, she makes it clear as day that after marrying me, her sex life was all downhill.

"The most aggravating thing of all is how she's turned the kids against me. I feel like an outsider in my own home."

An Actual Marriage: Are You Venters?

Frieda and David have all the benchmarks of the angry lovestyle of two venters; do you? In their day-to-day life together, they are reactive, volatile, and extremely sensitive to one another. Their anger intensifies and escalates—snap . . . snarl . . . shout—to silent fury. And they seem to be top-notch experts on hurting each other. *This is their actual venter marriage.* The one they know—and wish they didn't! Can you see a version of your own actual marriage in theirs?

- They fight over "nothing" . . . what to wear to a party.
- They level cheap shots . . . Mr. Know It All . . . jealous of younger women's careers.
- They can't restore the emotional balance . . . the "dress" ruins the whole evening; they're still angry on Monday.
- They engage in classical venter issues . . . money and jealousy.

Could the style of their actual marriage be reminiscent of yours? Do you blame your spouse rather than admit it takes two to dance this angry tango?

If you hear yourselves making pronouncements about each other:

he's difficult . . . she's impossible
he's a bastard . . . she's a bitch
he's worthless . . . she's hopeless

become savvy to this ploy so characteristic of venters—that is, if you want your marriage to change for the better.

Decoding Our Complaints: Making the Invisible Marriage Visible

Where do you stand? Are you rooting for Frieda, feeling that her anger is "correct," that she damn well has the right to be angry? Do you share her complaints? David is an insensitive brute:

"How can she be married to such a boor?"
"Fooling around right under her nose—in public no less."
"Old-fashioned male chauvinist. How humiliating!"
"He's just as bad as my husband."

You might come to such conclusions—particularly if you harbor similar feelings about your own partner. Or can you see David's point of view? Maybe his anger is legitimate; maybe he isn't so bad after all. Perhaps you share David's grievances. You know Frieda can sound like she's hard to take:

"That woman probably never listens to anything her husband says."
"I can see her spending, spending, spending."
"She overreacts to a little criticism."
"She turns his own children against him."
"She's just as bad as my wife."

Conceivably, the pendulum of sympathy could swing in favor of David—especially if you have a spouse who's not all that different or any less aggravating than Frieda.

Trying to figure out whose anger is more deserving, whose complaints carry greater legitimacy misses the point. The fundamental issue in this or any angry marriage is: *Why do we keep doing this and when are we going to stop?* To answer this question, we need to understand the real sources of their anger. We need to look beneath the complaints of the *actual venter marriage* of Frieda and David. And to do that, we have to analyze their grievances (decode complaints) and make their *invisible marriage* come into view.

What's going on? The battle might be over a dress, but the war is over the clash of their unconscious needs. And what are these? As we will discover, Frieda needs *to keep men at bay*. While David's hidden agenda is his need *to find approval*. We can uncover these needs, as you can your own, by analyzing the specifics of their frustrations with each other.

Remember, each grievance holds an insight into a spouse's inner emotional world. Each complaint contains a psychological clue that can offer insight into a partner's need. *Insight makes the hidden needs of an invisible marriage come clearly into view.* You only have to know how to peer inside.

HER COMPLAINTS = HIS NEED

Analyzing complaints to decode hidden needs is something Frieda, David, and I did together. Our starting point was Frieda's criticisms, which led us to uncover David's need for approval.

When we listened carefully, it was apparent that many of Frieda's complaints centered on David's behavior in public. To Frieda, it always seems that David is on display; he shows off, he loves a crowd, spends too much time socializing.

I asked why a person, David or anyone else, might put on a "performance"? Insecurity was Frieda's "obvious" guess: "He must need their attention."

Despite her quick response, Frieda was unconvinced that "difficult" David could be insecure. "It's ridiculous, he's well known, important. His life is filled with one accomplishment after another. If anything, he always acts sure of himself."

David would hardly be the first highly competent person who felt this way—steel on the outside, Jell-O on the inside. On the contrary, a quest for power and status is often driven by insecurity. Indeed, an endless appetite for achievement is invariably stirred by a longing more emotional than material. Isn't it possible that David's endless attempts to do better and better may be driven by a need to find recognition?

Frieda reluctantly agreed that this fitted in; indeed, it echoed one of her repeated criticisms—he never seems to have enough.

"We have to go to *every* social function. He's always got to have 'just one more' evening with a client. At the magazine, he pushes himself and everyone who works for him; nobody (especially himself) is ever able to do enough."

Still, Frieda could not shake her resentment of David's quest for attention. It felt "ridiculous" and "excessive." These words offered little sympathy and a fair dose of disdain, as if David's need for attention was some unacceptable failing on his part.

I asked Frieda to consider that the word "attention" had more than one meaning. "I need attention" could be, not only a clarion call to be noticed, but also a request for concern. A wound, I offered, by way of example, needs both sorts of attention: We have to notice it, but it also requires our care. When we are asking for the first sort of attention, we are also in need of the second.

Frieda was not entirely convinced, but she seemed to warm to the idea that David might not be a man with a weakness that she resented, but instead a person in a never-ending quest for approval.

YOUR COMPLAINT: YOUR HUSBAND'S NEED

Are Frieda's complaints echoes of your own? Perhaps the bell of recognition has already sounded. To zero in on this need for approbation, you can decode these additional complaints:

· Your Complaint

He ignores me—especially when we're out or other women are around.

· *Your Husband's Need*

Your husband's disregard may be defensive. If he feels he cannot get your approval, he might try the unwitting strategy of giving up on you and turning to others for the acceptance he desires.

He may also be using jealousy as a wake-up call: The message he's transmitting—"Pay attention to me. This (other woman) thinks I'm terrific!" The paradox is that he *does* get your attention, but it's the negative variety.

· *Your Complaint*

If I don't do something exactly the way he wants it done, he gets furious. If I have a different point of view, I'm the enemy. He can't take any criticism.

· *Your Husband's Need*

A person desperate for approval is often sensitive to any indications that we are not aligned with him. Differing opinions, criticism, even simple advice may be received as condemnations. "Are you for me or against me?" may be a constant way in which he unwittingly evaluates your relationship to him. Agree, and you approve of him; don't, and he may well read it as reproach.

Don't underestimate the power of words on someone who's sense of their own self-worth is shaky. What you might regard as the most innocuous of comments can evoke inner voices of self-condemnation in a spouse with shaky self-esteem.

· *Your Complaint*

He's so demanding. He's so impatient. He's got a temper. He'll fly off the handle.

· *Your Husband's Need*

Self-acceptance is in short supply (after all, if he accepted himself, he wouldn't need it from others). Emotionally he is probably demanding and exacting of himself. People with such inner taskmasters often get very irritated with themselves, angrily "beating themselves up" over how "no good" they are. They have a low tolerance for their imperfections and shortcomings. And they may well exhibit this frustration and intolerance not only toward themselves but to you as well.

· *Your Complaint*

He's impotent. He can't maintain his erection. Our lovemaking starts out fine but something always goes wrong. He's not that interested in sex.

· *Your Husband's Need*

There is nothing that gets in the way of good sex like the self-consciousness of a man with the need for approval. It keeps him from being able to relax and get lost in the experience of lovemaking. He may be watching "you" watching "him" make love.

· *Your Complaint*

He's so vain. He's always preening. Ten times a day I'm supposed to tell him he looks good for his age; if I don't, he gets angry.

· *Your Husband's Need*

When he looks in the mirror, your husband may see censure reflected back—"You're not handsome enough, young enough, successful enough." So he needs you to reassure him and disperse his self-doubt. Since nothing ever really does the trick to quiet his incessant question—"Am I any good?"—he comes back again and again.

Perhaps the last thing you might have considered is that you are married to a man who has a precarious sense of his own worth. It might strike you as odd that someone who seems so able is unable to hold on to good feelings about himself.

Yet many of us, husbands *and* wives, are trapped by this predicament. We walk around with an inner uncertainty about ourselves. It makes an individual outer- (and other-) directed—constantly looking to the outside to provide what is deficient on the inside.

But this is only one half of the story. If this is your spouse's plight, what is your own? We can return to Frieda and David to bring the rest of their (and your) invisible marriage into view.

HIS COMPLAINTS = HER NEED

Frieda has a need to keep men at bay. David and I worked at decoding his complaints in order to understand what Frieda's need was all about:

"She never asks my advice or takes it if I offer. She'll listen to anyone before she'll listen to me. It's so ironic; I have the respect of most people with whom I deal, except my own wife."

It seems when Frieda needs help, it's not natural for her to turn toward David. On the contrary, he seems last on her list. Disregard, indifference, disrespect may be a way to devalue her husband; it makes him unimportant and keeps him peripheral. In truth, it creates distance.

In Frieda's case, this "pushing away" seems quite extreme. Frieda not only rejects her husband's offerings but turns him into "the enemy."

I proposed an odd thought to David.

"Maybe the woman who loves you *needs* to turn you into her enemy? Maybe she needs to make you into an adversary rather than an ally? Maybe her need to keep you at a distance is so powerful, she has to make you her foe. After all, if you are opponents you are, by definition, on opposite sides, and that certainly creates a divide between you two. Could you be her beloved enemy?"

To David's surprise, it made sense.

"You know this could really explain a feeling I'm always running up against with Frieda. I often feel that she hears what I say as an attack on her. She makes me out to be an ogre and I don't like it."

As we continued to interpret David's complaints, it became increasingly clear that unconsciously Frieda was often in the sad position of pushing away the man she loved.

YOUR HUSBAND'S COMPLAINT: YOUR NEED

Enemies: A Love Story. This could be the title of Frieda's marriage; could it be yours, too? Indeed, while it may seem startling, there are many, many angry marriages where there is real love but also more than a fair share of an invisible agenda that makes a spouse an antagonist rather than an ally. Many of us can't stand the person we love most!

Perhaps yours is an angry marriage where one partner unconsciously keeps the other at a "safe" distance. These additional complaints may clarify this possibility:

> ### · *Your Husband's Complaint*

She is so involved with the kids. She works the children up against me. Sometimes she makes it sound like she conceived them alone.

> ### · *Your Need*

When we have this need to keep a man at bay, we may very well involve our children. How? You might have the children join in the devaluation of your spouse.

Or perhaps you close ranks and leave Dad outside the fold; you are *so* close with the children, there's no room for your husband to fit in. Shutting him out may be another distance-making tactic.

· Your Husband's Complaint

She never asks me about my problems. She isn't interested in what goes on at work.

· Your Need

You don't get into your spouse's head, his heart, or his world when you need to keep him at arm's length.

· Your Husband's Complaint

She isn't nice to me. She's not warm or affectionate. She'd never think of doing something special for me. Last on her list of priorities are the things I need.

· Your Need

A warm gesture, a special kindness is the way we reach out to a spouse. Nurturing a lover is a form of emotional embrace. Your need may make these efforts impossible. Likewise, being physically close, touching, hugging, caressing, may feel forced or even untenable. Your need makes such intimacies a struggle.

· · Your Husband's Complaint

When we have sex, it's as if she's doing me a favor. She never seems enthusiastic about making love. She never initiates lovemaking. I don't excite her.

· *Your Need*

We may fashion a psychological distance from our lover even if we allow our bodies to unite. Sexual indifference, apathy, anhedonia (an inability to feel pleasure) are often the ways we shut down emotionally in order to create this gap. Perhaps you have sexual union without letting your souls merge.

· *Your Husband's Complaint*

There have been men in her life with whom she's had great sex—I'm just not one of them. Her former lovers are her good lovers.

· *Your Need*

What better way to minimize your husband's importance than to make his overtures pale in comparison to others? Perhaps you achieve distance by putting a third person in bed; the ghost of your former lover may be sleeping between the two of you to keep you from getting too close.

THE INVISIBLE MARRIAGE AND THE CYCLE OF CONFLICT

The unconscious needs of David and Frieda create an invisible marriage, which ensnares them in a cycle of conflict. Just what is their inevitable angry tango about? Think about David's volatility, and Frieda's hidden vulnerability. His angry lashing out fulfills Frieda's unconscious desire to distance herself from men. David's attack confirms her subconscious belief that you can get hurt if you allow a man to get too close. So she reacts accordingly and proceeds to do anything and everything to keep David "safely" at arm's length.

Now consider David's reaction to being pushed away. Invariably he reads it through his unconscious perspective: "Frieda doesn't want to have anything to do with me because I don't meet with her approval; I'm unworthy." He feels rejected, scorned (after all, he's in the dark as to the idea that Frieda actually finds him frightening), and can only react negatively to what he regards as a rebuff. In the wake of this hurt, he has angry outbursts. Or he more urgently tries for approval with strategies (flirtation, workaholism, showing off) that inevitably backfire because they provide grist for Frieda's unconscious mill—they become more reasons to push David away. (Paradoxically, the harder David vies for approval from his wife, the less he gets.) Of course, we know what that means. David feels put down and the cycle spins on and on.

This is the vicious cycle of this particular venting duo, but its basic structure is the same for every couple in an angry marriage. As long as partners are unaware of their respective needs, they create a never-ending cycle of frustration because *a need determines our behavior toward a spouse* and *a need determines how we interpret and therefore react to a spouse's behavior.*

This is the powerful though invisible force that operates in an angry union: We see and react to a partner through the prism of an unconscious need. Fortunately, when couples begin to know of these secret forces, self-defeating patterns can indeed be laid to rest.

The Primal Marriage: Where the Anger Began

But how did Frieda and David get "stuck" with such needs? Their answer lies in the past, in their *primal marriage.* This first intimate relationship with parents is the model for all partnerships to follow, theirs and ours.

Long into adulthood, the inner child of this first union influences a marriage more powerfully than we can (or would like to) imagine. For Frieda, her need to keep men at a distance was the legacy of her primal marriage forcefully intruding on her present.

FRIEDA'S PAST: HER PRIMAL MARRIAGE

Frieda's mother and father haggled and bickered all the time. They were constantly at each other. What made things worse was that her father had a drinking problem. As Frieda recalls:

"My parents argued under the best of circumstances. Under the worst—when Dad drank—it could get really bad.

"A typical fight would start out with my father wanting to go out and my mother putting up a protest. Dad would get outraged—'Don't tell me what to do. What do you think I am? One of the kids you're bossing around!'

"He would slam the door and be off. Mom would bolt the locks, cursing at him and swearing that he would never 'step in this house again!'

"A few hours would pass and Dad would be at the door begging to be let in. (I heard everything. My sister and I could never fall asleep on these nights. We'd get into bed together and wait up.) He would sometimes start crying and calling for my mother. He'd call out, 'Pam, Pammy,' sounding so pathetic. It made me cringe.

"At that point, things would shift. Now she was in the driver's seat and she would stonewall him. He would quiet down for a while and then start his pleading again. Sometimes my sister or I would sneak downstairs to let him in and put him to bed just to get it to stop.

"He would put his arms around us and blubber on about how much he loved us and what good girls we were. I couldn't stand those wet drunk kisses, but they were better than hearing him carry on all night.

"The next day Dad would be back to his blustery self. But it was even worse; we all pretended that he didn't make a fool out of himself the night before."

Where did this chaos leave Frieda? The male model in Frieda's childhood, her father, was both frightening and pathetic. When angry, he seemed fearsome; drunk, he felt repugnant. In both instances he was someone from whom Frieda wanted to draw away.

In addition, forced to take over when her mother would "wash her hands" of her husband (Frieda, not his wife, would let him in, put him to bed, kiss him goodnight, etc.), Frieda found herself in an uncomfortable position with her father, especially when he became physical with her. It made her feel very awkward. These were not ordinary fatherly affections; they were the clumsy, embarrassing embraces of a drunken man.

This awkwardness, his fearsome and pathetic qualities, conspired to make Frieda repelled by her father. Instead of a protective fatherly relationship that engendered respect and intimacy, her father created a sense that a man is to be dreaded, best experienced at arm's distance.

Frieda's impression of men is indelibly marked by this experience. These feelings make themselves felt on into adulthood. Safety, reliability, attraction, comfort are not sentiments she feels naturally and easily toward men, including her own husband. The man she loves unwittingly becomes the man she cannot stand, and, like her father, she must push him away.

Might you have a primal marriage where your father offered a distorted model of what men are like? Often alcohol is the culprit that creates these problems, but it isn't always the case. Families free from this complicated disease may still create such distortions.

Did you learn when you were most vulnerable, most impressionable, to be disappointed, frightened, put off, by the most important man in your life—your father? Did you learn not to like or even hate the man you also dearly loved? Can this legacy of your primal marriage be the one you unwittingly carry into your own partnership? Perhaps your past can clue us into this possibility.

IS THIS YOUR PRIMAL MARRIAGE?

· Did your parents have a disagreeable or volatile relationship? · Did they argue? · Did your mother belittle your father? · Did your father threaten or intimidate your mother? · Did they lack mutual respect?

Parents may create a sense that marriage is a kind of warfare between the sexes. Their animosity may have an insidious effect: We don't learn from their mistakes, regrettably; we carry them on into the next generation. Their mutual disrespect for one another becomes the breeding ground for your distrust of men.

Was your father the "tyrant" and your mother the "softy"? · Was it, "Just wait till your father gets home"?

It doesn't necessarily take alcohol to make a father seem intimidating. Sometimes parents "split" their roles in the family. Mom is the good guy, Dad the bad guy. If this transpires, a father becomes larger than life; we see him as angry, frightening, punitive.

When this occurs, it perpetuates a little girl's vision of men as powerful and unreasonable. A man is an ogre (brute, monster, bully . . .), to be avoided, and these sentiments may continue to echo in your adult need.

· Was your father very physical (did you give him back rubs, sit on his lap, etc.)? · Once you were of school age, did you get in bed with your father? · Do you remember bathing together or seeing him nude regularly? · Was your father more affectionate to you than to your mother? · Did he like you "the most"?

Anger may not be the only thing that frightens us away from a father. Excessive physical contact may make a girl feel awkward and threatened. Feeling sexually stimulated by a father may also be disturbing.

A father's affections, especially when they are not being offered to (or welcomed by) a mother, may make a child feel uncomfortable and embarrassed. It is menacing, not comforting, to be the recipient of love when it feels more sexual than fatherly.

The consequence, later in life, is that the man with whom you are supposed to be close, your husband, continues instead to feel threatening. You push him away perhaps both physically and emotionally rather than let him get near.

· Did you have childhood fantasies, day or night dreams (especially repetitively) of men coming after you (hurting, kidnapping, following)? · Do you recall being frightened of male strangers? · Were you afraid of monsters?

These imaginings are often associated with children who feel unsafe with their own fathers. It is as if these dreams express what we fear about this real man in our life. This kind of early anxiety about men may dog us on into adulthood, where we unwittingly end up responding to our man as if he is the dangerous villain of our childhood imagination.

· Did you have a tough time during adolescence? · Were you rebellious? · Did you fight with your parents?

Often during adolescence when a girl begins to develop sexually, a need to push away first rears its head. If you had a fractious time during your teenage years, you may already have been burdened by the need—"Keep Away!"

Perhaps, as you ask yourself to explore your primal marriage, you hear echoes of your past in this story. You may be a woman who, unfortunately and unwittingly, drags negative feelings about her father (anxiety, fear, repugnance, sexual awkwardness) into her marriage. These sentiments give rise to a need to keep a man at bay, and intrude forcefully and unpleasantly on your love.

Once again your self-exploration is only part of your investigation. An angry marriage is fueled by *both* of you! In your husband's past there remains some unfinished business which has given rise to his need for approval. Examining David's primal relationships may be a starting point from which you can understand the origin and development of your own husband's need.

DAVID'S PAST: HIS PRIMAL MARRIAGE

"When I was four, my father, Vinny, got a lucrative job on an offshore oil rig in Alaska. It meant long stretches when he wasn't home, but he made the kind of money he couldn't have if he stayed in Texas; the oil industry was really off then.

"Every so often Dad would get home for a few weeks. When he had to leave, he'd give me a pep talk: 'No tears, boy. Your mamma needs a big man at home to take care of her.' "

David's mother, Pat, a self-involved woman, was more than content to have her husband away. Left alone with her, David was pretty much on his own.

"I think my mother had a good time with Dad gone. As soon as he was out the door she forgot about him—and me. I was a pest. I couldn't do anything right for her."

When David was six, an explosion on the oil rig badly injured his father. After months in a burn center, his father returned home.

"You would have thought my mother was the one with the

troubles. All she could do was bitch about how tough it was to care for Dad."

As her husband went from an asset to a liability, David's mother grew increasingly depressed and bitter. His father, though naturally good-natured, was often racked by pain, which made him irritable with David. David, attempting to be his father's good little man, did everything in his power to make things better. He desperately tried to make the unhappy people around him feel better, to no avail.

Eighteen months after the accident, David's father died. David, who was devastated, got no help from his mother through this ordeal. In fact, his mother, increasingly embittered by her "raw deal," showed an ever-dwindling interest in her son. Feeling only her own sense of injury and loss, whenever David made any attempts to help, she'd dismiss his efforts:

"I can remember one time when I had walked dogs for a neighbor without telling her. I came home with four dollars, which I gave to her as a surprise. I can remember her reaction like it was yesterday.

" 'What do you think we're going to do with this—run off to Mexico?'

"I was crushed."

How did all this affect a small boy? Since the very beginning, David has been trying to take care of things. After all, his father had given him the job at four! And David had, like any child, taken his "job" to heart. And in his unhappy family, taking care to David meant "I better make everyone feel better." The problem was, he couldn't do it successfully. His mother's depression and his father's death prevented him from ever succeeding.

Absorbed in their respective misery, his parents could not turn to him and say, "Yes, you've made things better. You're doing a good job." He couldn't make them smile at him.

And with his father's death David was left with the dreadful and desperate "realization" that he could never get his father's approval. Making it even harder on himself, he imagined—as small children are wont to do—that his father died *because* he didn't do a good job.

These childhood reactions left David with a terrible burden of guilt: He would have to be penitent and try harder. Since the age of six, David hasn't stopped trying. Though an adult, the desperate and frightened child in David is still trying to get approval and set things right.

There are many paths in childhood that may lead to an urgent need for approval. Loss and the burden of guilt may be the culprit; but as these additional questions indeed suggest, a childhood free from tragedy or trauma can still create such a desperate need.

IS THIS YOUR HUSBAND'S PRIMAL MARRIAGE?

· Was your husband's mother or primary caretaker a self-absorbed person? · Were his parents judgmental? · Were they quick to find fault? · Did they see the glass half empty rather than half full? · Were they unrealistic in their demands?

The personality of parents, not circumstances or emotional problems, can create a need for approval. Sometimes parents establish conditions where their child can't please them. They may be unreachable, demanding, or critical. No matter how hard a child tries, he can't get it right.

There is nothing that batters a child's self-esteem so much as the early and constant confrontation with a failure to gain recognition from parents. And we don't stop trying if we don't manage to get it from them. On the contrary, we incessantly seek their admiration. In truth, a husband hungry for approval may still be trying to jump through the hoops that his parents created in childhood. *There is no force more powerful in creating the insatiable drive for recognition than a withholding parent!*

· Did he have an ill parent? · Was there any family tragedy? · Was there financial upheaval (job loss, relocation)? · Was there a sibling who required special attention or care? · Was his primary caretaker depressed?

In families, circumstances can conspire that leave parents so exhausted there is little energy for a child—physically or emotionally. Perhaps parental preoccupation robbed your husband of acknowledgment and left him longing for its return.

Personal calamity is not the only thief to "steal away" a parent's involvement. The sadness and malaise of depression sap a person's energy, often rendering her emotionally unavailable to a child. Suffering this loss in childhood, we may grow into adults in search of attention and concern. Was this your husband's plight?

· Did his parents divorce? · Did he lose a parent through illness, death, abandonment?

Children often hold themselves responsible for divorce or family losses, blaming themselves for not being "good enough." This is a common childhood fantasy: "If I had been sweeter, smarter, better behaved, better in school, helped out at home . . . we'd still be a family." As adults, the desperate need for approval may be the legacy of this guilty burden. Maybe your husband is still searching for the pat on his head that says, "You really are a good boy—in spite of what you've done!"

How different a marriage begins to look when you know the unconscious needs, when you realize that an actual marriage is only the starting point. How different a marriage feels when you appreciate how childhood disappointments and difficulties of a primal marriage pursue us like unseen but powerful demons on into adult relationships.

Can we continue to dismiss David as an ogre now that we know of his futile struggle at six to make things better? Can we simply chide Frieda for being selfish now that we know how difficult those long nights of her childhood must have been? No. We can't be the same once we have insight. Insight brings the possibility of compassion and empathy, and that is the first step out of an angry marriage.

Taking Hold of the Problem: Getting Ready for an Adult Marriage

Empathy *always* makes couples less inclined to employ an old destructive style of anger, in this case, venting. Each person becomes sensitized to their own inner struggles and to the inner struggles of their partner. Psychologically more attuned, they see the self-defeating patterns clearly and realize the threat they pose to marital goodwill. This emotional clarity invariably makes couples more inclined toward change. In this way, understanding confers an extraordinary power. Above all it offers *the option to act differently.* Old, angry lovestyles may be relinquished as understanding heralds new possibilities.

As venters, perhaps you are feeling this promise, this hope. What can you do? We know that the biggest pitfall of this style is how very *reactive* venters are to one another. Above all, venters need to work on *resisting the urge to react.* Venters need to "grow up." Responses are heated, flashpoints are characteristically low—more like angry children than reasonable adults. These reactions have to be contained.

Consider these new possibilities: Try to become better at absorbing anger rather than simply hurling it back. Delay your responses, and learn to tolerate an urge to say or do something rather than letting it simply rip.

Venters need to exert more control, to think before they speak and shriek. This is absolutely crucial: introducing a moment of reflection, thought, consideration before dishing it out. It is, in fact, this interlude between an angry impulse and the urge to act on it that affords venters the possibility of not hurling anger like a weapon at one another. Delay a response until wrath ebbs and you have the space inside yourself to find words to express your hurt rather than launch an attack. *Thoughtful silence is a venter's most powerful agent of change.*

Venters need to replace their angry abandon with restraint. To achieve this, you can consider these new options:

I don't have to act on my impulse.

I don't have to say what's on my mind at the moment.

I don't have to be rude.

I don't have to keep on fighting.

I don't have to answer an accusation.

I don't have to throw in the past.

I don't have to raise my voice.

I don't have to threaten.

I don't have to respond in kind.

Try turning your Velcro insides to Teflon—don't let everything stick! Think about arguing more selectively. Consider whether it is possible to choose your battles rather than habitually fighting for every cause. Rather than letting every sling and arrow hit the mark—*duck!* If you can become a sturdier container for your anger, these different strategies will be possible.

There is no insurance policy that guarantees a venter new restraint, but insight does make us ever more able to improve. Especially since we know the promise—a marriage can be different and better.

PROVOKERS

A fter seven years of marriage to Malcolm, Cheryl was no newcomer to aggravation:

"Do you know what does me in every time? It's the empty milk carton in the refrigerator. I grab it in the morning and three drops dribble into my cup. I am a beast without coffee—I could *kill* him!

"And I believe Malcolm has really missed his true calling," she added with obvious sarcasm. "He has a gift which he has never truly exploited. He leaves every drawer open exactly one inch. Such precision must have its uses—maybe in the space program. Believe me, I sometimes feel as if I'd like to put him in orbit myself!"

While Cheryl knows she's exasperated, she doesn't realize hers is an angry marriage—*provoker-style!* Unlike a venter, she isn't always boiling over with venom. No. Instead, she lives with a man who drives her to distraction. And this is the telltale sign of this destructive lovestyle. A provoker feels as if she's been *made* angry; her spouse does it to her!

Provokers don't share anger equally. Only one spouse "owns" the marital anger. The other is "never" really all that angry. In a way, provokers are a hybrid: One of them feels anger overtly while the other doesn't express anger directly. Only one spouse is actively or apparently angry; the other is always playing the "innocent." One partner feels goaded, inflamed, incited, prompted by their spouse's actions (or inaction), and the other doesn't. So, while anger is very much part of a provoker marriage, there's a decided imbalance; just one spouse feels mad.

Malcolm, for example, is the "non-angry" spouse. He doesn't feel angry, just bothered. Cheryl's "drawer thing" is ridiculous: "She's always on my case. It can get to be a real pain." In a word, one partner is the provoker, the other the "provoked"!

The classic provoker couple is the "go-getter" and the "procrastinator." Beverly and Alfred are just such a pair. Only Beverly ever feels angry; Alfred can never see what the fuss is all about.

Articulate and attractive Beverly has little difficulty (and a good deal of acid wit) in pinpointing her frustrations. Alfred drives her "bananas."

"If I wrote a book, it would be called *The Sayings of Chairman Alfred,* and it would stretch on for six volumes. It would include such memorable lines as, 'I don't know. Can't it wait till tomorrow? I forgot. Gee, it was only a mistake. It's no big deal. Aren't you overreacting? Well, it doesn't bother *me* that much.'

"Need I go on? Talk about Teflon. Alfred let's everything slide off of him. The problem is, it usually ends up in my lap.

"I love him, but when he pulls this stuff I can feel so aggravated."

As with Beverly, the partner who "owns" the anger often becomes characterized as the chronic complainer, nag, or grouch.

Sometimes the split into go-getter and procrastinator isn't so amusing. When the provoker conflict centers on family finance, for example, it can mean serious trouble. A provoker who forgets to pay the mortgage, misplaces a bill, or loses the family checkbook can do serious damage. Careful Ian, who never paid a late charge on his credit card in his single life, found himself married to Jennifer, whose cavalier attitude to bills nearly drove him "over the edge" emotionally and economically. An unpaid homeowner's policy Jenny "forgot" to mail left them with $10,000 in bills after a spring hurricane!

We may not be equipped with Cheryl's sarcasm or Beverly's biting humor. We may never have gotten into the expensive predicament of Jenny and Ian. Yet those of us who are trapped by this style may well recognize their problems in our own liaisons.

Opposites Detract

As a rule, provokers tend to have very different temperaments, tastes, and styles from one another. We've already seen it in careful Cheryl and careless Malcolm, "go-getter" Bev and procrastinator Alfred, responsible Ian and slipshod Jenny; but there may be other variations. One spouse may be active, the other passive. One partner the leader, the other the follower. One the doer, the other the observer. One the athlete, the other the spectator. Or perhaps one partner is compulsive while the other specializes in the lay-z-boy, laissez-faire approach to life. Very, very often dissention rears its head over differences in habits; the neatnik finds herself living with a man who couldn't care less where his socks end up (we play Oscar to our spouse's Felix). In your marriage, which half of the "odd couple" are you?

Who's to Blame?

The aggravated half of a provoker pair always feel a similar sense of frustration no matter what "crime" a spouse commits. It's not the "sin," it's the attitude that drives him or her to distraction. As a result, the angered partner often reacts to every failing of the spouse with equal irritation. Sometimes this creates a situation where the passive spouse simply turns a deaf ear to a partner's protests. Feeling "here we go again," he or she tunes out, turns off, and basically ignores criticism.

While disregarding a spouse is one mode utilized by the "blameless" partner, it isn't the only reaction. Standard responses of the passive perpetrator include:

perplexed . . . What's all the fuss about?

defensive . . . Why are you pissed? I didn't do anything.

detached . . . Oh. You were angry with me? I didn't realize it made you so mad.

apologetic . . . Sorry, it wasn't intentional.

self-righteous . . . How dare you say that to me!

The passive provoker has an excuse for everything a spouse finds aggravating ("Could I help it if the bank closed just as I got there?"; "My secretary forgot to remind me"; "I was sure you'd bring the address"). In a variety of ways the passive partner declaims: "It's not my fault!"

In truth, this "innocent" partner is actually expressing anger indirectly using *passive* aggression, hostility obliquely expressed through inaction, forgetting, incompetence, inefficiency, neglect, "accidents," helplessness, or displacing blame. So, if you don't get mad but are maddening to your partner, you are probably a passive provoker, expressing your anger on the sly.

Although very different in their style of "getting angry," both provoker partners are quite irritable and not adept at tolerating frustration. Each of them has a short fuse emotionally and finds it impossible to achieve constructive ways to express themselves. The difference is that the active partner lets the frustration openly seethe, while the passive partner fumes more or less silently (showing their constant frustration in all the oblique ways that have been described). One provoker is always exploding while the other is constantly imploding.

Beauty and the Beast

Probably a good clue as to whether or not you are this angry duo is the extent to which you feel like a partnership in which there is a "good" guy and a "bad" guy. Frequently, it's an impression shared by outsiders, friends, and family, who see one spouse as the slob, bum, incompetent, shrew, bully, tyrant, or taskmaster, and the other as the slave, innocent, or victim. Friends may consider you a mismatched pair and think: "I sometimes wonder how a nice guy like that could get stuck with such a bitch," or, "She's such a sweetheart, I just can't see how she can stand to get into bed with the bastard."

Could you imagine your marriage described in these terms? If you play the beauty to your spouse—the beast—you may well be provokers!

Something's Gotta Give (I Can't Take It Anymore)

The visibly angered one in a provoker marriage tends to feel she "puts up with" or endures her mate. Often feeling her spouse is an affliction, her marriage a series of trials and tribulations, she grumbles and moans:

"I don't have the strength anymore."

"How does he expect me to take it?"

"I can't ignore it another minute."

This partner is likelier to mutter under her breath than shout, throw up her hands in exasperation, or gnash her teeth in utter frustration. As a rule, this provoked partner's ire foments and festers, seethes and stews until something, usually her temper, finally gives.

As a result, angry outbursts tend to come intermittently or in installments, once the straw finally breaks the camel's back! Typically, the angered spouse zeroes in on a specific failing of a partner, but her wrath has only a momentary effect; maybe the socks make it to the laundry bin for a day or two. Invariably, once the dust settles, the usual annoying behaviors return and the aggravation begins all over again.

Growing Apart

Whether a spouse grouses and the partner slinks away from the anger, both end up feeling as if they are caught in a rut. One laments, "I'm always pissed but it doesn't make you any different," and the other bemoans, "I'm not so bad but you never seem to be anything but angry." And the net effect is the same: a growing sense of futility and hopelessness.

Provokers tend to feel worn out by each other. In the extreme, they may end up feeling resigned at their mutual misfortune of being stuck with one another. All of these conditions create a real risk for provokers: *They grow apart because they feel worn down, exhausted, fed up.* Dora and Teddy are a pair of provokers coming close to this point of no return. Are you in this danger zone, too?

The Actual Marriage of Two Provokers: Dora and Teddy

Dora, a full-time mother of three-year-old twins, Jake and Leo, came to counseling with her husband, Teddy. In their seventh year of marriage, things were not going well. Teddy, who came late to the session ("Sorry, the traffic was really heavy on the bridge"), let Dora begin their story:

"Teddy is a really good father—when he's there. The problem is, he isn't around very much."

Teddy interrupted. "I happen to have a job that takes me to three different counties. I'm not off on a holiday leaving you home with the kids, I'm working."

It was Dora who spoke next, her anger mounting. "Then what about Saturday's golf game? And your monthly poker game? *And* last week's dinner out with friends that turned into an all-night affair? And you didn't manage to call home and let me know that. What's your excuse this time?"

Rolling his eyes in exasperation, Teddy answered, "I tried the house once. It was busy. I just forgot to try again. I told you I was sorry."

Trying to defend himself, he went on quietly, "Anyway, Dora, I tried to explain, you're the one who doesn't want to go out. You could have been there. We were just having fun. You don't like to party. You complain that my friends drink and carry on and you'd rather stay home and read a book."

Teddy's explanations did little to mollify Dora.

"And I suppose you just 'forgot' last week's appointment here, too? I came. I made arrangements to have my mother watch the kids and I managed to get here—and *be on time.*" Dora's angry reprimand was clear.

Teddy, who had sounded harassed until now, started to raise his voice. Irritation entered his tone for the first time.

"Coming here is your idea. Remember? Just like most things we do together." His voice dropped and he seemed to turn silent and stony. Dora went on.

"Yes it is. If I left things up to you, nothing would get done. You don't do anything unless you're pushed."

Dora turned to me as if she were looking for a sympathetic ear. Focusing her attention on me, she failed to notice that Teddy was no longer listening.

"Doctor, here is a perfect example. Teddy has promised to finish the basement. We need the space now that the twins are getting bigger. They really mess up the place."

Dora winced as she contemplated her "messy" house.

"Well, I know how well Teddy keeps his so-called promises, but I gave him a chance. Of course, he managed to find time to paint his friend John's garage, but at our house nothing happened for months. Then one Saturday, when the kids had torn the house apart, I just exploded, so he finally got off his rear end and bought it."

Teddy yawned. Dora never even noticed.

"Knowing Teddy as well as I do, I wrote down exactly how much we needed, the style number, the manufacturer. Everything. Of course he came home with the wrong color. And since it was cut to our specifications I have to live with this mistake for the rest of my life! My house is a shambles. I'm at my wits end!"

In spite of Dora's harangue, Teddy offered no rejoinder. In fact, it was clear his mind was elsewhere. More than once he had yawned. And now he looked as if his eyelids were heavy and he could use a good nap. Furious Dora and sleepy Teddy—provokers par excellence!

AN ACTUAL MARRIAGE: ARE YOU PROVOKERS?

In their day-to-day life, Dora and Teddy have many of the classical signs of a provoker pair. Their actual marriage is most certainly one in which Teddy's actions (and often his lack of action) are the fuel for Dora's angry fire. Look over the following list of telltale signs:

- They have differences in temperament; procrastinator vs. go-getter; he parties, she reads.
- He's passive/aggressive . . . he "forgets" to call; he misses the therapy appointment; he buys the wrong paneling.
- They have periodic blow-ups . . . she yells at him to finish the basement.

Is your actual marriage reminiscent of theirs? Might you be the passive/aggressive spouse who drives a partner to distraction by all the little stuff? Do you delay, forget, omit, neglect, obstruct, and then feel anything from mystified to annoyed that your spouse is pissed? Or might you assume the other role in this duo: the caricature of the aggravated mate who can so easily be tuned out? And does this role splitting put your marriage at risk of losing your love to a sense of futility and hopelessness?

Decoding Our Complaints: Making the Invisible Marriage Visible

What is truly driving this conflict—and driving a wedge between Dora and Teddy? The problem is not the unfinished basement; instead, it is the incessant drive of their unconscious needs. And ironically, as temperamentally different as Dora and Teddy appear, we will discover that they both experience one especially compelling need: *to prevent abandonment.* They both unconsciously grapple with the anxiety that they may be deserted, but they manage this anxiety in very different and conflicting ways. Dora nests and Teddy flies the coop! As you decode their complaints to get a look at the needs that drive their invisible marriage, you may indeed gain insight into your own.

HER COMPLAINTS = HIS NEED

When I suggested to Dora that she and Teddy had the same need—to prevent abandonment—she was more than mystified. She was confused.

"A month without a business trip and Teddy's chomping at the bit. How could someone who's running off to his golf game, his nights with the guys, who jumps at the chance to grab a drink after work or spend a Sunday watching football at someone else's house be anxious about being left? *He's* the one who's never around."

I offered a different perspective that might help decode this complaint:

"Which creates the more difficult target, a stationary or a moving one? For someone who is fearful about being left, the antidote may be never to stay in place long enough to let it happen. Anxiety over abandonment keeps your husband in flight. By being on the move, Teddy prevents himself from becoming too attached, feeling too rooted, too connected. It's a form of protection against being left. Perhaps what looks like an effort to escape from home is really an effort to escape from the full force of abandonment."

But Dora had other complaints.

"It just seems so selfish, *his* sports, *his* friends, *his* nights out. Teddy spends money on all his 'toys' without giving our budget a thought. Teddy is only concerned with Teddy. Believe me, he'll forget a doctor's appointment, but he's never forgotten a time he tees off on the first hole."

Dora's frustration at Teddy's self-absorption was intense, but I suggested another very different way of analyzing his apparent selfishness.

"Selfish people are actually people who have little trust and confidence in others. Selfishness is an attempt to 'take care of oneself' because you lack the conviction that anyone else cares. This is the surprising paradox—the unconscious psychological motive for selfishness is an overwhelming fear that *no one will be there for me, therefore I must take care of myself by myself.* Could Teddy be so focused on himself because he has little faith that someone will be around to care for him?"

For Dora, it was difficult to think of Teddy as someone suffering with this anxiety over abandonment, especially since her patience had worn perilously thin. Theirs was a provoker marriage in jeopardy.

YOUR COMPLAINT: YOUR HUSBAND'S NEED

Are you feeling as exhausted as Dora? Are her frustrations similar to your own? Perhaps these other decoded complaints may help you discover whether the husband who is wearing you out actually has a hidden need—to prevent abandonment.

· *Your Complaint*

Sure, he did the laundry, so now all the white underwear is pink . . . He's ready to drive me to my job interview and he's locked the keys in the car . . . I stood waiting in the rain for an hour because he "forgot" which movie theater we were going to.

· *Your Husband's Need*

Your husband may be verbally agreeable or compliant, but in spite of his "words," in his "deeds" he never quite does as you request. In effect his lips say yes but his actions (or inaction) say no.

What does this have to do with a need to protect himself from abandonment? Unconsciously, he doesn't believe you would stick around if and when he displayed his own desires openly and they were in conflict with yours (i.e., I don't want to do the wash, drive you to work, go to the movies). Declaring an angry *no* feels too risky. So he goes along with you overtly—and refuses you covertly.

· *Your Complaint*

No matter how many times I've mentioned it, he still leaves the toilet seat up. Why doesn't he clean the hair out of the sink—he knows it revolts me? He knows I can't stand Japanese food so why does he bring it home for dinner.

· *Your Husband's Need*

Your husband cannot express full-blown anger. An eruption would be far too dangerous; you wouldn't stay around if he got really mad. So anger has to be let out in small and indirect ways. Your pet peeve is just made to order, he gets *you* through it!

· *Your Complaint*

He dumps decisions in my lap. He doesn't take charge of things around the house. He doesn't manage our finances. He doesn't give any input into decorating the house. I have to be the responsible one in the family; he just plops himself down in front of the TV.

· *Your Husband's Need*

What looks like a failure to take charge or assume responsibility may actually be an unconscious reluctance to invest himself in home and hearth. The more he invests in you and his family, the more he stands to lose.

· *Your Complaint*

We have sex infrequently but I'm pretty sure he masturbates.

· Your Husband's Need

Sexual self-reliance may be what his need demands. This way if you abandon him, he won't suffer such deprivation—he still has self-love even if there comes a time when he doesn't have yours.

· Your Complaint

He's not very demonstrative. He's not the sort of man to say, "I love you." He isn't romantic; sometimes I feel he doesn't love me—deeply.

· Your Husband's Need

Withholding emotionally may well be prompted by fear. If he let go and was totally devoted, what would happen to him if you were no longer around? The prospect of loss always looms on his emotional horizon and keeps him from becoming completely attached to the person he loves most—you!

Does it come as a surprise that the "easygoing guy" who manages to drive you crazy is a man hiding his aggression, his power, his anger, because they feel dangerous? Perhaps you share your life with a man for whom love is a high-risk venture; intimacy, emotional dependency, might make him feel far too vulnerable. Many of us do!

HIS COMPLAINTS = HER NEED

Teddy and I worked on decoding his complaints to see how Dora's need, to prevent abandonment, revealed itself in their actual marriage. This was no easy task. Teddy was as passive/aggressive in a therapist's office as he was in his marriage.

As we began, Teddy wearily admitted to only one wish: that Dora get "off his back." Things weren't good, but he was convinced it was primarily because Dora felt dissatisfied with him. Not vice versa. I told Teddy that he seemed sullen and wondered if now he must feel as if he had two women bugging him: me and Dora! I added that

I wasn't at all interested in debating the validity of Dora's complaints, but that here we would use them to discover things about Dora's mind and *not* about Teddy's alleged shortcomings. With a rueful smile and a nod of acknowledgment he reluctantly continued. Dora's reaction to money matters came first:

"If I buy something I want—just for fun—she gets so upset. She watches our money like a hawk. Dora's always talking about having a nest egg. We do well; we don't have to be as tightfisted as she is."

Teddy's list grew longer. Dora wasn't generous with gifts. She often took economies that weren't necessary. Teddy's trips to the supermarket were always a bone of contention.

"I come home from shopping and I get the third degree: Why didn't I go to the other supermarket that was having the sale on toilet paper? Why did I buy Perdue chickens? Don't I know the name brands are more expensive? And on it goes."

I suggested that we could decode Teddy's complaints by trying to understand the meaning money might hold for Dora.

"Money may very well mean security, but not just in the usual sense. Dora is anxious about abandonment. She fears that there will come a time when she is deserted and will have nothing. That being the case, Dora can't relax and have fun with money. Dora isn't cheap; rather, in her mind, she's stockpiling against the day supplies run out."

Teddy had other grievances. Dora was stubborn.

"Dora makes up her mind about something and that's it. She gets an idea that something has to be done and she doesn't give it a rest for a minute."

Teddy was surprised when in order to decode his complaint, I asked a question that sounded more biological than psychological:

"What happens to your body when you're terrified? You become 'stiff with fear.' Even our language acknowledges this physical response. You feel petrified, frozen, paralyzed, turned to stone. Fear can stiffen our minds the way it paralyzes our bodies. After all, isn't that really what 'stubborn' describes? It's about being rigid and closed; our mind locks solid around an idea.

"When people are highly anxious, they often become intellectually rigid. I think Dora's fear of abandonment may have robbed her of mental flexibility."

YOUR HUSBAND'S COMPLAINT: YOUR NEED

Have you begun to see how an analysis of Teddy's complaints leads us to Dora's need to prevent abandonment? In decoding the additional complaints that follow, you might get a better idea as to whether you, like Dora, are anxiously struggling to prevent abandonment.

· *Your Husband's Complaint*

She's a perfectionist, a stickler for details; the littlest things that go wrong bother her; if I make a mistake, it's the end of the world; bringing home the wrong brand of detergent is a crime; if she can't clean up after a party, she can't sleep.

· *Your Need*

For you, anything less than perfect is the end of the world. Your need to prevent abandonment leaves you feeling: Don't do things just right and out you go! Disorder, especially on the homefront, is very threatening. It feels as if your personal world is unraveling, coming apart. Unconsciously you are reassuring yourself that if everything is securely in place, you will be, too.

· *Your Husband's Complaint*

She's so pushy; she's always on my back; the woman doesn't know how to relax; she's always on to the next project; as soon as I finish something, she's got the next assignment ready.

· *Your Need*

Fear of abandonment creates an insatiable anxiety monster that resides within you. You need to appease it—constantly. So you never stop trying, you never let down your guard. Your husband feels pushed, but only because he doesn't understand the fear that relentlessly drives you.

· *Your Husband's Complaint*

Every time I want to go to a ball game (golf, fish, play poker . . .), she's miffed . . . She really resents any trips I make for the job . . . If I don't call home when I'm out, she's furious.

· *Your Need*

Separations are trying. In your unconscious, when someone departs, you imagine that they'll never return. Your husband feels tethered because he doesn't understand that you are always fighting the possibility of losing him, so you hold on for dear life.

· *Your Husband's Complaint*

She asks me to do things, but she's happier if she does them herself; when she gets involved in work (kids, charity, housekeeping), there's no room for me; I never walk in the door and find her excited or really happy to see me—she's either pissed off or busy.

· *Your Need*

Controlling your emotional attachments to your husband is a theme of your need—not just his! The paradox is that you need him around—to reassure yourself that he's not abandoning you—*but* you don't let him get too close emotionally or sexually in case he does leave.

· Your Husband's Complaint

Sex is always exactly the same; she gives me directions on how to make love to her; if we're not in the right position, she can't have an orgasm. She has to feel "just right" to make love.

· Your Need

People with abandonment anxiety are often highly controlling and controlled, in bed and out of it.

THE INVISIBLE MARRIAGE
AND THE CYCLE OF ANGER

Because of their unconscious needs, Teddy and Dora have an invisible marriage in which they are locked into a cycle of conflict. Dora pushes Teddy's buttons and Teddy certainly pulls Dora's strings. Together, like two marionettes they do an endless angry two-step. Dora's need to prevent abandonment exerts a powerful hidden force. It makes her controlling. That's all Teddy's unconscious needs. Dora's domination panics him. He can't be that tied in to someone; they might leave him. After all, he is unconsciously terrified of abandonment as well. So, to be safe and protected from that possibility, Teddy pulls away.

That does it for Dora's unconscious, which reads Teddy's distancing as, "Uh-oh, I'm losing him." Insecure, Dora naturally gets increasingly anxious and depressed, so she angrily demands more from her husband (time, attention, togetherness). In response Teddy gets nervous and pulls away (remember, intimacy puts him at risk), or perhaps at other times, frightened by Dora's anger, he compliantly says yes though he feels otherwise inclined. Both of these reactions are the very behaviors that make his wife more anxious.

And so the cycle of the invisible marriage spins on and on. Might this be the predictable path your invisible marriage takes as well?

The Primal Marriage:
Where the Anger Began

How on earth did two grown-up adults become so anxious about abandonment? To find the answer, we need only look at their past. For each of them their insecurity originated, as it does for all of us, in their first union—*the primal marriage*.

DORA'S PAST: HER PRIMAL MARRIAGE

"I remember it like it was yesterday," Dora said. "I was away, at summer camp—it was my first time at Camp Cejwin but my second summer at sleepaway. I was seven. I wasn't keen on going—but I went. I was always the kind of kid who listened; my parents wanted me to go, so I went. I felt homesick for weeks. But I stayed. My parents wanted me to.

"Nobody came for Visiting Day. My mother told me my father was going to be away on business and she couldn't make the trip herself.

"I stayed two months. I don't remember many letters. Once I got a care package, but I think that was it.

"Then I came home, on a plane from Vermont. Only my mother was at the airport. I don't think I even asked her where my father was—maybe I already knew something was wrong.

"My father was at the house when I got there. He was sitting in the living room as if he were a guest waiting for us. I walked into the living room with her—I had a sick feeling in my stomach.

"My father spoke first. 'I'm not going to be living here anymore,' he said. 'Mommy and I are getting a divorce.'

"If he said anything after that, I can't remember what it was. He left immediately after his 'speech.' I just remember feeling that my whole world had ended. And believe me, in a lot of ways it did."

Dora's father, who had been a remote figure in her first seven years, played an even smaller role in her life after her parents' divorce ("I never spent loads of time with my father before the divorce, but I know I didn't spend a single holiday with him once he left the house. He was very busy with his import business and I guess he just didn't have time for me").

Her mother was something else. High-strung and nervous, she became overinvolved with Dora after the divorce. "My mother who was always pretty pushy, put all her energies into me once Dad was gone. (Dad remarried but Mother never did.) I think she meant well, but she guided my every step. Especially when I got a bit older.

"I couldn't walk out of the house without giving her every detail about where I'd be. Then I had to dress just so. She watched my weight; I went to a dietitian at sixteen because she thought I wasn't losing my baby fat. She made sure I acted properly—I even went to a kind of etiquette class taught by a Miss Manners/Emily Post sort of lady. Mother left no stone unturned.

"And I was the perfect child. Always. The nice young lady."

At seven, with her parents' divorce, Dora's predictable world was wrenched from her without warning or notice. This was especially devastating because Dora was far from a secure child well before the divorce. Her mother, herself anxious, created a sense that the world at large was a dangerous place. Her father, who might have offered his little girl some protection by buffering her mother's nervous tension, was just not around very much.

The divorce itself, as well as Father's absence, fueled Dora's sense of insecurity. Dora understood her father's absence through her own pain—"If he loved me he would be with me."

Ironically and regrettably, her parents, who had not done a skillful job at providing Dora with a sense of confidence, made decisions that further undermined her sense of security. For example, sending her away from home, at six—to summer camp—when she was too little and too frightened to manage this long separation. Repeatedly in her primal marriage Dora learned an equation between being loved and being left. The divorce, in particular, left the sad but indelible impression that she had been forsaken by her parents.

The legacy of this primal marriage is that Dora is always grappling with anxiety. The abandoned little girl in her is easily revived. She manages this anxiety in much the same way her mother did. Feeling that the world is veering out of control, she tries to manage it by imposing order.

Might you be carrying the legacy of a primal marriage in which you too felt uncertain and insecure?

IS THIS YOUR PRIMAL MARRIAGE?

· Did you have a parent who was obsessed with your appearance (weight, size, attractiveness, dress). · Did you have a perfectionistic parent? · Did you have a fearful or even phobic caretaker?

Relaxed, calm, reassuring caretakers are crucial to a child's sense of security. We develop a comforting voice within ourselves when we have heard that voice in our primal relationship.

But the drive behind obsessive or perfectionistic parental concern is anxiety. Regrettably, what parents transmit to a child with their excessive involvement and vigilance is a sense that something is terribly wrong. If apprehension pervaded the atmosphere of your primal marriage, perhaps you were a worried child who grew to adulthood robbed of that inner comforting voice.

· Did you have an early, frightening, or unexpected separation from your family? · Were you hospitalized? · Did you live apart from your family for a time (i.e., spent time with relatives)? · Did your parents travel frequently? · Did they divorce?

A child's sense of time and distance is different from that of adults. Separations that may seem of little consequence to an adult ("It was only a week you spent with Grandma when your brother was born") may feel unending to a small child. Particularly to a small child, an absent parent (even due to illness or divorce) may indeed feel like one lost forever.

· As a child did you have rituals—at bedtime, for example (looking under the bed, door open just so, light on, favorite pillow, etc.)? · Did you have any object that you hated to be separated from (a blanket, pillow, teddy bear)? · Did you suck your thumb for 'a long time'? Were you distraught if you were denied these?

Anxious children seek ways to comfort themselves and may become overwrought if deprived of them. Repeated rituals may be a necessary and even indispensable attempt to achieve calm through predictability. A soft object that becomes an inseparable "friend" can be another path to reassurance. And the soothing consolation of a thumb is yet another way a child may seek relief from anxiety. Perhaps you were a child in dire need of such comforts.

PROVOKERS

• Were you a "clingy" child? • When you were small, did you have trouble separating from your caretaker? • Were you unduly frightened about going off to school? • Did you resist sleepover dates with friends? • Did you shy away from risk taking (i.e., sports, daredevil games)? • Did you get fixated on a "favorite" food?

A secure child can go off and explore the world, take chances, develop curiosity, because he or she is certain of the home base. If we live with the fear that what we have may be gone, that we will return to find nothing, we have that much more difficulty letting go of it. If as a child you suffered these inhibitions, it may be that you were afraid to let go of the little you felt you had.

• Were you a really "good" child? • Were you always dutiful, obedient? • Were you very neat and particular (i.e., about your toys)? • Did you hate to get messy or dirty?

It is a common childhood fantasy to associate being messy, disorderly, or dirty with being bad. Sometimes anxious children work overtime at making sure they are none of these "bad" things— they can't risk it. The fantasy is that if they are good (clean, neat, orderly, obedient), they won't be deserted.

Though your story may not be exactly like Dora's, the underlying issues may still reverberate in your primal marriage: You don't necessarily need to endure a personal calamity to develop a need to protect yourself from abandonment. Sometimes it is a climate of uncertainty that leads to feeling unanchored. The threat of abandonment can be as frightening and influential as an actual episode of desertion.

Now let's explore Teddy's primal marriage and how it created his fear of desertion. It might indeed cast light on your husband's inner emotional world as well.

TEDDY'S PAST: HIS PRIMAL MARRIAGE

"There are five of us—I've got two older brothers and two younger sisters—and still to this day Dad's point of pride is that he's never shown favoritism: 'You all got treated fair and square in my book' is the way he puts it.

123

"Mom really held down the fort but Dad ran the show—Mom took her orders from him. He was big on discipline. If we acted up at the dinner table, let's say I didn't want to eat something I didn't like, we had to leave. And then in this stern voice he'd instruct my mother—'No dinner.' And believe me, we didn't eat!

"If we really acted up, let's say we talked back to him, he'd give us a swat, or think up some really 'creative' punishment to teach us respect.

"Dad was big on self-sufficiency. We had a family game—a sort of wilderness version of hide-and-seek. He'd take a hike with one of us and have us mark the trail. Then he'd leave. And we had to find our way back, relying on the markers we'd put up. 'If you do a good job going out,' he'd say, 'it's a piece of cake getting back.'

"I don't remember much about myself when I was very young, but I do remember when my youngest sister was small—and I suppose she was treated just like I was. I remember very clearly that Joanna would be crying and my mother would make a move to pick her up. 'It will spoil her if you're always jumping up to save her,' he'd say. So, instead of picking her up, my mother might close the door or even turn on the radio so as not to hear Joanna.

"Actually, I think my mother was relieved. She wasn't one for cuddling kids herself. In spite of having five of us, she was not a 'baby person.' More than once she's told us that 'children improve with age.'"

What was going on in Teddy's primal marriage? Both of Teddy's parents were rigid and cold, not that interested in or capable of giving their children the individual time, attention, and warmth they needed—not that this was something either of them could admit to! Actually, they never needed to make these admissions, since they created a family system which made it possible and legitimate for them to hold back. How so? Under the guise of trying to build character, enforce discipline, and instill moral values, Teddy's parents relieved themselves of the more emotionally complicated aspects of parenting—sensitivity, responsiveness, understanding. In truth, they made a virtue out of their own shortcomings (Mother's awkwardness about touching Teddy became "cuddling spoils children"; Father's difficulty with being personal and intimate with Teddy became "I treat each child exactly the same").

How was Teddy affected by all this? From his infancy, Teddy's parents did not tune in to him. To a child, particularly a very young child, this absence of responsiveness is experienced as abandonment. From a child's point of view, when a parent is not there to respond (even if they're just next door in the living room listening to the radio), they are just not there at all. And this creates anxiety and uncertainty in children. Ironically and sadly, his parents who never left his side still left Teddy feeling deserted and unprotected.

But another problem developed in Teddy's primal marriage. The reliance on rules (dictated by his tyrannical father and rubber-stamped by his mother) left little room for self-assertion. Teddy wasn't allowed to object, have his own opinions, or be angry—especially at his parents. As any act of his developing autonomy was an act of defiance (risking punishment and banishment from the family), Teddy learned to express his contrary feelings covertly.

The net effect is that the legacy of Teddy's primal marriage is twofold. He carries around the fear of abandonment and the need to protect himself against it. But he is also dogged by a need to hide his overt anger and express it only in the most indirect fashion.

Maybe you have a husband who, like Teddy, seems to come from a rock-solid family but is indeed a person who has been left emotionally oppressed and wanting. These further questions may help you analyze your husband's primal marriage to see if this family system is at the root of his need.

IS THIS YOUR HUSBAND'S PRIMAL MARRIAGE?

· Were his parents disciplinarians? · Were they "old-fashioned" when it came to child rearing? · Did they have a lot of directives about how he should manage his life (object to girls who weren't good enough, assume he'd go to his father's alma mater, insist on a particular profession)?

Discipline, especially when it is rigid and harsh, is often a cover for a parent who is really being a dictator and wants to control children. Old-fashioned often means "we aren't interested in listening to our children, we want to run the show." And endless parental advice is often not about the sharing of wisdom but an attempt to domineer.

This kind of parenting forces a child's natural frustrations and anger underground. If this happened to your husband, it may explain the passive/aggressive aspect of his need.

· Did his parents push toward self-reliance? · Did they pride themselves on how self-sufficient he was at such an early age? · Did they like their children to act "grown-up"?

The faster children mature, the less a parent has to be involved. Sometimes caretakers push for maturity because it makes life less complicated for them. The difficulty is, a young child may feel he is being thrown out of the nest before being ready to fly. Perhaps this demand to be an adult before his time contributed to making your husband feel as if he lost his home base.

· Were his parents against "babying" their children? · As an infant, did they put him on a timetable (feeding, sleeping) right away? · Do they claim he was toilet-trained "right on schedule"?

Parenting, especially in a child's early life, requires following a child's lead and gradually shaping behavior to the schedule and demands of everyday life. This flexibility makes a child feel their world is responsive. Rigidity, forcing a child to fit a mold, might be a way in which your husband's parents failed to tune in to him. This failure to connect when a child is in need is a form of abandonment.

Taking Hold of the Problem: Getting Ready for an Adult Marriage

We now have a very different view of a pair of *provokers,* Teddy and Dora, than when we first met them. Ironically, these two people who seemed at first glance so opposite have all too much in common—*a need to prevent abandonment.*

Teddy's family seems such a contrast to Dora's. While her family foundered in a sea of anxiety, his seemed rocklike and substantial. But we discover that an authoritarian home, just like a broken home, may be the spawning ground for a fear of abandonment, albeit with the passive/aggressive twist.

All of this background changes the way we see things. Nagging Dora can become transformed when we learn she has an anxiety monster lurking inside her that needs appeasement constantly. And Teddy, who can be so annoying, is cast in an altogether different light when we see how little warmth and tenderness he received from his family.

This sort of mutual empathy reduces the likelihood that a couple will simply reemploy their old destructive style, provoking. But that isn't enough. With what we now know about this style, there are several things provokers can do to take hold of their problem and set the stage for change.

In the provoker style, we know the biggest problem is that couples are off balance and only one owns the anger. The challenge is to encourage *joint ownership of anger*. Probably the most effective way to accomplish this is to make anger the problem of the *relationship* rather than the problem of an individual *spouse*.

Instead of the actively angry partner making pronouncements ("I am so angry that you didn't . . . "), it is possible to offer anger as the problem. A question such as "I wonder why we get into these situations where I end up feeling angry with you?" can begin to lay the groundwork for seeing the anger as a joint dilemma.

You can "attack" the problem of anger rather than use the anger to attack the "problem" spouse. When you do so, you are issuing an invitation to your partner rather than hounding him or her. And you don't let your spouse off the hook. It's his/her anger, too!

And if you are the Dora, the actively irritated partner, in this duo, there are several things you can try to do that will help break the pattern of your destructive anger. You can remind yourself to try these different strategies:

- I don't have to react the moment I'm provoked; that plays right into my spouse's passive style and makes it easy for him to regard me as "the nag."
- I can talk about what irks me once I have some distance from the feeling; the more I talk about anger rather than appear irritated, the more my spouse will actually be listening. In this way I assert the legitimacy of my frustrations.
- I can choose my aggravations wisely. My constant state of

anxiety makes everything seem equally terrible. I need to stop and prioritize what I need my spouse to do based on reality, not on my own inner anxiety.

· I can let my spouse take over, on his terms. My perfectionism means I often do everything because I do it "perfectly." I can try to tolerate less than ideal conditions when trying to get something accomplished.

· I can say less critical things and more positive things. My anxiety colors my perceptions and keeps me from tolerating my frustrations. I generally see the glass half empty. I can remind myself to tell my husband all the things I appreciate about him.

And there are options that you can entertain if you play Teddy in this provoker pair. But probably none more important to remember than these:

· I can practice saying no. I am entitled to express my preferences in my marriage. My lifelong habit of denying my own assertiveness means I say yes without stopping to admit to myself or my spouse if that is my inner truth. I can stop and listen to my secret self. I can listen to my inner voice and ask my spouse to respect my wishes—once I know them myself!

· I can legitimize my anger through my directness. If I feel angry, as I often do, I can reveal it candidly, explicitly, openly. As I am increasingly straightforward about my anger, I will no longer have a need to be passively aggressive.

· I can own the anger in my marriage equally with my partner if I assert myself, and if I am forthright and open about my own angry sentiments.

You now have these new possibilities for handling your anger. They are possibilities that can help the imbalanced anger of a provoker-style marriage achieve greater alignment. When this happens, you will invariably feel a greater alliance with your spouse. Standing shoulder to shoulder rather than fuming in opposite corners of the room is the moment when you start making your marriage all it can be.

What's to come? So far we have met two couples, venters and provokers, who though very different in their angry lovestyles share a common bond: both know that they are in an angry marriage. Next, we meet four couples who share another quite different tie—they are in angry marriages and don't have a clue![1]

Instead of my office we'll have a change of venue, catching a glimpse of them through a typical moment in the actual marriage they share.

This switch is not arbitrary. Presenting each lovestyle as if every dissatisfied couple trotted into a psychotherapist's office would give quite the wrong impression. It just doesn't happen like that at all, particularly for those couples who don't even know they're angry.

In my experience, these couples are more likely to find their way into my office because one of them comes for a particular problem, such as depression, rather than both partners coming together for marital difficulty. Fortunately, what often happens is that the work of individual treatment changes the marital system so that the second spouse seeks help . . . eventually.

One of the couples we will learn about next—Laura and Jason, are enactors. We will meet them in the moments before they say goodnight. You won't be a fly on my office wall but you will be one in their bedroom! But before this detailed analysis of their enactor marriage, let's look at the more general features of this style. Perhaps you will begin to see the pattern of your own marriage taking shape.

Seven

ENACTORS

E very six months, for the last two and a half years of her six-year marriage to Art, Linda has regularly headed to the posh Golden Door Spa.

"It's hard to describe. I start feeling antsy. I just have to have the time off. I go to the spa for a week. Then I feel better. Art isn't thrilled; but he's got his golf game every week that he can't live without, so I have my spa."

Regrettably, the calm that settles over Linda is short-lived. In a few weeks she's setting her sights on her next visit to the Golden Door. As for Art, his golf game is not just a sport but an obsession.

It may be hard to work up sympathy for Linda and Art, an affluent couple who spend more time in saunas or on putting greens in a week than most people spend in a lifetime. But such trappings of "the good life" shouldn't fool us into missing their mutual misery. In spite of mudpacks, massages, herbal wraps, and holes-in-one, for the last two and a half years Linda and Art haven't had much fun together. This isn't lost on them. They know their marriage is not quite paradise, or even close to it. What they don't know and would be surprised to learn is that theirs is an angry marriage—enactor-style.

A Few of Their Favorite Things

While anger is at the root of their marital discontent, enactors like Linda and Art manage to keep their anger hidden. How do they get anger to perform its disappearing act? Enactors distract themselves from anger by using action in order to prevent feeling. These activities intended to dispose of emotional discomfort are "enactments," actions that are not just personal pleasures or pursuits but instead serve to prevent the expression of angry feelings. (Remember, as with any covert style, this is neither a conscious nor a deliberate strategy; instead, it is the unwitting and necessary way anger is banished.)

As a rule, enactors are compelled to do something to feel good in order to avoid feeling bad (read "angry"). For example, enactors may gratify themselves outside their partnerships in order that full-blown frustration with their spouse never comes to a head. And it isn't simply the spa or the links that can serve this purpose. In fact, for most enactors the escapes from anger are far more prosaic.

Pursuits, from shopping to gambling, sports to eating, may actually be an enactor's required escape. Yet every jogger, fan of football, and lover of vanilla fudge is not in an angry marriage. Obviously there are a fair number of happily married people who do many of the things just attributed to this covertly angry lovestyle. How can you tell if these aren't just run-of-the-mill events of married life but instead the dodges used by enactors?

Enough Is Never Enough

One telltale sign, the extent to which actions exist and anger doesn't, has already been suggested. Enactors who carry on their diversionary pursuits don't feel they're in the happiest of marriages, but they don't feel angry marital frustration, either. Ironically, they often feel quite the opposite; marriage is made easier and conflict-free because of the enactor behavior.

Typically, enactors are excessively involved with their distractions to a point where this significantly reduces the time available for marriage, spouse, and family. An "obsessed" golfer like Art who spends more of his free time in a golf cart than his bedroom is standard.

Enactors also expend a significant portion of their energies and resources, often money, on their pursuits. In short, enactors spend more time at and get greater satisfaction, pleasure, and reward from their chosen activities than they do from a marriage.

Time, effort, and energy aren't the only markers of enactors. Compulsion can be added to the list. Constantly attempting to fend off anger, enactors can never give up on the behavior that has unwittingly become their "protection" against feeling mad. For an enactor, enough is never enough. The woman who can't give up her endless shopping sprees, the man who can't miss his workouts no matter what, the workaholic who can't pass up the next deal may all be enactors. Actually, what they can't relinquish—though they haven't a clue as to the real motivation—is the behavior that chases anger away from their front door.

Separate Tables

Rather than bringing a couple together, enactor enterprises enable partners to go their own way. Pursuits are not common or shared, fostering distance instead of exchange. Art and Linda fell victim to this, admitting ruefully, after two years of spa visits and golf tournaments, that they were indeed leading "two different lives." This is the real trap for enactors: distance leads to lack of interest. Over the years, enactors may find they have little in common and end up conducting parallel lives. In the extreme, diverging interests may leave "two strangers living under one roof."

Not every enactor ends up feeling isolated, though many do. Nonetheless, emotional reactions certainly run more toward boredom than wrath, indifference than ire, apathy than antipathy. Enactors are likely to find each other and their marriage tiresome, dull, tedious, unstimulating. Marriage is not all that appealing. Sometimes lack of interest sours into revulsion; any feeling from distaste to disgust is possible.

Enactors are creative folk. The most ordinary aspects of married life can be turned, albeit unwittingly, into tools for defusing frustration. Let's take a closer look at the most typical ways enactors go about enacting.

There's Someone Else

In order to evade frustration over a lack of companionship in a marriage, enactors may substitute a same-sex friendship for the friend they don't find in their own partner. Finding intimacy outside a marriage may deflect angry disappointment about this deficit inside the partnership.

Generally, when it comes to quashing anger, female and male enactors use friendships quite differently. For a woman, more often than not, it means finding one very best friend who becomes confidante, comrade, counselor—all the things her husband fails to offer. In doing so, she doesn't have to face angry disappointment because her husband lacks the willingness to pay attention.

Men don't use friendships quite the same way. Rather than singling out one person to help them deflect frustration, they generally count on a group of friends for diversion. As a rule, male enactors herd rather than pair. Perhaps a husband spends endless hours "with the guys" shooting hoops, having a few beers, or bowling, where he feels uncritically accepted and admired.[1]

And the corner bar may no longer be the favored retreat; it may now be the computer. Nightly, Susan's husband, Joel, "meets" his hacker buddies on an international computer network, rather than the local bar and grill. Joel spends more time caressing his keyboard than his wife.

Friendships are not the only replacement relationships that enactors create. Substitute companionship may originate on the homefront, as near as the nursery. Enactors, dads or moms, may throw themselves into the lives of their children. The dad who spends more time coaching Little League than talking to his wife, the mom who's up all night typing term papers (not making love), may be using children as an unwitting ploy to dodge anger. Bear in mind, enactors are not just interested parents. They are overinvolved, vicariously deriving from their children's lives the excitement, pleasure, gratification they don't find in their marriages. A child-centered life obscures the deficits and deficiencies of a marriage, obliterating frustrations and keeping anger in check.

An Affair to Remember

An affair may be an enactor's activity of choice. But we need to remember that an enactor is using the affair in order to avoid experiencing ill-will. Therefore, for example, enactors do not use a lover as a weapon against their spouse the way an overtly angry venter might. Instead, a lover becomes the "good partner" to offset frustrations with the disappointing spouse. In a way, enactors make one good relationship from two people—lover plus spouse. For example, a married man might leave a good mother to his children at home while he has a good sex partner during lunch! By including both women in his life, an enactor has everything satisfied and avoids frustration.

Typically, enactors don't reveal affairs; on the contrary, they may even keep them a long-term secret. Confrontation is not in an enactor's best interest. It could upset the critical status quo that keeps anger in check.

So, if you find yourself "mad" about someone other than your spouse, you may be using an extramarital romance to keep from feeling mad. An affair to remember is often the way an enactor tries to forget—anger!

Keeping Busy—Body and Soul

Hobbies, civic projects, charities, sports may be some of the myriad ways enactors deflect anger. But some enactors go in very different directions, turning to spiritual pursuits. Having a guru, a healer, or a psychic may be an attempt to fill up a spiritual vacuum that exists in a marriage. If we get solace this way, we don't have to pay close attention to the emotional deficiencies of a marriage.

Many, many enactors use food in order to stifle anger. Covertly angry, they seek oral gratification when marital gratification is wanting. In other words, they eat instead of eating themselves up with rage.

Getting "filled up" is an enactor dodge that isn't limited to food. Some enactors "shop till they drop," filling up a closet instead of a stomach. These spending sprees work to camouflage anger in much the same way eating binges do. Giving in to the pleasure of an impulse ("I *must* have that dress") may supply a person with gratification. Then an individual is less susceptible to facing up to a lack of marital fulfillment.

Although women are often stereotyped as "spenders," men easily take to this kind of enactment, buying themselves "toys." The latest stereo equipment, a state-of-the-art computer, a new five iron may be the playthings men indulge in as anger avoidance.

But working is probably the single most common enactor strategy. And nowadays the workaholic enactor may as easily be the wife as the husband. (In the couple to follow, the husband, Jason, is the perfect prototype; he's too busy being enmeshed in the next deal to get mad.) So, ironically, as we will soon see, the spouse stuck nightly in an endless commute from work may actually need and welcome this as part of his diversion.

Paying the Price

Enactor behavior is often self-defeating, even self-destructive. For example, a workaholic enactor may sacrifice his participation in the life of his family, risking stress, high blood pressure, even a heart attack. The eater may sacrifice her health and figure in becoming less attractive to her spouse. The shopper may blow the family budget and financial stability. Unfortunately, enactors may even resort to seriously harmful behavior in order to find relief from anger:

"Let's do a line or two after the kids are asleep."

"Do you have any Valium?"

"It's only a weekend junket to the casinos."

"Why don't we have any beer in the house?"

These refrains are often sounded by enactors whose efforts to subdue an inner storm of anger may put them at risk (a marker of just how awful it must be to let the anger erupt).

Alcohol may be an enactor's attempt to douse the fury. Using liquor to unwind, to feel mellow, to relax, to forget may actually be an unwitting attempt to take the edge off wrath.

Stemming the tide of rage through drugs (cocaine, marijuana), improperly used medication (tranquilizers, sedatives, sleeping pills), or even compulsive sex (one-night stands, prostitutes) may feel necessary, even urgent. By providing an enactor with a surge or rush of pleasurable feeling, a potentially bad mood is altered to the point where anger "ceases" to exist, at least for that moment.

Gambling, which provides thrills and excitement, may provide another potent "rush," offering a special escape hatch: If there ever is any anger, it is directed toward "lady luck" rather than a spouse.

It's important to point out that enactors are not necessarily falling-down drunks, drug addicts, sexual predators, or gamblers who have mortgaged the house. While the risk is that an enactor's behavior may take on a life of its own and begin to dominate the enactor's existence, these are the extremes.

What we are really focusing on is the person who may not be addicted but still needs the drink, drugs, sex, or gambling to make married life more palatable. That's the yellow flag!

Jason and Laura are enactors. Jason overworks; Laura overeats. Neither of them has yet used an affair as a defense strategy against anger, but one of them is certainly considering the possibility.

The Actual Marriage of Two Enactors: Jason and Laura

Laura sat in bed watching *The Late Show*. Jason was in taking a shower. As on so many other nights, he had come in from work after 10:00 P.M. After finding himself something to eat he had finally come upstairs and headed directly for the shower. So, even though it was late, Laura still had a good half hour to herself.

Laura didn't much mind. Actually, it made life easier; Jason didn't like to see Laura cozily eating in bed, and as usual she was in the mood for ice cream.

Unfortunately for both of them, as Jason emerged from the bathroom he spotted Laura shoving the ice-cream container into the wastebasket. "It was such a 'turn-off,' " Jason mused. "Too bad I didn't come home after Laura was asleep."

Laura had been a good-looking woman when she first came as a "temp" to his office. His first marriage was already history, even if it did take a few years for him to move out, but Laura had certainly been an important reason for making the final break. Things had been so much better with Laura, especially in bed, that it made his divorce seem right.

Just four years later and what a difference! Jason felt slightly revolted at the idea of making love to Laura. Now, noticing the ice cream, he just had to say something.

"Don't you think you should hold off on this ice-cream routine? Couldn't you try another treat to break this habit?" he commented without any rancor in his voice.

Laura hated her battles with weight, but she just couldn't swear off the treats she loved to indulge in from time to time. She kissed Jason goodnight and mumbled something about trying harder.

Before he turned out the lights, Jason reminded Laura of his upcoming plans for the next few days.

"It looks like that bank merger is coming through," he said in a suddenly animated voice. "I've been sweating this one. And believe me, it will be another feather in my cap.

"I can't wait until the Rotary Club meets. The timing is perfect. The guys will be drooling."

Laura didn't make a comment. She just couldn't get into Jason's excitement over a big deal; it would hardly make her "drool."

As quickly as he began Jason ended his monologue, turned over, and fell asleep. And Laura was left awake thinking about something, the new gym instructor, that did indeed excite her.

Laura closed her eyes and Mat's dark, lean body came into view. Today, he had made her feel so at ease, even about those extra pounds—"I hate those young scrawny women. Can you imagine Rubens painting those broads? No way! It's a woman like you he'd be after."

Laura wasn't certain, but she thought Mat's hand brushing against her breast as he said this was no accident. Even now her nipples got hard, once again, as she remembered his touch. She imagined making love with Mat the way she and Jason used to when Jason was still married to his first wife.

Laura smiled. Thinking about Mat was more relaxing than a Valium. She'd have to get to the gym more often. Maybe Jason's advice was worth taking—"Try another treat to break the ice-cream habit." She laughed to herself as she fell off to sleep. "I might just try Mat; at least he'd be a lot less fattening."

An Actual Marriage: Are You Enactors?

Jason and Laura are in a typical enactor marriage. Jason isn't overtly angry and neither is Laura. Rage and wrath are just not part of their *actual marriage* but action is—both *enact* in order not to feel. Jason works. Laura eats. Both have affairs (remember that was how they met). Is this the state of your marital union as well? And are these additional telltale signs indicative of yours, too?

- Both find married life more palatable thanks to their enactor behavior . . . She finds a cozy night alone "easier"; he prefers his late nights at the office.
- They are indifferent . . . She's not interested in his deal; he doesn't ask about her day.
- They have a distaste for each other . . . sexually.

As you run a check of your marriage against that of Jason and Laura, you might find that your actual marriage is reminiscent of theirs. Or you might discover, regrettably, that alcohol, drugs, sex, or gambling are part of your more self-destructive enactor marriage.

Two for the Price of One: Burying Anger/Burying a Need

Every angry marriage has its hidden driving forces, unconscious needs. But an angry marriage where anger must be hidden (like that of enactors Laura and Jason) is burdened by a second set of hidden forces: Not only is our unconscious busy burying needs, it's busy burying anger, too. For those couples in covertly angry marriages, enactor or otherwise, the mind is working overtime.

As we go on to decode the complaints of Laura and Jason, we will discover that for enactors some of the very same behaviors that keep them from feeling their anger may also reveal the nature of their needs.

For example, as we will see with Jason, work may prevent anger from taking hold, but it might also be a way to fight sadness (his unconscious need). And what about Laura? Food might keep her anger in check, but it might also be her attempt to combat inner emptiness as well (her unconscious need).

For each participant in a covertly angry marriage, two processes are served for the price of one. Therefore, the task is twofold: uncover the anger; unearth the need. We've addressed ourselves to the first. Now, by decoding the complaints, we can tackle the second.

Decoding Complaints: Making the Invisible Marriage Visible

What buried needs are driving a wedge between Laura and Jason? Jason the workaholic is actually a man grappling with depressive feelings. Along with his need to defuse his anger, he has an unconscious need—*to fight sadness*.

Laura is unwittingly engaged in her own painful struggle. Not only is she loathe to experience anger but she has an unconscious need—*to fill her emptiness*. These inner battles are at the root of their angry marriage.

As we explore the grievances of their *actual marriage* and decode the complaints, this powerful but *invisible marriage* will come into focus. Perhaps yours will, too.

HER COMPLAINTS = HIS NEED

First, we can consider the complaints Laura has about Jason. Each of her grievances can help piece together his need, to keep sadness at bay.

While Laura doesn't mind the "time off" from Jason because he's so busy with work, she does have something to say about the hectic pace it creates in their life.

"We never have time to relax. He's always got another poker in the fire, a new building that has to be seen, a location to be scouted. Just when he's planned to spend a quiet weekend at home, he'll find something at the office that he just *has* to do."

Jason, who is always active and busy, hardly fits the stereotype of what most of us (including Laura) imagine as a depressed person. Probably most people think of depression more conventionally: someone cries, feels "blue," and suffers from inertia; he can hardly get out of bed to face the world each day. That is one way sadness strikes us, but it isn't the only way.

Actually, the very opposite may happen. Depression can rev us up. Depression can keep individuals on the run as if they can outpace the sadness that seems to chase them down. A person looks active but is actually agitated.

The man who can't stand still, listen to music, take time off, read to his children before bedtime, or ever welcome any other low-key activities may be a person who, like Jason, is dogged by sadness, and is on the run from it.

Laura also complains that leisure time with Jason is a big problem. And vacations become impossible: Jason is on a cellular phone to the office even on the beach!

With the need to keep away sadness, relaxing for a man like Jason is just too threatening. It creates a quiet which allows his depressive feelings to catch up with him. Jason can't lie on a beach listening to the surf because peacefulness gives his sadness an opportunity to wash over him like a wave.

YOUR COMPLAINT: YOUR HUSBAND'S NEED

Do you have a restless, intense, driven husband? Perhaps you might begin to rethink this perception and consider the psychology behind his relentless chase. Maybe it is sadness that is stalking him, after all. These other decoded complaints can help you get closer to understanding your husband's need.

> · *Your Complaint*

Nothing holds his interest for very long; he's out of one thing and into the next; he gets bored so easily.

> · *Your Husband's Need*

It isn't that he grows tired of an activity. Rather, he needs to keep himself involved in *all* absorbing pursuits at *all* times so as not to have room for the sadness (or his anger).

> · *Your Complaint*

After a big deal he's elated, for about a minute. If he finishes a project and there isn't another immediately in sight he's restless. I think he's secretly disappointed when everything goes well and things are ready to wind down.

· *Your Husband's Need*

When the intensity let's up at the close of the day or the close of a deal, he faces an emotional letdown. When things come to a rest, he finds himself dropping back down into the depressive feelings.

· *Your Complaint*

He's always bragging; he broadcasts his success to everyone; he even shows off to our own kids.

· *Your Husband's Need*

He may unwittingly try to enlist everyone around him in helping to lift his spirits. It isn't showing off; he's fighting his demons.

· *Your Complaint*

He's always got to have that drink before dinner. He likes to do a line or two of coke every weekend. He sometimes takes diet pills to perk himself up.

· *Your Husband's Need*

Alcohol, drugs, and misused prescription medications are often resorted to by people who are struggling with depression (as well as anger) and don't know it. Because they may have a momentary effect of blocking a mood, these substances are a way unhappy people attempt to fight their sadness. Regrettably, they don't eliminate the sadness but in the end actually make things worse.

If your hard-driving husband uses alcohol or drugs, he might be attempting to self-medicate against depression. Self-medication for depression is behind many, many people's use of alcohol and drugs.

Remember also that such substances tamp down the angry fires: two for the price of one.

These insights may help you cast a new light on your husband, though it may be difficult for you to consider a man who appears so dynamic as one who is also depressed. His outer life may, at first glance, give little inkling to the quiet sadness that envelopes him. Perhaps with what you now know you can see things, not as they seem, but as they really are.

HIS COMPLAINTS = HER NEED

Laura's complaints offer a window on Jason's need. And the reverse is true: Decoding Jason's grievances enables us to have insight into Laura's need—to fill the emptiness. And this analysis may provide guidance for insight into your own behavior.

Much of Jason's criticisms center on Laura and other men:

"Laura's always flirting. She's invariably got some young 'protégé' (an artist, a dancer, an unemployed carpenter) in tow. We have some lousy paintings and a lot more furniture than we need because she has to 'support' them."

If a person feels meaningless and empty, she may use attention to fill an inner void. For Laura, the admiration of a man makes her feel bathed in good feelings. But she needs an endless supply of adoration to fill a virtually bottomless pit; therefore, she must have an endless parade of "admirers."

Laura's inner hunger makes her very susceptible to being taken advantage of. Her need clouds her judgment. An unscrupulous man, sensing her need, showers Laura with admiration not because he sincerely feels it but because he knows it's a way to manipulate her: If he fills her empty heart, he can empty her pocketbook!

While Laura may not yet be having a full-fledged affair with Mat, Jason is aware that she's inclined in that direction:

"I'm no fool. I know Laura has a lot of sexual drive and it isn't being used in our bedroom. But I think she gets bored easily."

Laura turns away from what she has with Jason (especially since marriage has put a damper on their "mad passion"). Looking as if she's grown "bored," she is actually in a desperate search for more and more outside affirmation and stimulation to banish the inner void.

Why does she resort to sex to plug the void? It's as if the physical act of having someone inside her could fill the emotional vacancy. What's more, the bodily sensations of lovemaking, the surge of unbounded pleasure, offer Laura a respite from her inner deadness. And remember, too, if she's having good sex outside her marriage, her angry frustration is doused. Again, two feelings buried through one enactment.

YOUR HUSBAND'S COMPLAINT = YOUR NEED

You may not be quite like Laura. You might be more inclined to express your need through your relationship to your children or perhaps friends rather than an extra man or scoop of ice cream. These additional decoded complaints may help you see yourself and your need to fill the emptiness, even if sex is not part of the picture.

· Your Husband's Complaint

She's always cooking up a storm. She overeats. She can never stick to a diet. She stuffs the kids. She's got a terrible sweet tooth.

· Your Need

Food is the way many, many people cope with inner emptiness. Trying to soothe themselves, they feed the body as if it could fill up the soul. Since the longing is never sated, they keep on eating. With an inner void you have an endless task on your hands (no wonder you can't diet!).

· Your Husband's Complaint

She's got everything and she still wants more. She's spoiled and she wants to spoil the kids.

· *Your Need*

When feeling empty, people often turn to material objects erroneously (and unconsciously) believing, if I have what I want I will feel better. Maybe this (car, dress, jewelry . . .) will do the trick. But it doesn't work. We get what we think we "want"—and we still feel hollow and bereft. So we try again and again, appearing ungrateful when what we are is empty. This unhappy insatiability is often mislabeled as "spoiled." Does your lover mislabel and misunderstand your misery?

· *Your Husband's Complaint*

She overdoes it with Valium. She uses sleeping pills. I think she takes the diet pills because they give her a buzz.

· *Your Need*

It is often frightening to feel emotionally barren and empty. When the silence and the loneliness become unbearable, some people resort to substances that chase it away or put them to sleep. Conveniently, such efforts also banish anger! Again, two for one!

· *Your Husband's Complaint*

She's a real princess. She hasn't done anything with her life. She only wants to be richer than we are.

· *Your Need*

Outer life is a reflection of inner feelings. If a person feels filled up with goodness, she has an inner reserve into which she can dip—for herself as well as others. She can give, she can do, she can accomplish, she can achieve, she can feel "rich" only if she possesses inner resources. Emotional emptiness invariably gives rise to a barren life (ironically, when a woman suffers such emotional impoverishment, she often gets the title "princess").

Perhaps these insights may make you and your spouse far more sensitive to each other. And with that sensitivity you can move forward to see just how the cycle of conflict spins on, depriving your marriage of the joy and pleasure it could certainly hold.

THE INVISIBLE MARRIAGE AND
THE CYCLE OF CONFLICT

Looking back on the relationship of Jason and Laura, we can see how their needs keep them locked into their enactor marriage. Perhaps through them you can get a fix on your own unhappy cycle.

Unlike venters and provokers, enactors in conflict don't spend time being openly angry; they do more of what they do best—*enact!* And that is what puts an enactor marriage at risk.

How does it "work" for Jason and Laura? We can start with Jason. His need to fight the sadness makes his work all-consuming; he doesn't stop for a moment (that behavior is determined by his need). Laura, unable to appreciate Jason's real motivation, instead feels unattended and neglected. She doesn't get the fueling she desperately craves. So she goes off to find it in other places (like Mat and the refrigerator).

Where does that leave Jason? With Laura more removed, less involved with him, Jason finds cold comfort on the homefront and no relief from his sadness. So, in order to prevent being engulfed by despondency, he throws himself that much more into work. And the cycle of enactment spins on.

But another spin can be put on it if we begin with Laura and a behavior determined by her need. She "cocoons": coziness helps combat her emptiness.

To Jason, Laura's "refueling" feels like inactivity, and for Jason that's deadly; inactivity pulls Jason down into his depressive feelings. So Jason, driven by his need, finds something to take him up and away (for example, another "new deal").

Then where does that leave Laura? On her own. With Jason emotionally unavailable, she feels emptier than ever. And she's back to fulfilling her need in her usual enactor ways (please pass the Häagen-Dazs!). The cycle spins on. *Unmet needs make Jason and Laura enact over and over and over again!*

The Primal Marriage: Where the Anger Began

Why is Jason so sad? How did Laura end up feeling so emotionally barren and lonely? Where did such powerful needs originate? And why are these two people carrying another burden, hidden anger? The answers lie in their past, in the primal marriage where the pain first took shape.

LAURA'S PAST: HER PRIMAL MARRIAGE

Laura still remembers her first party dress:

"I think I wore it for my fourth or fifth birthday. It was a green velvet dress with small pink satin roses around the neckline that my mother, who always dressed me to the hilt, had bought.

"I remember it scratched me terribly but my mother insisted I wear it—'Every little girl dreams of a dress like this,' she told me. So I wore it.

"It was a big party. There was a magician doing tricks and a bunch of children having a great time. I wasn't one of them.

"My father as usual wasn't there—and my mother only stayed long enough to greet the guests. I remember watching her go upstairs and asking her to stay. Actually, I don't think I said it. I just held onto her skirt.

"She pushed me away. 'Don't be difficult, darling. I have a terrible headache. Jeremy is a wonderful magician. I am sure all the children are envious.'

"I started to whimper. Mother got stiff and her voice got stern. 'Laura, stop this carrying on at once. You are so dreadfully ungrateful. And you look so red and ugly when you cry.'

"I tried to stop, hoping she'd stay, but she just looked disgusted and retreated, as she always did, to her room.

"My mother, always picture-perfect, only emerged from her bedroom when my father came home. She spent an enormous amount of time on her looks. I could never kiss her because I'd mess up her makeup.

"Melva [her nanny] would put me to bed while my parents would have a late dinner together (I usually ate earlier with Melva). I'd sneak Twinkies into my bedroom. My parents would have killed me, but they never came into my room. And if Melva did see them, she never ratted on me. I think she felt sorry for me."

Perhaps Laura's life seems the virtual prototype of the poor little rich girl. Laura had parents who gave her many material things. But they had a much more difficult time giving her what she needed most—themselves! Their love, attention, and affection were in short supply. In fact, when Laura did turn to them, they felt put upon, as if her childlike needs were a stream of unreasonable demands.

They didn't like being parents, and having a child didn't really suit their temperament; they dealt with their own shortcomings by turning over much of their responsibilities to others—nannies, housekeepers, "magicians," tutors, instructors. But always under the guise that they were giving everything to Laura that her heart could desire.

Parenting of this kind engendered enormous loneliness in Laura. Denied the basic connection of generous loving kindness from her caretakers, Laura felt empty inside. But she was also confused because, at least on the surface, "she had everything."

This behavior created an emotional contradiction: Laura felt emotionally starved while she looked completely well supplied materially. The angry hurt and disappointment that she might have felt toward her parents for giving so little emotional sustenance was cut off at every turn ("Why are you crying? No other child has all the things you have").

Laura had "no cause" to get angry; Laura had "no right" to her anger. Indeed, she was sternly reproached if she even whimpered in protest. In effect, Laura learned that her anger had *no legitimacy*. As a result, she was forced to deny its very existence! It is here in her primal marriage that Laura's anger was first forced out of the emotional picture. Anger denied is anger buried.

Thus the legacy of Laura's primal marriage is twofold: It gives rise to a painful sense of inner loneliness, and it is the place where her anger first gets banished.

Could this be the double burden you carry from your own primal marriage right into your adult partnership? You needn't be the poor little rich girl to feel the disparity between what your parents gave you materially as opposed to what they shared emotionally. Might you be a person who had the appearance of receiving plenty while feeling emotionally starved? Could this be at the core of your primal marriage?

IS THIS YOUR PRIMAL MARRIAGE?

· Do you have few if any memories of your parents playing with you or joining in on any school activities? · Did you rarely have kids to your house? · Did you prefer to go to other people's homes?

Children who miss their parents' deep involvement often have a paucity of memories of shared happy times together. Unable to put their finger on what they are lacking, they feel drawn to homes where parental warmth and interest are in more abundance.

· Did you have tantrums? · Did you whine or cry when you wanted something?

Confused and miserably unhappy children often have tantrums. They feel uncontrollable frustration because they see something they want and can't have it. What they don't understand is that the frustration of not having what they need emotionally is at the bottom of their unhappy outbursts. Perhaps that's what you really wanted and couldn't have.

· Were you told you were "spoiled"?

Happy, fulfilled children with inner contentment don't struggle with this chronic dissatisfaction, while children who feel empty and deprived do. It's also worth remembering that something "spoils" when it has not been taken care of properly. Maybe on an emotional level that happened to you.

· Did you ever steal things from other kids or want to? · Were you envious of other kids? · Did you ever sneak food behind your parents' backs? · Did you have any eating-related problems? · Did you make up stories or lie?

Children who feel empty and bereft often try to fill in the missing spaces and make up the deficits. Unable to put their longing into words, they take action. Sometimes they actually take things that belong to others. Sometimes they try and fill the hole inside them with food. Sometimes they make up for the deficit by making themselves someone else through fabrication or fantasy.

No two primal marriages are exactly alike. Your family may seem worlds apart from Laura's. Nannies and extravagant birthday parties might not be part of your personal history, but you may have suffered emotional deprivation nonetheless. If your need to dispel the emptiness (and deny the anger) took root in an emotionally ungiving family, the next task is to see how your husband's need to dispel sadness came about. Jason's primal marriage can be our point of departure.

JASON'S PAST: HIS PRIMAL MARRIAGE

"My mother was always angry. She woke up angry. She went to bed angry. For the most part she was angry at my father. He didn't make enough. He didn't get the promotion. He wasn't rich like his brother, Larry.

"I can't say I remember a lot of these episodes because I didn't spend a lot of time at home. I was pretty independent from an early age. I always stayed in the school yard shooting hoops or something. Most nights I wasn't home until dinnertime.

"My father was a really bright man. He was always up on politics (he loved all those current affairs shows on TV). He was the nicest egg. He would give someone the shirt off his back (that would infuriate my mother, too—'Charity begins at home,' she'd snipe at him).

"Dad did not fight back. Never. 'You just have to learn to take your mother with a grain of salt,' he'd confide to me after one of her tirades, or he'd joke, 'She doesn't sound so bad if you're watching a football game and having a beer.'

"I wasn't angry with my father, but I do remember after I visited my uncle Larry in L.A. that I wished we had a house with a swimming pool.

"For a while when my father got laid off, Larry sent us money. And believe me, my mother didn't let my father forget it. She could be a real ball-buster. I remember once, during that period, we were eating dinner and my father didn't seem to like it. My mother let Dad have it:

" 'If you were paying for it, you'd have the right to complain. In the meantime only your brother has that right, and he's in California.'

"My mother had some mouth!"

Jason could not take his father's advice: "Take your mother with a grain of salt." On the contrary, she had an enormous impact on him. Jason loved his father and it hurt him to see the incessant belittlement and humiliation against which his father never took a stand.

This pain of seeing his defeated father is a sadness Jason carries with him from his primal marriage. But there are other things that conspired to create the melancholy mood that dogs him in his adulthood.

What Jason could not appreciate was that passivity was a marker of his father's own depression. Handicapped by depression, Jason's father had little ability to take hold of his own life: Depression robbed him of his assertiveness, his get up and go, his aggressiveness. It crippled his capacity to work. It even prevented him from defending himself and standing up to his wife's barrages.

As a result, Jason is not only saddened by his father's plight, he also unconsciously identifies with him. Jason has taken on the depression of his father. But Jason's efforts to manage the sadness are different. If his father gave himself up to the sadness, Jason throws himself into activity to try to escape it.

If this is the origin of his need, the question remains as to why the absence of anger? All children (especially boys) want a father to be heroic, larger than life. When he isn't, when he instead seems a crashing disappointment, it makes them sad *and* mad—how dare my hero fail me! Therefore, in addition to feeling sorry for his father, Jason, like any other little boy, was also angry with his dad.

But his father's sad quality made it impossible for Jason to express his frustrations openly. His father acted like a wounded bird, and Jason's anger provoked far too much guilt in him to be expressed at a man who was already down for the count. So, while Jason was feeling sorry for his father, he could not permit himself to feel irate. Jason's anger was buried under a mound of guilt.

Perhaps in some way your husband shares Jason's primal history, a father who evokes both overt sadness and covert anger? Was his father a model for his own depression? These additional queries may enable you to understand the nature of your husband's primal marriage and how it impacts on your marriage.

· Did he have a passive father? · Was his dad a "loser"? · Did his father have trouble holding a job? · Was there a disparity between his father's talents and his accomplishments?

Men who have capacities that they cannot realize often suffer from depression—the real and insurmountable obstacle to success. Ironically, your husband's workaholism may be his effort to "prove" he will not be the failure his father was. Unfortunately, your husband may still be fighting the same demon as his dad.

· Are his childhood memories sad? · Does he think of his family as joyless? · Was there little excitement or pleasure in his home? · Does he think of his parents' marriage as unhappy?

The problem of sadness may not lie with one member of the family alone. Families can be depressive. A pall of gloom may have enveloped everyone, including your husband. And he may carry that burden on into your marriage.

· Was he the sort of kid who barely came home? · Was he always on the go (sports, friends, school activities)? · Did he run around with a crowd (a gang)?

Perhaps your husband had to escape an unhappy home and attempt to chase away the despondency in himself as well. Activities as innocent as "shooting the hoops" till sunset or more self-destructive pursuits such as running around with a fast and wild crowd could have been his attempt to cope. As an adult, his style of dealing with the gloom may not have changed.

Taking Hold of the Problem: Getting Ready for an Adult Marriage

How different two enactors like Jason and Laura can seem once we possess insight. It is as if we are meeting two different people. The workaholic and the spoiled princess are labels we can only apply if we fail to appreciate their emotional struggles against sadness and loneliness. But once we know about Jason's depressed father and Laura's unsuitable parents, we can feel empathetic rather than write them off out of hand.

If you make these same connections in your own enactor marriage, you offer yourselves the same possibility for mutual compassion. The more you understand, the less likely it is that you will kick in to your habitual enactor cycle. And in turn, the likelihood of boredom, apathy, or antipathy in your marriage is diminished by creating the opportunity to care about each other.

But specifically, as enactors, there is one thing couples can and must attend to in order to take hold of the problem. If you are enactors, you now know your biggest problem: action substitutes for feelings—you *do* in order not to *feel.* And here is an important warning: No enactor marriage can change until enactments are curbed!

In an enactor marriage, insight is crucial, but it can only go on to transform a partnership if the behaviors that defuse unpleasant and unacceptable feelings are eliminated. There is no way around this. If you have, for example, substituted a best buddy, a favorite child, or a pet charity for a full-blooded (and therefore frustrating) marital relationship, you will have to reduce your level of involvement with those people or activities. And in other situations, in order to allow anger into your marriage, where it belongs, you will have to eliminate or markedly curb your enactments:

If you binge . . . you have to stop bingeing.

If you drink . . . you have to stop drinking.

If you have affairs . . . you have to stop having affairs.

If you do coke . . . you have to stop doing coke.

It is self-deception to suggest that a person can hang on to enactor behaviors and break out of this self-defeating style. The two are mutually exclusive, contradictory:

· Enactments prevent us from feeling.
· If we don't let ourselves feel, we can never learn to put our feelings into words.
· And words are the only way out.

An angry enactor marriage can only change once pain and unhappiness are put into words. Angry marriages (enactor or otherwise) only change through communication that is grounded in insight. We will detail this insight-based exchange in a later chapter on using insight and the new language of love (chapter eleven). Such communication ultimately transforms our angry marriage into an adult marriage.

While transforming action into words is crucial, it is also, especially for enactors, enormously difficult. After all, think about it. When an enactor stops doing the very things that help him or her chase away intolerable feelings, he/she is going to experience those warded-off feelings! For example, Jason will feel the brunt of his depression and Laura the anguish of her emptiness.

This hardly makes the prospect of giving up enactments enticing. But there is something crucial to remember. Jason is not a sad little boy and Laura is not a lonely little girl. They may feel emotional pain once they relinquish their enactor pursuits, but since they are no longer vulnerable little children, they possess what it takes to survive even their most overwhelming emotions. And what's more, they have each other.

Enacting is an old solution, resorted to because people had no better way to solve the problems of a primal marriage, the pain of sadness and the heartache of emotional emptiness. It is time and it is possible to find a better way. And never forget that with your most intimate and loving partner, your spouse, you can relinquish your enactments and help each other heal.

DISPLACERS

Surprisingly, we can probably understand displacers most easily if we think of politics, not love: find an external opponent
and divert disquiet on the homefront. Unconsciously, in a
word, that is the displacer's strategy. Displacers are very angry
people, who don't get angry with one another. In order to feel safe,
displacers divert anger to targets outside their partnership. In this
way, anger rears its "ugly head"—but at a secure distance from their
marriage. Displacers need outside enemies because they unconsciously assume that the rage they feel, if allowed admittance into
their own union, will turn them into mortal enemies.

In fact, the more displacers feel angry frustration outside their
own union, toward a mutual adversary, the less they feel it for each
other. If displacers do happen to feel the glimmer of their hidden

rage emerging, they can always shift frustration back to where it "belongs"—the enemy!

Actually, while displacers are among the last people to feel angry *within* their marriage, they are often couples whose angry (albeit covert) lovestyle emerges very early on in their partnership; it may well emerge even before they "tie the knot." (Displacers are often planning an engagement party while railing against their prospective in-laws!)

Us vs. Them

Displacers are couples who form themselves into a basic unit, a sort of closed system. There is a definite sense of "us" and "them" that goes along with this angry lovestyle. Displacers seem to have a chip on their marital shoulders, often resenting the way they are treated by others. Arguing with their outside foes or in the extreme irately cutting off relations altogether ("How could they do this to us; to hell with them!) is typical. This latter reaction can leave displacers with a sort of phantom enemy, for example, the sister they actively detest but haven't seen for twenty years (one displacer I know refers to her sibling as her "ex-brother"). Holding grudges, nursing wounds are well within the repertoire. Displacers have a long and unforgiving memory. And they need it to ensure an ever present target for their wrath.

Angry: Nine to Five

Family members are typically the first and foremost displacer enemies. A mother-in-law continues to be the "perfect" foe on all counts. If open antagonism against the family hasn't erupted by the wedding, as it often does (classically, displacers find wedding plans a fertile breeding ground for family enmity: "Your mother will wear chartreuse over my dead body!"), it surely emerges around other marital milestones—for example, the first grandchild. Displacers, when they are new parents, don't argue with each other over child rearing; it's too perilous. Instead, they get mad at the new grandmas and grandpas, aunts and uncles ("Maybe in their day you didn't pick up a crying baby, but *we* don't believe in that nonsense"; *"They* have no right to tell us how to raise our child! *Their* kids are no prizes!").

Displacers may also shift their anger in directions that extend well beyond family. A friend, boss, employee, or co-workers may be the person onto whom anger is jettisoned. Ed, an X-ray technician, and Katie, a paralegal, are displacers who unwittingly transpose their "dangerous" marital anger to less threatening territory, the office. From their shared perspective, Ed is surrounded by the most impossibly demanding doctors: "They give everything to me at the last minute and then they want the results yesterday."

Katie meanwhile is in an office brimming with incompetents: "I know twice as much as most of the high-priced lawyers. You should see the mistakes they make and expect me to correct."

When couples like Ed and Katie unknowingly shift their anger away from each other and onto others, it often has a specific quality. The anger that is displaced is not volatile rage or open, aggressive hostility. It is more in the vein of angry impatience, disgruntled disappointment, suspiciousness.

Displacers tend to be judgmental and critical—not of themselves, of course; Ed wouldn't suggest Katie might be impatient, nor would Katie intimate that Ed might be inefficient. That could stir up antagonism between them. They have a different sort of joint venture: They find fault and often tend to look down on *other* people, even those they claim to like. (As one "friend" of Ed and Katie once quipped, "They even hate the people they like.")

A Complex Superiority Complex

Displacers probably gossip with one another, commiserating about all the injustices, the injuries, the things people do and say that they can't abide. And displacers do it behind closed doors—it's just between the two of us.

Their angry irritation with others can sound as if displacers are backbiting and disloyal, suffering from a jointly held "superiority complex." But this conclusion misses the essence of what it means to struggle with this covert style and the enormous need displacers have to protect their partnership from rage. By feeling "superior," displacers bind themselves securely together, forming an exclusive club to which only two people belong.

But turning inward has its consequences in married life and is often misinterpreted by those they turn away from. Margo and Sam felt the jolt of this misconception intrude on their displacer marriage:

"Around the holidays, I knew people in the office were planning a New Year's party. I overheard a comment about Sam and me. They said we were snobs and even if we did come, we wouldn't talk to anyone. It really hurt."

Irene and Roger didn't need to eavesdrop to feel the sting of this typical misinterpretation:

"When I told my sister we wouldn't be coming to her picnic, she lashed out, 'You two are so full of yourselves you'd never lower yourself to be with me and my friends.'"

Regrettably, displacers are often seen by outsiders as aloof, unsociable, retiring, unapproachable, removed, brusque, stuffy, haughty, conceited, and cold.

Isolation is another major repercussion. Displacers separate from the world rather than join in and become part of things. Their social life is affected; as a rule, displacers' homes are not bustling, cheerful, sociable meeting grounds for friends and/or family.

The quality of friendships is also influenced. Displacers' social life tends to be superficial; as a couple, displacers probably do not have one other "special" couple with whom both feel very close. Less likely to have buddies, comrades, confidants, pals, or intimates, displacers may never have a best friend—other than their spouse. Difficulties around feeling open and trusting (even with people displacers believe they like) is a hallmark of this style.

Displacers: The Next Generation

Of all the angry lovestyles, displacers have the distinction of revealing themselves through their attitudes toward children, even if they don't quite realize it! Remember, displacers deflect anger by being an impenetrable duo. Baby, as the saying goes, makes three. The addition of a child profoundly affects (and sometimes threatens) displacers. Therefore, reactions to the next generation can help us pinpoint this style.

For example, displacers may seal themselves so tightly in their "togetherness" that it becomes impossible to make room for children. So displacers may delay childbearing or opt out of parenthood entirely ("We can't see ourselves having kids"; "We like our lifestyle too much to change it").

If displacers do make room for the next generation, they may make their child part of the idealized inner circle ("Frankly, other kids don't hold a candle to our son/daughter"). A child becomes a charter member, so to speak, of the displacers' exclusive and exclusionary "club"—joining with "us" against "them" ("Our boy/girl doesn't have much to do with the other children in the neighborhood").

Or it can go quite the other way—unfortunately. Unconsciously this style may force displacers to cast a youngster out, joining the ranks of "outsider" ("We don't have much to do with our son/daughter"). Blaming children for marital frustrations may also be part of this picture ("Frankly, the only problems we have are because of our son/daughter"). Regrettably, to keep marital harmony, displacers sometimes need to make their own flesh and blood into the "enemy."

But there may be a variation on this unconscious tactic if displacers have two children, "splitting the ticket": one child is brought into the fold and the other is not. This is unconsciously a most effective tactic for enabling couples to continue deflecting anger. Joined by the "good" child, the displacer parents fortify an anger-free union by having the "bad child" as the scapegoat for displaced ire ("Our son is an angel, but our daughter—that's another story"). Families with a black sheep of a child may actually be displacers at work.

Moving Targets

When displacers lose their external enemy, they often turn on each other (for example, when a reviled parent dies, or when a family relocates to a new town, leaving old enemies behind). This is not the most common occurrence because displacers work fast unconsciously to find a scapegoat who is actually a "displacement replacement." If circumstances conspire against finding a stand-in, the anger may indeed come home to roost.

Some displacers get angry with each other on vacations when they "get away from it all" and find that the nearest person at hand is their spouse—and only their spouse. In that confinement, heretofore displaced anger can sometimes end up, temporarily, in the displacer marriage. Considering the risks, displacers probably don't go in for long vacations!

Paying the Price

While displacers have found an unconscious mechanism for deleting anger from their marriage, they pay a price (in every covert lovestyle there is always a price to be paid). Anger goes, but misery doesn't; it just wears a different, tamer look. While displacers at first feel snug and cozy in the small and insulated world they have created, it can eventually feel wearing and lonely.

Displacers tend to feel the excitement and liveliness go out of their marriage. Dinner after dinner with "just the two of us" loses its allure and vitality if it is really the result of the isolation that invariably becomes part of this style.

At some point the isolation of displacers may create more than marital tedium—it may hurt, especially at holiday time when they see others surrounded by family. (Though, in a pinch, to defend themselves, displacers may leave town for the holidays or even declare celebrations overrated.)

Nonetheless, displacers don't feel marital anger and instead might feel sad, lonely, cut off; marriage begins to feel desolate and barren. These and any other sentiments of regret are likely to be felt only intermittently and only once displacers have been married for a time.

Age takes its toll on displacers: The sense of regret over what they have "missed out on" or "given up" because of their marriage becomes more prevalent, more pronounced, and regrettably, more painful with time.

With time, "I'm sorry that we didn't have children"; "I miss having contact with our son/daughter"; "I wish my children were closer to each other," may also be the laments echoed by displacers.

But displacement may end up being so very effective in rerouting anger that it creates an interesting and disquieting possibility. In theory, it is possible that displacers may be so good at displacing that they never feel as if they themselves have a problem! This is a possibility, though a slim one. Life has a way of catching up with us, even if we have worked overtime at externalizing anger.

At some point even the best-defended displacer misses the friendships, the family, the camaraderie at work. Even the best-defended displacer gets tired of hating, weary of blaming, enervated doing battle. The moment comes to virtually all displacers when they lay their heads down on the pillow in the dark of night and know in their hearts of hearts that something is amiss.

Hansel and Gretel

Perhaps the saddest feeling displacers may encounter is the conviction that they live in an unfriendly and inhospitable world. Needing external targets (foes, adversaries, opponents, enemies), a pall of distrust descends on their lives. Displacers unwittingly transform themselves into Hansel and Gretel—alone in the dark woods surrounded by ever present danger and people who are up to no good.

Ironically, displacers may be caught in the odd (and to them inexplicable) predicament of being in a "good" marriage in a "bad" world. They feel reasonably happy with each other, but generally miserable nonetheless. In the end displacers have each other but that, sadly, may be all they have.

Catherine and Andrew have been married for eleven years. And while nothing has shaken their displacer alliance, their lives are deeply affected by this angry lovestyle. Perhaps yours is, too?

The Actual Marriage of
Two Displacers:
Catherine and Andrew

Catherine closed the front door and sighed with relief. It was after nine; the last guests were gone. Thank goodness they only had to give the office cocktail party once a year.

"The invitation said six to eight. You'd think people would have the good taste to leave on time. Instead, they hang around and eat you out of house and home."

"How many people do you know with manners?" Andrew responded. "I don't see why you're so surprised. Remember when we first met, you gave me a badly needed crash course in etiquette."

Andrew's mind flashed back to the days when Catherine used to elbow him at a dinner party if he did something wrong. Whatever annoyance he felt melted away when he realized Catherine was merely putting him on the right track, something his ill-bred parents had never done. In the end he could only feel grateful.

"If it wasn't for you," Andrew continued with obvious devotion, "I might have been one of 'them.' "

Catherine added her two cents:

"And speaking of manners! Did you talk to the man Janice brought tonight? Maybe he has money, but he's so crude.

"By the way, Janice brought you a present (probably something she had in the closet from her 'ex'). She knows you're forty tomorrow.

"Your boss and that lackey he's grooming are so pompous," Catherine went on.

Andrew's head nodded in absolute agreement.

"Yes. They share the same management philosophy. Let the guy under you do all the work and you take all the credit."

"What a shame," Catherine thought. She had really helped Andrew climb that corporate ladder. If only he had pushed for Karter's job. But how could she really get angry with Andrew? Was it his fault that promotions were all about politics rather than hard work?

Actually, she thought to herself, what really made her angry was having to put up with Andrew's parents.

She and Andrew tried to steer clear of the O'Dells. But since she'd turned thirty-five, three years earlier, her mother-in-law had been whining about not having grandchildren. Repeating Catherine's words, Andrew had made it very clear how the two of them felt: "Catherine and I do not have the same mentality as you and Father. We do not think we need children to make ourselves complete. Catherine is all I need!"

Catherine knew Andrew admired her. He had from the very beginning. She recalled their first date, a tennis match. Andrew couldn't get over Catherine's form. He had even called the pro over—"She's only a beginner. Isn't she a natural?" he had said excitedly.

Catherine had been attracted to Andrew from the start not so much by what he was (he was a little chunky, he didn't know how to dress, and he didn't have the greatest job), but by his potential. After eleven years he had shaped up a lot (Catherine bought Andrew's clothes, watched his diet, encouraged him to get his degree, so for the most part those things were under control). But getting Andrew to eat right was still a chore; all those bad habits Mrs. O'Dell had instilled were to blame.

Andrew's voice snapped Catherine out of her thoughts.

"What are you thinking about?"

"Oh, just how your mother is still pushing the grandchild thing. You'd think she'd lay off already."

Andrew's expression changed. Tomorrow he would be forty, and he wasn't very excited about the prospect of entering middle age. Suddenly, Andrew heard himself saying something he never imagined he would say: "You know, Catherine, maybe we should think about children."

Catherine felt an angry shock to her system.

"Your mother is such a witch. Look how she can get to you. Any contact with her is too much. That's it. As far as I'm concerned, she's not ever putting her foot into this house again!"

Andrew listened to his wife and suddenly had a new thought.

"You know, my mother really does get in the way. Maybe her carping is the reason I can't feel too excited about this birthday."

Agreeing that Mrs. O'Dell was the culprit, Andrew and Catherine closed the living-room lights and climbed the stairs to bed.

An Actual Marriage:
Are You Displacers?

In their everyday life together Andrew and Catherine have all the earmarks of displacers. In their actual marriage they are not overtly or actively angry with each other, but they are mad as hell at any number of other people!

Their displaced anger builds the wall that seals others out and themselves into their marriage. And whenever the possibility of anger enters their marriage, it makes a quick exit by being displaced onto others. It's *their* (friends, family, bosses) fault they're unhappy!

But there are many other specific markers that they possess:

- They have outside "enemies," us and them . . . the in-laws, Andrew's boss.
- Antagonism emerges around a life transition . . . their biological clocks are winding down and they get angry at Andrew's parents for reminding them.
- They gossip, are judgmental, superior . . . "post-party pick-apart".

Do you see any of these qualities in your actual marriage? If you are not especially unhappy in your marriage but you are not intimate with friends, feel alienated from family and isolated at work, it may be that the real problem lies not with "them" but with your angry displacer marriage.

Decoding Complaints: Making the
Invisible Marriage Visible

As with any angry marriage, even a covert one, unconscious needs are the force driving the invisible marriage. In this case, Andrew has an unconscious need—*to have an idealized protector,* while Catherine has a need—*to remake a man* (to turn a weak man into a strong one). But decoding complaints to clarify this invisible dance takes a slightly different twist in a displacer marriage; after all, displacers

164

don't believe there is anything wanting in each other. In keeping with their "tight union," displacers don't complain. Observe, notice, comment, offer "constructive criticism"? Yes. But complain—about each other? Not really. Remember, at a pinch, there's always someone on hand to fault in place of a spouse.

Perhaps sometime in the future comments will turn to grievances; observations will erupt into objections. But for Catherine and Andrew, that has yet to occur (and frankly, for some displacers in an extremely "tight" relationship, it never does take such a turn).

To the question, "What are your complaints?," true to displacer form, Catherine or Andrew would have a neutralizing response—"Well, I wouldn't go so far as to call them complaints . . ." So we won't either. Instead, a partner's "observations" will be our window on hidden needs.

HER COMPLAINTS = HIS NEED

Catherine's "observations" can become the window into Andrew's need—to have a perfect wife in order to feel perfectly protected.

"What I've noticed is how Andrew hangs on my every word. We can discuss something and the next time we talk about it he's spouting my ideas. Actually, it can feel quite good."

The old saw goes: "Imitation is the highest form of flattery." Behind such admiration is adulation. And Andrew unconsciously needs to have that high regard, even reverence, for his wife. His need drives him to this idealization.

Catherine also notices that Andrew seems more self-assured and certain when that happens.

"He's always much more forceful and convincing when he's repeating the sorts of things he knows I feel. Like the time he could be so clear about the grandchildren issue."

Catherine's ideas seem better to Andrew than his own, and therefore he latches onto what she says. Andrew feels safer cloaked in Catherine's ideas. They are more than mere words; they are a protective shield that she magically offers him.

It makes him feel stronger and more confident. Catherine knows best; therefore, if he is an extension of her, he knows best. And he can stand up to anyone.

Ironically, the sense of protection she affords him allows Andrew to be more aggressive (toward his parents, for example). So his behavior is not only a sign of his need at work; spouting the words of his idealized protector enables Andrew to keep displacing his anger. One behavior can serve two psychological masters—hidden anger and hidden need. As has been said before, the mind can be very economical. Two for the price of one!

YOUR COMPLAINT/OBSERVATION: YOUR HUSBAND'S NEED

Do you feel unrestrained admiration from your husband? Does he follow your lead and look up to you for it (and therefore, down on most everyone else in his world)? Are you the source of the strength he has and then uses aggressively toward others? It might be that behind his observations lies his need to idealize you.

If you are not yet clear on your husband's unconscious inner workings, perhaps these other decoded "comments" will bring you to the point where you are able to uncover this need.

· *Your Complaint/Observation*

He tells me I have impeccable taste in clothes; he let me decorate the house because he completely trusts my judgment; he tells everyone I'm a gourmet cook.

· *Your Husband's Need*

You're good, but you're not that good! No one can be. But your spouse needs to see you as flawless, so that's what he does. Also bear in mind that his idealization keeps you so perfectly wonderful he has nothing about which to become angry (on the contrary, everyone else looks bad by comparison). Thus his admiration serves two masters: it makes you into his perfect protector and it keeps him from getting angry with you to boot!

· *Your Complaint/Observation*

He always looks to me for the decisions; I'm the final word on things; there's no doubt he defers to me.

· *Your Husband's Need*

Your husband gives himself up and over to you because he needs you to take care of things—and him. He puts himself into what he believes is your perfect care.

After a time, having a husband who relinquishes himself to your better judgment can get to be a drag. For now you both blame it on his mother, who didn't allow him to have a mind of his own! With her as the fall guy, the anger of feeling burdened is vanquished.

· *Your Complaint/Observation*

He tells me I am all he ever wanted. He says he doesn't need children to make him happy. I think I'm more important to him than the children.

· *Your Husband's Need*

Children may feel threatening. He needs your protection and they could take you away from him.

HIS COMPLAINTS/OBSERVATIONS = HER NEED

Reversing our strategy by looking at Andrew's "grievances" in order to decipher Catherine's hidden need, we find that Andrew also "really has no major complaints." As the other half of the displacer pair, that is just what we should expect. Nonetheless, through Andrew's observations we can still get a grasp on Catherine's need to remake a man.

A good deal of Andrew's commentary on his wife is about how much of his success is owed to Catherine:

"Catherine came from a better background than I did. She was a much better student. She was much more sophisticated. I was lucky she fell in love with me."

Is Andrew "lucky in love," or is he Catherine's "raw material" to fulfill her need to remake a man? Andrew, "below" her educationally and socially, feeling less worldly, is the sort of diamond in the rough her need requires.

This sense of disparity that Andrew feels leaves him open for Catherine's "renovations":

"Coming from my family, I never set high goals for myself. Of course, I never realized this until I met Catherine. She set her sights high for me, especially at work. And she really made me 'go for the gold.' She showed me I had a lot over the other guys around me."

Finding her diamond in the rough, Catherine's need to remake a man—to make him better, stronger, more powerful—causes her to exert pressure and turn her "lump of coal" into a gem. And each time he reaches a plateau, Catherine needs him to go on.

Catherine is not simply an ego booster; she's really like a coach getting her "fighter" into shape. The stronger he feels, the more Andrew can take on his world of work and climb the ladder. Catherine stirs the fires of angry competitiveness to keep Andrew on the move up. Remodeling Andrew into the more powerful, forceful, commanding version of himself is her need at work!

The double payoff here is that Catherine also turns Andrew's aggression toward his co-workers—it's those "assholes" he wants to KO. Officemates become opponents. Andrew doesn't get angry at Catherine for pushing him; instead, they both team up against the foes at work who make all these efforts necessary. Satisfying her need to remake a man and at the very same time enabling Andrew to keep diverting his ire, Catherine is a true displacer!

YOUR HUSBAND'S COMPLAINT/OBSERVATION = YOUR NEED

Do you build your husband's confidence with a hidden agenda—to remake him—one that is hidden even from yourself? Could you "work him up" in order to "move him up" and make him more powerful? Perhaps you do it differently from Catherine. If so, these further observations may bring you closer to uncovering whether this is indeed your contribution to your invisible marriage.

· *Your Husband's Complaint/Observation*

I never understood how interfering my parents were until I married. Nowadays, I don't take crap from my brother (sister, mother, father) anymore.

· *Your Need*

Reworking a man's attitudes toward his family is a typical feature of this need. You can't tolerate the status quo he has with his family. You need him to "stand up" to them; it's a proof that he's been remade into a power to reckon with. And that's the goal of your hidden need.

His future complaint may revolve around a feeling of resentment—you alienated him from his nearest and dearest, but for now you both agree (and keep displacing) that "they" are the culprits!

· *Your Husband's Complaint/Observation*

My wife put me on a diet. I never paid much attention to my clothes until my wife got me to understand the concept "dress for success." She's the reason I went back to school.

· *Your Need*

Encouraging or even insisting upon our husband's self-improvement is often a way we act when we are driven by this need. You need him leaner, cleaner, chicer, smarter. With a need to remake a man, progress is your most important business!

For now, with your assistance, he's actively displacing his

irritation—grateful to you and angrily resentful that he didn't get these things at home, the first go round.

· *Your Husband's Complaint/Observation*

I've become much more outspoken; I don't let people walk all over me anymore; I've stopped being Mr. Nice Guy . . . since I met my wife.

· *Your Need*

Assertiveness training is a specialty when you have a need to remake a man into a powerhouse. Bashful, shy, diffident, timid are not acceptable qualities in a man. You need him transformed into someone who has backbone and bravado.

In getting him to speak up, he also is more likely to "talk back." Then he's better at displacing his anger onto others. Another case of two for the price of one!

Sometimes a man has a rude awakening and discovers that he's so aggressive that he's not liked. It may never happen, but if it does you might eventually take the heat—"Before I met my wife I was a nice guy." Right now you are still his hero.

· *Your Husband's Complaint/Observation*

I learned how to be a good lover from my wife. I was sexually naive when we met. I was a virgin; she wasn't. I wasn't very experienced but my wife was.

· *Your Need*

What better way could you serve your need than by making your spouse a better lover? Taking a man who is sexually naive, uninitiated, inept, and turning him into a sexual force is the ultimate renovation.

YOUR INVISIBLE MARRIAGE AND THE CYCLE OF DISPLACEMENT

Looking back at the partnership of Andrew and Catherine, you can see how their needs keep them locked in their displacer marriage. And perhaps by exploring their pattern, you may discern your own.

Before we go on to look at this cycle, we must restate an important point: The cycle of Catherine and Andrew is *not* a cycle of angry conflict. That only happens to openly angry couples such as venters and provokers. This is not the case for displacers.

Displacers are in a marriage that keeps them bound to each other, that hermetically seals them into their relationship. Hidden needs must "collude" and "conspire" to bring a couple closer, making them more dependent, reliant, involved, symbiotic. And for a very important unconscious purpose, the tighter they are, the less room there is for anger to intrude. And this in turn means anger goes elsewhere.

Andrew and Catherine hear the rumblings of unhappiness (around the issue of children), but they are still well enmeshed in their tightly woven cycle of displacement. Just how do their needs work in concert to create this sort of impenetrable invisible marriage?

We can begin with Andrew. His need to believe in an idealized protector makes him admire his wife and look to her for his well-being. Catherine by virtue of her need to transform a man interprets this elevated regard as a sign that Andrew is weak and unworthy. Unconsciously she surmises: "If a man looks up to me and needs me, he must be inferior." With this unconscious presumption, her need to make a man strong springs into action. Catherine pushes Andrew onward and upward.

But remember, Catherine is never angry at "unfortunate" Andrew for his shortcomings; she's only furious at the people who were responsible for his deficits. (Just as Andrew is never angry at "perfect" Catherine for her pushiness, only disdainful of the "idiots" who stand in his way.)

And once again the cycle spins on. *Not* a cycle that splits them apart but a cycle that draws them ever closer and keeps them in their displacer mode.

The Primal Marriage:
Where the Anger Began

Why is Andrew in need of a perfect protector? How is it that Catherine must make a man stronger? And why are they carrying another burden—hidden anger that at all times must be banished from their partnership? Why must they become Hansel and Gretel, holding hands tightly in an inhospitable world? The answer lies in their past, in their *primal marriage*.

CATHERINE'S PAST: HER PRIMAL MARRIAGE

Though she relates it as if it were the most matter-of-fact event, Catherine describes what must have been an excruciating experience for her.

"My mother is a nut. She always has been. One day when I was nine, she found out I had eaten candy on the way home from school; my sister must have said something. Candy was forbidden (a lot of things were).

"I came home and found the door locked. There was a note: 'If you like candy so much, then stay outside where you can eat it all the time.'

"She didn't let me in. I rang and rang but then gave up. I sat on the doorstep for hours. Finally, when my father got home—I bet it wasn't until eight or nine o'clock—I was allowed inside.

"I can't say I remember my father saying anything to me or to my mother (he usually didn't say much of anything—he's the quiet type). I just went up to bed."

In Catherine's life this was not a single event.

"Then when I was fifteen, that witch pulled another stunt. With my allowance I had bought a dress for a formal dance. I hid it from her because it was low-cut.

"Two days before the dance, the dress was missing. Again I found one of her famous notes—on my bed: 'That dress is now where it belongs—in the garbage.'

"I remember telling my father what had happened. It was pretty clear that he knew about her antics, but he just let it ride."

Catherine's mother was brutal. Malicious, spiteful, and competitive, she did not refrain from treating Catherine—a young, helpless child—harshly.

She frightened, hurt, and enraged her daughter, but to give vent to these reactions was, for Catherine, out of the question. After all, if eating a candy bar brought down her mother's wrath, what price would her mother extract if Catherine were to get angry?

Catherine feared that her anger would bring about her own annihilation. Being left on the doorstep, having her clothes discarded, it was no wonder she had this worry and no wonder she buried her anger.

There is another reason Catherine's anger went underground. Her mother offered a model of anger that was ruthless and unmerciful. As a child, Catherine feared that her own anger, once it emerged, would take that same form (after all, she unconsciously reckoned, "I am my mother's daughter"). Frightened that she would also have a ferocious temper, she had yet another powerful reason to steer clear of her ire.

But we can't leave Catherine's father out of this primal scenario. *He never came to her rescue!* Quiet, passive, insipid, he never interceded to prevent or even curb her mother's nastiness. Hurt and disappointed by her father's failure to defend her, Catherine has spent her life trying to right this wrong. She is forever "working" on a man to make him strong, adequate, and able. At the same time, she struggles to manage the rage that she still carries around inside.

This is the double legacy of Catherine's primal marriage: She has an unconscious need to remake a man. If she can make him powerful and effective, then she is safe from the harshness and cruelty of her mother. But she must also rid herself of annihilating and ugly anger.

Might you have this painful history that intrudes on your marriage? Did you have a cruel mother and a father who stood by and let you be her victim? Was your mother ferocious and your father docile? Did your primal marriage leave you enraged but unable to air your anger toward the person responsible for your pain? Perhaps this lies at the heart of your primal marriage.

IS THIS YOUR PRIMAL MARRIAGE?

· Did you have an angry mother for whom you were the nearest and likeliest target? · If something didn't go right at home, did she take it out on you? · Were you the "bad" kid?

A parent who uses a child as a whipping post takes advantage of a child's weakness. It's no wonder you grow up needing a strong man at your side.

· Did you hate your mother but never do much about it? · Do you think of her as a "nut," "witch," "bitch," but not feel very emotional about it?

Parental abuse has to create intense ill-will. The absence of this appropriate effect means you may manage the injury by denying the rage. You may minimize the damage done to you but still desperately need protection. As an adult, you continue to deny the rage, redirecting it to a safer target—often someone else's mother, your husband's!

· Were you frightened of witches? · Did you have dreams about sorceresses? · Were your favorite stories about wicked stepmothers, evil fairies, spell-casting witches?

In your case, these fantasies, dreams, and fairy tales may have had a particular painful meaning because you identified strongly with the characters who fell into such cruel hands.

· Did minor infractions bring down your mother's wrath? · Did she have a temper? · Was she jealous of you or competitive? · Was she spiteful?

Sometimes parents are so unhappy, they turn mean and ugly. Instead of creating an atmosphere of trust, they damage a child's sense that the world is a safe and welcoming place. If this was your childhood, is it any wonder that as an adult you continue seeing the world as an inhospitable and unfriendly place?

With this cruelty as the only face of anger you knew, is there also any wonder you need to keep from showing it to your spouse? The child in you must imagine that your anger will be as monstrous.

Each primal marriage is unique. Yours may be quite different from Catherine's. Perhaps your mother's cruelty was more subtle. Might she have treated you unkindly through silent disdain rather than inflamed actions? Perhaps, regrettably, it was even more brutal and involved physical abuse?

Perhaps your father failed to protect you because he was absent, not insipid. Could the roles have been reversed? Might you have been the victim of your father's wrath and the failure lay with your mother? Unfortunately, there are any number of ways we may have been treated cruelly as children.

Catherine's primal marriage may give you a new way to understand your own childhood and the baggage you carry along into your marriage. Now how can we understand Andrew? His primal marriage is our starting point.

ANDREW'S PAST: HIS PRIMAL MARRIAGE

"My mother was always crying, most often because of my grandmother, a real angry witch. She was German. Very tough and very exacting. Grandmother made my mother's life miserable. I can remember Mom trying to make these really nice Sunday dinners when she would invite my grandparents.

"Mother would start preparing a week in advance. By Sunday, she'd be a nervous wreck. During the dinner Mom would be all thumbs: Without fail she would drop a dish or burn the roast. And that would give Mother O'Dell the opening she was waiting for.

"She was too refined a lady to call my mother an idiot, but she could shoot her this irate look that just turned Mom to Jell-O.

"After these fiascos my mother would put me to bed and tell me how terrible she felt (my father didn't have the patience to listen; he never had the patience for my mother's whining)."

Andrew's grandmother was not the only person who could turn his mother into a helpless puddle of tears.

"There was a time when my parents split for a while. I must have been eleven. Dad moved out of the house. My mother fell apart.

"I'd hear her pleading with him on the phone, threatening suicide. There wasn't one dinner during those six months at which I didn't hear how awful she felt. Sometimes I'd wake up at night and she'd be pacing around the house crying and pleading with my father, and he wasn't even there. She'd lost it!

"I think my father was scared Mom might go off the deep end. Finally he came home."

As a child, Andrew felt sorry for his mother, who always seemed so wretched. But his feelings went beyond pity. His mother could become so overwrought and distraught that it became frightening. She even scared his father! Andrew's mother did not simply lose her composure; she became unglued, hysterical. She seemed utterly defenseless and incapacitated.

Her incompetence and vulnerability made Andrew feel unsupported and unprotected. In fact, it was not simply that she appeared incapable of caretaking; she reversed the roles, seeking comfort from Andrew in times of distress.

Though unintentional, this was too great a burden for a young child. It left Andrew with a desperate need—to have a perfectly competent protector. In this way he could leave the threatening and overwhelming feelings behind.

But why did he have to ditch his anger? While Andrew often felt sorry for his mother, he also felt embarrassed and angry. He hated his mother for her pathetic helplessness. But could he yell and scream at her, shake her and shout, "Stop!" as he secretly wished? No. His mother was far too fragile to tolerate his wrath. In his child's mind, he even suspected it could destroy her. Her threats of suicide made the danger of his anger an even greater risk—she might take her own life in its wake. Andrew's anger couldn't stay in his primal home.

Might your husband have struggled with this sort of primal family? Did he have a caretaker who regularly "fell apart"? These additional questions may enable you to gain a clearer picture as to whether your husband and hence your marriage are burdened by this history.

· Did his mother or father confide in him? · Would he/she discuss their marital or family conflicts? · When he/she had problems with someone, did your husband hear crying, pleading, begging?

If parents are having problems, it is sometimes appropriate for children to know, in order to be reassured ("Daddy and I are angry with each other—not you"). But children *must* be spared front-row tickets to their parents' troubles and misery. It is too frightening to see parents self-destruct. If your husband saw and knew too much too soon, he may be an adult who craves an ideal protector in you.

· Was there any calamitous event (divorce, illness, death, job loss, fire) that "undid" his parents?

Sometimes a traumatic experience robs a parent of his or her confidence and competence. Even if your husband's parents were relatively well put together most of the time, seeing it happen in the extreme just once might have been overwhelming. As an adult, he may need you as a perfect protector, believing unconsciously that you have the power to guard against such an occurrence.

Trauma may also cause children to inhibit their natural anger. It may have felt too risky to get angry in a fragile or wounded family.

· Did his parents have drinking binges, become hysterical, or fly into rages? · Did one parent have emotional breakdowns, severe depressions, threaten suicide?

Parents who are unable to cope, who fall apart or become unhinged (because of alcohol, temper, emotions), are very threatening. It is a dreadful, even terrifying feeling to believe that our parents are that fragile and unable to protect themselves. As an adult, perhaps your spouse tries to escape these unbearable feelings—by finding a perfect guardian in you.

Taking Hold of the Problem: Getting Ready for an Adult Marriage

Andrew and Catherine must seem so different now. Can we dismiss them as snobs once we have insight into their past? No, not when we understand that their marriage is a fortress built to keep out the pain and the anger. This seemingly aloof couple are really frightened children who hang on to one another because the world is not to be trusted. And they cannot trust themselves with their fury. They have learned (and still believe this "primal premise" of their respective childhoods) that anger is too risky, ugly, and powerful to have a rightful place in their marriage.

Challenging these long-held assumptions about anger is the first task of displacers as they prepare for a truly adult marriage. Displacers need to know that anger is only a feeling. As children, they have been misled into believing that it is a dangerous weapon because:

- Some caretakers give themselves permission to act cruelly when they feel angry (i.e., a vicious or abusive parent).
- Some caretakers don't allow others the feeling or expression of anger claiming it to be an act of cruelty (i.e., a suicidal or overwrought parent).

Displacers need to know that their adult marriage can be different from their primal relations, in which anger and cruelty were joined as if one. They are *not* one and the same. And the power to draw the line forever separating the two is in a person's own hands. Sadly, it is a line all too many parents fail to draw.

Above all, displacers need to know the real facts about anger, so they can relinquish their primal fantasies and permit this forbidden emotion into their marriage:

- Feelings—specifically anger—cannot make bad things happen.
- It is not the angry feeling that is dangerous but what people do because they feel angry.
- Angry people are only dangerous if they use anger to abuse power over another weaker human being.
- Anger does not beget cruelty.

As their own rage emerges, as it will and as it must (for every displacer is indeed a wounded and enraged soul), displacers must put anger into words and demand from themselves the restraint they could not get from their parents. Displacers need to be different from the example set for them. They must try language rather than brutal and heartless action as a way to dissipate their frustrations. This is no small task, to develop a new and kinder model for managing frustration—especially since there was no such model in the individual's primal past. Nonetheless it is essential preparation for an adult union.

Perhaps now that you know something of this history, you can extend compassion to yourselves. Each of you has endured a wounding primal marriage where parents failed to create safety and instead created chaos and terror. Closed in your inner sanctum, the two of you avoid the world as if it still offers you the pain and treachery of childhood. The two of you are "the walking wounded," hanging on to each other for dear life.

These insights and the compassion they allow are absolutely crucial for displacers! Why? Displacers face an enormous challenge as they prepare for an *adult marriage:* They must let down their guard. Why is this such a daunting task? Remember, displacers are deeply frightened people (in no small measure frightened because of the seemingly inevitable link between anger and cruelty).

Only if displacers understand their primal fears can they risk coming out of the fortress they have erected in their marriage: We cannot stop displacing our anger until we know we are safe. Displacers discover through insight that it is the past, their primal marriage, from which they are truly seeking refuge.

Insight can enable you to learn what every displacer must know before venturing forth: The witch is dead! The tormentor who through misuse of anger made life unbearable no longer holds your life in his or her hands.

Displacers must try to be brave. But it is a bravery born of self-knowledge—and this makes all the difference. If you are a displacer who can find the courage, you need to remind yourself that things can be different, that anger can make its way safely into your marriage. As a displacer, you must offer yourself these reminders of how things can be different and better:

I can break open the hermetic seal on my marriage.

I can include important others in my life.

I can make loving space for children.

I can have deeper friendships.

I can have greater satisfaction at work.

I can have warmer and closer family relations.

Bravery delivered through insight is amply rewarded. In the end, displacers can have both the safe haven of their marriage and fuller, richer, more rewarding lives. You can have both, and you deserve to lay claim to it all.

Nine

SYMBOLIZERS

I f we are symbolizers, anger makes its appearance in symptoms instead of words. We can't get openly angry, so our bodies give vent to the emotion our minds can't tolerate admitting. Anger gets unconsciously rerouted and symbolically aired.

In this way, symbolizers are not unlike displacers. Displacers reroute anger by severing it from its original connection in their marriage and attaching it to a substitute person outside their partnership. Disguised in this way, anger can be more safely expressed.

Symbolizers also deflect anger from its real sources, but the target for this deflected anger is surprisingly their own bodies! Unacceptable anger is made tolerable by converting it into pain or discomfort. This is the startling feature of symbolizers: Disguised anger is turned against the self.

In a married couple, both members may convert marital malevolence into a physical malady. But this is not usually the case. Generally, only one becomes afflicted with a physical infirmity; the other becomes the caretaker—the "nurse." Together, with one "infirm" and the other attending to the affliction, this strategy serves a single purpose: Anger is concealed. Instead of feeling angry, the nursing spouse may end up feeling guilty (if he doesn't caretake properly and constantly). On the other hand, the afflicted spouse may feel hurt (if she doesn't get taken care of properly and constantly).

This can be another clue; symbolizers pay a lot of attention to what ails one of them. If you play Florence Nightingale to your partner (or vice versa), you may actually be nursing anger symbolically.

It's the Real Thing

While symbolizer maladies are really physical equivalents of anger, it does not make them "unreal" ailments. Regrettably every ache and pain, every moment of discomfort and distress a symbolizer registers is the real McCoy. Symbolizers are not feigning illness. Rather, it is as if our bodies have a point of vulnerability through which anger, converted into a physical form, is expressed.[1]

This notion of real ailments brings us to an important point. First and foremost, physical symptoms should always be evaluated medically. No one should ever assume that an ailment is the conversion of anger until the possibility of a disease process is clearly ruled out. Dismissing recurrent headaches with "You're just angry at your husband," is misguided.[2]

Second, symbolizers often need medical help. Physiotherapy may be required for an "angry" back. Painkillers may be helpful for a "raging" headache; medication may be necessary for "boiling" blood pressure. Though emotions may be the starting point for an ailment, symbolizers may very well end up needing an internist as well as a therapist.

Is There a Doctor in the House?

The life of symbolizers frequently revolves around the joint search for a solution to their physical problem. Backaches, headaches, fatigue, gastrointestinal problems, anxiety attacks, vertigo, pain—any of these ills might befall a symbolizer. There is no one symptom that is the "symptom of choice."

Conventional medicine is usually the first route. Typically, it brings the symbolizers to several different physicians or moves them through one specialist to another. Ironically, doctors may end up colluding with a symbolizer's efforts to keep anger under wraps. Wishing to be thorough or, perhaps, to avoid a future lawsuit, the doctor who finds nothing medically wrong with a symbolizer doesn't confront her patient but simply orders another battery of tests.[3] And that becomes another telltale clue; symbolizers rarely say no to the idea of being prodded, poked, monitored, X-rayed, scanned.

But symbolizers don't stop with the medical approach. Alternative nonmedical methods are pursued: acupuncture, massage, spas, chiropractice, macrobiotics, the Alexander Technique, Rolfing, vitamin therapy, nutrition, and biofeedback may be on the symbolizer's list. Specialized clinics (allergy, headache, sleep disturbances, PMS, etc.) become way stations in a symbolizer's search for relief.

The symbolizer's quest may seem decidedly unorthodox as he or she turns to faith healers, gurus, astrologers, aroma therapists, Rolfers, or physics when anger becomes a physical problem. (Unfortunately, symbolizers can be patsies for a charlatan's latest cure. If you don't feel "teed off" in your marriage but you've taken to reading tea leaves or drinking herbal teas for what ails you, perhaps you're a symbolizer!)

Have You Thought of Seeing . . . ?

Symbolizers may extract another clue from their relationship to the medical world. Dr. Asch, an experienced internist, put his finger on a telltale sign:

"Over my years in practice it's happened more than once. I evaluate a patient and all signs lead to an emotional basis for their problem. I suggest they see a colleague of mine, a psychologist. And that's the last time I ever see them in my office."[4]

Symbolizers don't want to hear that they need their "heads examined," unless it means taking yet another picture of their brain. But there are important reasons for this reluctance.

Perhaps symbolizers resent this suggestion because they are frightened of losing their symptoms and fearful of finding themselves in a place (read "therapist's office") where their anger may be unearthed. If you've ditched a doctor who's been brave enough to suggest that your marriage and your ailments could benefit from insight instead of X-rays, you are certainly symbolizers!

It may not be doctors alone who make symbolizers angry. Symbolizers feel injured by anyone who treats the illness matter-of-factly, with indifference, or skepticism. And they may, indeed, get miffed at this "unsympathetic" person (bear in mind that the caretaking spouse gets as angry as the partner who is afflicted; the "nurse" can't afford to lose a patient and find marital anger).

What Ails You?

The course of the symbolizer's ailment is a revealing aspect of this angry lovestyle. If illnesses have a beginning, middle, and end, an individual is probably not a symbolizer. It takes more than a single bout with a malady to rate the interpretation that anger is the true culprit.

The ills of symbolizers are chronic ("I take the Geritol every day"; "I'm never without Bufferin"; "The pain always hits me in the same spot"). While persistent, the maladies are not life-threatening; they don't make a person sick as much as they render him or her "unwell." A person is not in danger but incapacitated: rundown, under the weather, not up to snuff, not ourselves, indisposed, feeling low or poorly—all aptly describe a symbolizer's condition and mark this covert lovestyle.

In addition to sustaining a chronic ailment, many, many symbolizers also suffer from periodic episodes where they feel extreme physical distress and panic about it: Their hearts race, heads pound, blood vessels throb, palms sweat, and stomachs turn. During these anxiety or panic attacks they may hyperventilate, feel dizzy, even disoriented. Feeling as if they are having a heart attack or that something is dreadfully wrong, they often make that frantic mid-night call to their doctor or head for the nearest emergency room.

No Can Do

No matter the nature of the ailment, for symbolizers, illness be-comes a theme, a preoccupation, illness-as-lifestyle. Couples work their lives around "the problem." A symbolizer marriage is full of do's and don'ts, can's and cannot's. If you are the one who suffers, it may make you demanding. Suffering in silence is not part of this style: "You *know* how sitting in those stadium chairs always makes my back go out" (so the two of you miss the big game); "You *know* my stomach's acting up; I think we have to say no to the dinner party" (so the two of you don't socialize); "I feel a migraine coming on; I'm going to bed in the spare room" (so the two of you don't make love . . . again).

This brings us to another important feature of this covert love-style. The limits imposed on a marriage may eventually make a couple angry: After all, you might hate to miss the game, the dinner, and the sex. But symbolizers don't get irritated at each other; they get aggravated at the ailment—those damn headaches, that misera-ble allergy (in this respect symbolizers bear some resemblance to displacers, though instead of complaining about the mother-in-law who's a pain in the neck, they *have* the pain in the neck to complain about). If in your marriage you bear ill-will only toward an illness, and not toward your spouse, you might be symbolizers.

Paying the Price

It is not that difficult to understand the price paid by symbolizers in their unconscious efforts to banish anger from their partnership. As one symbolizer quipped, "It's a lot like living under a big wet blanket!" This lovestyle puts a damper on married life. Symbolizers worry rather than have fun. They pay for stays in hospitals instead of hotels. Their social life and their sex life suffer. Often both come to a halt!

In the extreme, they may end up feeling life together is just no fun at all. The caretaking spouse gets fed up, sick and tired, even disgusted. Dispiritedness, listlessness, and depression are frequently the "patient's" legacy when anger is unconsciously transformed into illness (ironically, it is these feelings that might finally get a couple into therapy).

Symbolizers achieve and accomplish less, losing hours out of a day, days out of a week, weeks out of a year. For example, vacation days and insurance benefits are exhausted tending to an ill partner.

The sun and brightness, the excitement and joy, drain themselves from the symbolizers' union. The symbolizers' marriage may indeed begin to feel "under the weather," as if it could use a generous dose of Geritol. For Maxine and Jim, a pair of symbolizers, their marriage certainly seems in need of some pep pills.

The Actual Marriage of Two Symbolizers: Maxine and Jim

Maxine called Jim at work. She was doubled over on the kitchen floor in pain; it was her back again. Fortunately, Jim's boss was on vacation. Getting out of the shop would be easier today than it was the last time when Mr. Andrews had balked: "Jim, if Maxine needs help you're going to have to make other arrangements. This is our busy season. I need you here."

Jim had been miffed and had related the episode to his wife. Maxine in turn was outraged.

"He's got a lot of nerve asking you to put your job before an ill family member. But you'd better be very careful," Maxine warned. "Plenty of guys would jump at your job in a second. And if you lose your job, we're in a mess. I can't go back to sitting at a typewriter with my back the way it is."

Fortunately, this morning there wouldn't be that risk.

Now Jim was home. The hydroculator he'd bought was in a pot of water on the stove. He watched it carefully. Last time he overheated it and nearly burned Maxine.

Poor Max—these backaches were the devil. And tonight they were going to cost him a bundle. It was too late to sell the tickets to the country music show.

"Damn those backaches," he thought. "I'll have to give the tickets away."

This was starting to be the story of their life. Since Maxine's first attacks, they had been forced to cancel more dates than they went to. Their social life was at an all-time low.

Still peeved about the tickets, Jim carried the hydroculator wrapped in a towel into the spare room; Maxine slept on the floor in there when she had an "episode" (their sex life had also died, thanks to his wife's fourth lumbar vertebra).

Maxine didn't look too uncomfortable. Jim wondered if she could make it to the concert.

"Max, if the muscle-relaxant pills work, maybe you'll be up to going to the show tonight."

"How can I go? Those pills Dr. Colwin gave me are worthless; they do nothing for the pain. Anyway she had the nerve to tell me I should go talk to 'someone.' I'm not taking her pills and I'm not going back to her, either. I hear there's a clinic at the university run by that Dr. Meltzer who wrote the book you read. That's where I'm going."

Maxine remembered the tickets. "Why don't you go alone?"

She winced, feeling her back tighten. Seeing her face, Jim jumped in her direction, offering the heated pad.

"Not when you're in this kind of pain. How would you manage without me?"

Maxine answered that question silently. Jim could get so flustered trying to help it often made things worse. He wanted her to get going when all she needed was not to move a muscle. This back thing was awful. Maxine started to cry, and now to make matters worse her heart started to race; it was becoming difficult for her to catch her breath. She felt queasy. She hated when this happened.

Jim saw her distress but he felt at a loss. What could he do? So many of the things that looked promising had failed to help. Yet they couldn't stop trying.

"Look, Max. Forget about the tickets; you don't even like country music that much. And the hell with Andrews. I'll take a day off and take you to the clinic. I'm sure it will help."

Maxine could barely get the words out as she nodded in agreement.

"Yes, they say Dr. Meltzer is a miracleworker. I'm sure it will help."

If only they could both believe it.

An Actual Marriage: Are You Symbolizers?

Maxine and Jim are symbolizers. Are you? In their everyday life together, their *actual marriage*, they have more than a few markers of this covert angry lovestyle.

First and foremost, they are not directly angry with each other. They don't get mad—one of them gets ill and the other gets busy! If and when anger does rear its "ugly" head, it's vented on the "damned" disease, the "damned" doctor, or the callous, uncaring, insensitive people who "just don't understand."

But there are other signposts of the symbolizer marriage in their partnership. Perhaps you share them as well:

· Both participate in the ailment; it brings them together . . . he comes home from work, takes days off, drives her to clinics.
· Their life is limited; they underfunction . . . missed concerts, no social life, no sex, no typing work.
· The illness is chronic and she has "attacks" . . . bouts of back pain; shortness of breath, heart pounding.

Is your actual marriage reminiscent of theirs? Remember, the roles may be reversed. Perhaps you play Florence Nightingale to your husband, the invalid. Or perhaps you take turns having the marital malady. If you don't get bent out of shape with your marital anger but your back gets bent out of shape, if you're not spent with rage but just tired out, if your stomach never gets tied up in knots from fury but is just tied up in knots (or the same can be said of your spouse), you are symbolizers.

Decoding Complaints: Making the Invisible Marriage Visible

What are the unconscious forces behind this relationship? Jim has an unconscious need—*to rescue*. While Maxine has her own unconscious agenda—*to maintain control*. Through an analysis of their complaints, the needs driving their invisible marriage will come into view.

HER COMPLAINTS = HIS NEED

Since a clue is embedded in every grievance, we can analyze Maxine's complaints about her husband and decipher Jim's hidden need *to rescue,* to save someone.

Maxine is most disturbed by the way in which Jim reacts to her problem.

"Even when he sees I'm immobilized and I tell him I can't move a muscle, he'll ask if I can manage to get up and go. It's as if he doesn't hear what I'm saying."

Because of his need, what Maxine says and Jim hears are two different things. Maxine says, "I can't move off this floor," and Jim unwittingly hears, "I'm in trouble. Save me!"

Jim pushes Maxine, not because he's insensitive but because he can't bear seeing her helpless anguish. If she gets up and resumes her life, then she's okay; he's come to her rescue. He can't take no for an answer because that will mean he didn't do his job—to save her; he would feel far too guilty.

This leads to another issue for Maxine:

"Sometimes I think I'm more composed than he is, even though I'm the one in pain. Jim tries, but he's not exactly cool, calm, and collected when these problems crop up."

This points out something crucial: Jim's need to rescue is driven by dread and apprehension. After all, if someone is there to be rescued, it means there is something dire from which they must be spared. It is the dread of these unknown but imagined consequences that generates his nervousness. People with a need to rescue are generally quite anxious. And anxiety can certainly get in the way of a cool, calm, collected demeanor.

YOUR COMPLAINT: YOUR HUSBAND'S NEED

Does your husband harbor a nervous impatience with your problem? Does he push you to be up and at it when you feel down and out? A man with an unconscious urge to come to the rescue may very well respond in such high-pitched ways.

But these are only a sampling of reactions; there are indeed others. Perhaps what follows will illuminate your husband's unconscious agenda to come to the rescue.

> *· Your Complaint*

He's constantly asking me if I'm okay. Sometimes he's too solicitous. Half our phone conversations start with "You sound different. Are things all right?"

> *· Your Husband's Need*

With a need to come to the rescue, your spouse cannot afford to be casually interested in your well-being. He has to know where you stand in order to know when he has to come to your aid. His scrutiny is directly related to his need to be on alert.

> *· Your Complaint*

I asked for the thermometer and he dropped it. Driving to the emergency room, he almost had an accident. He came home from the pharmacy with the wrong painkiller. When I'm in pain, he looks dumbstruck.

· *Your Husband's Need*

With a need to rescue, the simplest of tasks become of paramount importance. Flooded with anxiety, he may become flustered or paralyzed. As a result of this internal pressure to come to your aid, he is much more likely to foul things up and appear incompetent.

But remember, it is hard to get angry at a guy who's just trying to be nice and help with what ails you. Once again, *two psychological purposes are served for the price of one.* His need is at work and it likewise helps to subvert anger.

· *Your Complaint*

Whenever he hears about a doctor (clinic, medicine) that someone recommends, he wants me to go. He's always clipping articles, reading books, watching shows to help me.

· *Your Husband's Need*

He's full of suggestions, ideas, possibilities because his real though unconscious task at hand is to spare you. To your husband, to "heal" you is to save you.

· *Your Complaint*

When I cry because I'm upset over my situation, he can't stand it. He hates to see me in pain. If I can't sleep, he's up all night.

· *Your Husband's Need*

Of course your husband is both concerned and disturbed by the difficulties of your condition. But your tears, pain, and anguish are exceptionally trying for him; they are signs that you are desperately in need of a savior. Unconsciously designated as your rescuer, your distress signals alert and alarm him.

These thoughts may enable you to develop an altered view of your spouse (and his responses to you and your malady). Perhaps your physical frailty stirs up your husband's anxieties. The need to deliver you from your suffering may be the unseen but ever present burden he carries into your marriage.

HIS COMPLAINTS = HER NEED

We can reverse our strategy and analyze the grousing and grumbling of Jim in order to bring Maxine's need *to maintain control* into view.

The complaint that lies at the core of Jim's unhappiness is the fact that Maxine's back problem puts a "very big dent" in their social life. When Maxine's back goes out, everything changes: Maxine, who's no social butterfly to begin with, is even less inclined to be social.

"But it's not just the big things we miss. Even a movie or a hamburger at the diner are too much for her," says Jim.

Maxine's ailment dictates the tempo of their life. And that can reveal something about her need: Through her infirmity she regulates (read "controls") the level of activity in their marriage.

Maxine unknowingly uses her body to impose and dictate the terms of her relationship. She doesn't like to socialize and she effectively, though unwittingly, makes sure that they don't. Her back says, "No, we're not doing this, that, and the other thing." Maxine grabs the reins of her relationship by being incapacitated. Her infirm body commandeers her marriage.

Of course, it becomes impossible for Jim to get angry with Maxine for exerting such control. After all, it's not her fault her back went out again or that she gets these "attacks." Maxine garners sympathy rather than ire. Plus she has a built-in defense against any angry frustration ("I'm not crazy about basketball but I'd go if only I felt better"). Maxine's bad back works overtime keeping her in control and keeping anger out of her union. Two for the price of one—again![5]

It's crucial not to shift into thinking that Maxine's need for control is willful or deliberate. She doesn't consciously want control.

But unconsciously, she needs it and "pays" with a high degree of physical and emotional suffering. There must be a reason—and there is. Control is so important that no price (even her health and well-being) is too high. Control at any cost!

YOUR HUSBAND'S COMPLAINT: YOUR NEED

Perhaps you're ready to consider the possibility that your physical foible is actually an unconscious ploy to take and maintain control.[6] If so, this further decoding might be of help in revealing your need at work.

· Your Husband's Complaint

We stop having sex when she has her bad back (irritable colon, headaches, dizzy spells, panic attacks).

· Your Need

Sex means excitement and loss of control. This can be an uncomfortable state for someone hell-bent—unconsciously—on keeping things regulated.

But control also means taking charge. Your infirmity enables you to say no to sex and take little or no heat for spurning your spouse's advances. "Not tonight, dear, I have a headache," is the stuff of bad jokes because there are a lot of symbolizers out there trying to exert control in the bedroom.

· Your Husband's Complaint

She gets these attacks where she can't catch her breath, her heart races and she thinks she's dying (having a heart attack, going crazy). She can get so frightened and panicky.

· *Your Need*

These "attacks" are not physical but emotional in origin. They are panic or anxiety attacks. But for you it feels as if your body is reeling out of control, and that is frightening beyond belief. *Anxiety or panic attacks are a classic sign that someone is struggling with the problem of control!* (Remember: These attacks are real and medication can prove very useful in alleviating these frightening symptoms. Panic attacks are a potent reminder of how emotions may affect the body).

· *Your Husband's Complaint*

She got angry with the internist when he suggested she see a psychiatrist. She stopped talking to the friend who told her "it was all in her head."

· *Your Need*

You are angry because you are threatened by anyone hinting that your ailment may be manipulative. But outrage at these others is also a not-so-veiled warning to your spouse: Don't take my symptoms away or I'll be furious. Since he doesn't relish your getting angry with him, he takes the warning seriously and never makes such suggestions. Once again anger is successfully kept at bay in your symbolizer union.

· *Your Husband's Complaint*

Even if she says I should go out, I feel bad leaving her alone. She tells me I don't have to drive her to the clinic (come home early, leave the party with her), but I just can't bring myself to do it.

193

$$\boxed{\cdot \textit{Your Need}}$$

When we have the need to control, a tool of the trade is guilt, and an ailment works perfectly in creating it! Guilt over your "condition" makes your husband do a dance around you. Remember, too, a husband who feels guilty has difficulty getting angry. After all, you didn't force his hand; his discomfort did. Again, two for one.

THE INVISIBLE MARRIAGE AND THE
CYCLE OF SYMBOLIZING

Now that we understand the unconscious agenda each partner brings to their relationship, we can finally see how Maxine and Jim get trapped into their symbolizer cycle. In laying out the cycle of their invisible marriage, you might begin to construct your own.

We can begin with Jim and his need to rescue. This need creates a sort of nervous energy which Jim directs toward his wife. Urging, nudging, cajoling Maxine to "get up and go" are reactions determined by his unconscious state.

Maxine does not, however, see Jim's efforts as an attempt to carry out his rescue mission. No. She reads the prodding as "He's rushing me. He's pushing me. Things are getting out of hand. I better take over." And she does.

As a symbolizer, that means something very particular. Maxine's body becomes the vehicle through which she exerts the control. So, for instance, she declines to do things because it "would be too much for my back." By virtue of her physical ailment, Maxine takes the reins of their partnership (she doesn't "get up and go"). Where does that leave Jim?

He can't appreciate the fact that this is Maxine's unconscious attempt to take over. He only interprets her inactivity, her under-functioning via his need. "She's really in trouble. I must come to her aid." So what does he do? Of course, compelled by the need to rescue her, he nervously pushes. And the symbolizer cycle spins on!

Now let's see the shape their invisible marriage takes if we start with Maxine. Maxine's need to take control makes her back go out. Yes, she may have a weak fourth lumbar vertebra, but it is the need to take control that is served by her back "going out."

Jim reads her breakdown the only way he can: It sounds an alarm for him to "come to her aid." As a result, his need has him hurtling into frantic action (buying books, searching for cures, running with overheated hydroculators and the wrong painkillers).

How does Maxine interpret all this? Maxine misses the fact that Jim's frenetic actions are determined by his need to be her savior. Instead, she can only interpret his behavior through her own unconscious assumptions. She experiences his heightened level of activity as loss of control. There is only one possible response to that unacceptable situation: Maxine must take command. And she does; her back flares up. Here we go again. The symbolizer cycle spins on and on.

The Primal Marriage: Where the Anger Began

How did it come to be that Jim has to rescue and Maxine to control? And why do they both need to transform their anger in this symbolic, somatic way? The answer lies in their pasts. It lies in their respective *primal marriages,* but it is buried deeply in barely remembered memories or in memories so dreaded and dreadful they are *completely repressed* (blocked out). And that makes our exploration of these two symbolizers and their primal marriages different from that of the other angry couples we have met so far.

MAXINE'S PAST: HER PRIMAL MARRIAGE

Maxine has some vivid early memories of her childhood. But at some point her memories grow dim.

"I remember the house in Ironweed very well. But once we moved into my grandfather's house in Flint (the summer before I started fifth grade), I don't remember a lot of details.

"I think we moved because my mother got sick. I'm not exactly clear on it, but she had some kind of kidney problem that kept her in the hospital quite a while."

Maxine's memories grow dim because she does not want to remember. Or, more aptly, she does not want to let go of her secret—her primal family secret. With time, Maxine admits more details into her memory. It is not easy.

"When my mother came home from the hospital, she wasn't herself. She was very edgy. She stopped being active in PTA and civic organizations. Grandpa had an explanation; it was because of the move. 'Your mom doesn't really know people in Flint,' he'd say.

"Dad also offered his 'theories.' 'Those doctors with all their tests took the wind out of your mother's sails,' he'd say to account for Mother retreating to her room or staring blankly out a window.

"At first I believed them. But not for long. I knew it was all a lie. But we all kept up the pretense.

"After a time Mom got better. It lasted about a year. Then I got a call at school that Mom's 'kidney' was acting up and I should come home right away to take care of my little brother.

"Throughout my childhood I got a good number of those 'kidney' calls. They would usually come after my mother had these bouts of insomnia. She'd be tense, argumentative for days. Then she'd snap.

"It was awful, worse as I got older. When I was a teenager, I lived in dread someone would find out the truth. At school I just kept telling the kids that my mother was real sick. They believed me and I got a lot of sympathy.

"To this day, there is hardly anyone outside my family who knows that my mother's 'kidney problem' was manic depression."

Periodically, because of her mother's mental illness, Maxine's life as a child went reeling out of control. But something made this especially devastating: It was a terrible secret as a result of the adults around Maxine lying to her. This magnified her confusion and anxiety. Even when the lie became evident to her, the family tenaciously clung to the myth.

What did this mean for Maxine? The legacy of this secret lie was, *as it always is for children,* isolation in an unmanageable, frightening mess. She could confide in no one and found no solace from the adults around her. The lies, pretense, myth made that impossible. Is it any wonder she developed a need to take control?

But why does that need get expressed through her body? The lie about her mother's "illness" took its toll in other ways. It made Maxine very vigilant and worried about her own body. She became quite focused and preoccupied with her physical well-being.

What's more, Maxine connected illness with attention and control. From her child's-eye view, a "sick mother" became the center of attention. After all, when Mother "took ill," normal routines came to a halt. As Maxine saw it, the family's very conduct was determined and dictated by her mother's illness: it made them move, made Grandpa cook, made her come home from school, even made them lie! Maxine came to her own childlike conclusion: Be sick and run the show. She learned to equate illness with the power to control.

But now we need to add one more piece to this fascinating and complicated primal marriage: Where did the anger begin and why was it banished? Maxine, like any other child in her predicament, was furious with her mother for "getting all the attention" and for "ruining" Maxine's life.

But in spite of her fury she could not express her rage because Maxine harbored a frightening fantasy—one that is common to many children, but especially those with mentally ill parents. If you get angry, you lose it and go crazy. (As an adult, her panic attacks are a re-creation of this worst childhood fear about control; when her body seems to go haywire, she comes close to feeling she's "losing it.")

Remember, she didn't know her mother suffered from manic depression. Maxine only observed that her mother grew edgy, argumentative (read "angry"), and then "snapped." For Maxine, getting mad and going mad were one and the same.[7] Is it any wonder Maxine can't ever get angry?

The legacy of Maxine's primal marriage is complicated indeed. It leaves her an adult with a need to take control and control her anger. Her own body is the battleground on which these struggles meet.

Do any elements of this primal marriage resonate with your own? Do you have memories of childhood cast in the shadow of a family lie or myth? Was your childhood confusing, even chaotic, because of the things you couldn't quite understand or believe? Perhaps these or similar predicaments are the burden you drag from your primal into your current marriage.

IS THIS YOUR PRIMAL MARRIAGE?

· Did your mother explain your father's hangovers with "Dad isn't feeling well today"? · Did your disturbed sibling's tantrums get excused with "He's just out of sorts." · Did your mother tell you her bruises were "because she fell"? · Did your sister go in for "surgery" when she was actually having an abortion?

Families often struggle with problems like alcoholism, drug abuse, mental illness, unwanted pregnancy, sexual and physical abuse by lying. Frequently the falsehoods involve the fabrication of a more acceptable "illness" (a headache vs. a hangover).

Family chaos explained away by this sort of deception and lies is enormously frightening to children. They frequently grow into adults who need to take control. But they are often confused by the deceptions and continue to mistakenly attribute their emotional problems to physical ailments. Perhaps you grew up with these confusing connections and still continue to make them.

· Were you a "delicate" child? · Did you often go to the school nurse or stay home from school? · Do you have fond memories of being home sick with Mom? · Were your parents hypochondriacal?

There are some families in which children learn that they can get the attention of their family most effectively through physical complaints. Perhaps that was the only or best way to engage your parents and you still unwittingly carry on this "tradition"—using what ails you to take charge and get what you want and need, love.

· Did you lose a parent to illness? · Did you have an ill sibling? · Did you have a parent who was hospitalized, institutionalized? · Did your parents "split" for a time, even if you can't quite remember?

These are only a few of the calamities that can throw a child's life offtrack and create chaos. Your need to take control may have taken hold in such family turmoil.

· Did you have an alcoholic parent, given to irrational outbursts? · Did you have an emotionally disturbed family member who had an uncontrollable temper? · When your father/mother got angry, did they seem to go crazy? · In a fit of temper, was anyone destructive, violent? · As a child, did you have tantrums?

Children subject to irrational anger and uncontrolled rage in others (or themselves) may often struggle for control over these frightening forces. They may also live in dread that to get angry is to fall apart, go over the edge. Could this be your terror, and is it relived every time you have an anxiety attack?

Your primal marriage may be a carbon copy of Maxine's but it need not be. Your path to your need to control may be quite different. It may not have been a shattering or devastating event that created your helplessness. Could it have been more subtle, a result of your parents' personalities rather than a pivotal incident?

Work backward from what you know to what you don't know. But rest assured, if you are a symbolizer, there are things in your past, in your primal marriage, that made it so.

The next undertaking is to discover the roots of your husband's need to rescue. Exploring Jim's primal marriage is the first step. But there is something else to bear in mind here.

Maxine's memories were vague. Only with time could she allow herself to look squarely at recollections of her primal marriage, which were exceedingly painful. Maxine had the memories, but she kept them just outside her reach. When she was ready, she could grab hold of them.

This is not so with Jim. In Jim's primal marriage, there are particular recollections from which he has been completely cut off. This happens to many of us. We endure something so unendurable that we entirely block out or repress the memory. As children, such forgetting is a way we save ourselves. As adults, remembering is our salvation.

JIM'S PAST: HIS PRIMAL MARRIAGE

Jim recalls his childhood with quiet revulsion.

"My house had a white picket fence around it, green shutters, and a golden retriever, Skipper, on the front lawn. My two sisters, Lilly and Kate, one older, one younger, were leggy blondes. My baby brother Evan was a little angel and I was a great athlete. My mother and dad were college sweethearts, both came from the right part of town. We were a picture-perfect family on the surface.

"You only had to stick around to see it all unravel. Dad stayed away a lot. He had a boat and after work he would go there, not come home. Sometimes he would let me come to help him varnish or do some chores. But mostly he didn't want the family around.

"Maybe I was only nine or ten when I figured out that it was his hideaway and he must be meeting women there. I saw some under-wear in the cabin—the black lacy kind—and I got the picture.

"Meanwhile 'back at the ranch' my mother was a piece of work. She was a prim and proper matron—until cocktails. She convinced herself that as long as you drank after five, you didn't have a problem with alcohol.

"Mother was not very demonstrative. But with a few drinks it was 'Come here, sweets, give me a kiss.' When she got this way, I headed upstairs to my room.

"I'll never forget one evening when she was feeling particularly affectionate. I must have been eleven. It was Christmas break and my older sister Lilly had brought her boyfriend, Henry, home from college. I was on my way upstairs and I heard my mother talking to Henry in that silky voice of hers.

"I went down and spied on them in the living room. The room seemed bathed in a glow of light. I don't remember a lot of what went on, but I see myself sitting on the stairs (almost like I was floating over the room) watching my mother kissing Henry. It made me sick.

"I never told my sister. I couldn't bear to ruin her vacation and she had such a crush on Henry. Instead, I just made sure that Henry never got to be alone with my mother for the rest of his stay. I just pretended that because I only had sisters, I liked hanging around with a 'big brother.' By the end of the holiday Henry was calling me his Siamese twin.

"Frankly, I didn't blame Henry one bit. My mother threw herself at him. He was completely helpless. I wasn't even mad at my mother. She was pathetic. I felt sorry for her."

There is enough dysfunction in Jim's primal marriage to explain many difficulties with which he might struggle. But as unpleasant as these memories are, they are only a partial picture of his primal marriage. To understand him, we need to see more. What "more" is there?

While the revolting episode with his mother and Henry is actually something Jim witnessed, it is also a screen for another more difficult memory that Jim has buried beyond active recollection.

Sometimes when we are forced to erase our most horrible experiences from our minds, we unconsciously rewrite them in a milder, more acceptable form. When this happens, there are several identifying markers that can alert us that what we actively remember is a cover for things we can't bear to recollect.

A memory that is without many details, where we recollect ourselves as an observer to a scene, and where we recall our images bathed in a glow or aura of light, are the signs that there is a darker memory that lies beyond our active recollection.[8]

This aptly describes Jim. And it is no accident that he recalls Henry dubbing him his Siamese twin. What Jim can't bear to remember is that the "identical" experience happened to him!

When he was very young, Jim's mother, while drunk, was sexually overstimulated. On the pretext of being lonely she would take him into her bed, fondling him and rubbing her nearly naked body against his. It was an experience that flooded Jim with sexual excitement, leaving him in a frenzied state of helplessness.

He was panicked by this bewildering experience and he longed to be rescued from this bedlam as he had rescued Henry. It was this sexual abuse at the hands of his mother and his desperate wish to escape her that gave rise to his anxious, panicky need to rescue.

And this is what draws him to his incapacitated wife. Unconsciously, when Jim sees his helpless wife, it is as if he is seeing himself. In trying to save her, *he is symbolically trying to save himself.*

But again there is one more piece of this puzzle to put in place. Why no anger? Jim's helpless rage at his mother's assault got buried along with the entire experience. He can't dare feel the rage because it might unearth the reason for it. The secret must stay buried, and along with it the anger; a hateful anger at her violation, and betrayal so intense that the child in Jim fears its deadly force.

Might your husband's primal marriage be one in which he was a helpless victim? And could the terrible recollections be so deeply buried that they resurface in a less sinister form?

· Did he see one parent abuse the other? · Were his siblings abused, sexually or physically?

Parental abuse is about the misuse of power. The power of the strong over the weak. Even if your husband was not the target, he would still be profoundly affected by the experience. Witnessing abuse, he may have ached desperately to make it go away. But he was as powerless as were the victims. Perhaps the guilt of not having come to the rescue of a sister, brother, or mother is the origin of his need.

· Were his parents cruel, vicious, sadistic? · Did they taunt or tease him? · Were they harshly punitive? · Did they have extreme or peculiar ways of punishing their children?

Regrettably, there are many ways a parent can abuse the privilege of power they hold over their children. In word and deed they can render a child their helpless victim. Forcing a petrified child to jump off the high diving board to show he's a "real man," making the child who hates spinach eat pounds of it so he'll "get used to it," locking a child in a dark cellar to "teach her a lesson" are just a small sampling of "inventive," nonviolent methods. Could your husband have been subject to this variation of abuse? If so, you can of course understand how rescue became his need.

· Did he believe he was adopted, or have childhood fantasies that he was the child of someone rich or famous? · Did he have dreams of running away from home? · Did he invent magical heroes or magical lands where he "lived"?

We can get a hint of unacceptable and, therefore, repressed memories if he cherished a wish to escape from home. Escape is a form of deliverance. Perhaps, what he can't remember was that he was in need of such salvation and thus created it through his imagination.

· Did he ever look into the mirror and feel as if he wasn't looking at himself? · Did he ever feel detached from his own body? · Did he ever have the odd sensation of being in a crowded room and feeling very detached, or as if he was floating off in space or was the only person there? · Did he ever have momentary amnesia?

Children who have had traumatic but forgotten experiences may suffer from odd sensations in which they feel unreal. It's almost as if they must split themselves off from the real memory by becoming unreal. This is a way his mind may have sought protection from the recollection of intolerable thoughts.

Taking Hold of the Problem:
Getting Ready for
an Adult Marriage

Don't you feel quite different about Maxine and Jim now that you've seen their primal families? Can you dismiss Maxine as an unbearable hypochondriac? Is Jim still the bumbling nursemaid to his impossibly demanding wife? No. They are two people who carry the burden of primal secrets and primal shame. And it is because of their respective secrets that anger is exiled from their marriage. One of them believes that anger will push them over the edge; the other that it will push them into confrontation with painful memory where hateful deadly anger is also waiting to be found.

Before symbolizers can put insight to work in order to forge a truly *adult marriage,* they must rework their deep-seated fears about anger. For the symbolizer who believes that getting mad is tantamount to going mad, she needs to take an adult look at mental illness. Agitation, tension, and outbursts are the symptoms of the problem, not the cause. As children, we understandably get confused and reverse the order. We don't comprehend that emotional instability alters our parent's mood and instead believe that an angry mood alters their stability. This was how we understood it as a child in a primal marriage. It is time to replace the logic of childhood with the reason of adulthood. Simply stated, anger cannot and does not make anyone go crazy. The challenge of a symbolizer is to believe this!

(The panic attacks of symbolizers often make this a daunting challenge; that is why medical assistance is frequently necessary and extremely beneficial. For example, medication to bring panic attacks under control can be crucial in taking hold of the problem.[9] Once a symbolizer is spared the terror of such episodes, she can work more calmly and diligently on developing these new adult beliefs about anger.)

The second symbolizer has another sort of undertaking. As a small, dependent, helpless child, the truth of memory and the hateful rage that accompanied it were too much to bear. Your mind did a wonderful thing: It protected you. Repression was your rescue, your salvation, your deliverance. Forgetting put a thick wall around the ugliness, the pain, the fury. It locked it away so you could go on with your young life.

But your guardian has done its job and is now working to protect you when you no longer require such safeguards. You are an adult, you have the power today that you did not have then in your primal marriage. You can remember because you will not only survive the shame, the guilt, the rage, but you will become free from the darkness and dread that haunt you. In your primal marriage, forgetting was your escape; in your adult marriage, remembering is your road to freedom.

From all this it is plain that symbolizers have a significant undertaking when it comes to their marriage and their hidden anger. To make these transformations possible, they must share their dark and frightening secrets. If you recognize yourself and your symbolizer marriage, perhaps you can begin to do that sharing now with one another. Perhaps with what you now have discovered you will both see what needs immediate attention—not the bad backs, the headaches, but your troubled souls.

Yet secrets are a daunting burden to unload alone or even with the help of a spouse. That is why symbolizers need to consider getting outside assistance in this struggle. The single most liberating thing for you to do is to join a group where other people can share your secret. In a therapeutic setting with other people who were abused, molested, who have alcoholism or mental illness as part of their primal marriage, you will find it much easier to lay these demons to rest. When the secrets see the light of day, anger can take its rightful place in your marriage.

T	e	n

SUPPRESSERS

uppressers are people who bury their anger by *suppressing conflict*. They will do "everything and anything" to make sure dissension doesn't enter their marriage. Division, discord, disagreement, opposition have no place in this union. Arguments, altercations, battles, rows, spats, quarrels, squabbles, and contests are ventures into forbidden territory. They all mean unleashing anger, and that is an anathema to a suppresser. The unwritten motto of this marriage: *"Without conflict, there is no anger!"*

Suppressers can be an ingenious lot. Their creative instincts mean that there is a great deal of variety in their partnerships on two accounts. For one, there are simply a significant number of ways people can detour around conflict. And second, while suppressers may rely more heavily on one mode of conflict avoidance than another, they rarely choose a single way around a conflict. Suppressers often take the smorgasbord approach: a little bit of this, a little bit of that. Such diversity makes suppressers an interesting style to explore and a most challenging one to identify.

Mixed Marriages

Suppression is a coping style that easily dovetails with other angry lovestyles, overt or covert. Suppressers may marry out of their "kind." A venter, a provoker, or an enactor may well have vowed, "I do," to a spouse who has unconsciously vowed, "I don't," want conflict. A husband who lashes out with an angry and biting tongue may have a wife who "bites her lip." A passive/aggressive wife might live with a man who passes over her provocations. And a man who enacts may love a woman who "acts" as if nothing is wrong in the face of his misdeeds. When it comes to angry lovestyles, suppressers are frequently in "mixed marriages."

This prospect of the mixed marriage adds yet another fascinating and challenging dimension to the suppresser style. But there is something else that confers a compelling aspect to suppressers. When it comes right down to it, even for those in the best of marriages, there is a little bit of suppresser in all of us. As you explore this lovestyle, you are bound to see your marriage and yourself.

Before we detail this style, something needs to be clarified. Suppressers often behave in ways that, on the face of it, seem reasonable, even commendable, in a marriage; they may be apologetic, for example. But suppressers do the right things for the wrong reason. They do what they do in order to suppress conflict. And it is this motive for the behavior, not just the behavior itself, which we must include in order to pinpoint this self-defeating style.

It Hurts to Be in Love

As is always the case when I'm at work on a new book, I talk it up with good friends. But no discussion of the angry marriage struck more pay dirt than when I described my ideas about suppressers.

My friend Paula's dinner table on a blustery subzero evening in January was typical. The stories came tumbling out. I felt as if I was chairing a regular meeting of SA—Suppressers Anonymous. Carol, who "never fought" with her husband, Bob, began with a classic "1950s housewife" example: She would "slave over a hot stove all day" only to find Bob preoccupied and unappreciative over dinner. Hurt, she'd retreat to bed (not at all in the mood for sex). The next morning she'd get up "feeling a little blue," but by midday she'd manage to be back in the kitchen "cooking up a storm" (but never stormy with rage).

Though most women are no longer stay-at-home moms "slaving over a hot stove," many, many women are still suppressers, turning anger into hurt. When they feel pressure, harried, ignored, left out, unappreciated, and particularly when criticized, suppressers don't object, argue, or lash out. They don't get mad; they get sad.

"Anger to hurt" is a typical mode of suppression, and it isn't confined to women. Although it may fly in the face of our long-cherished stereotypes, there are many men who feel injured when they are actually angry. For every woman slaving over the stove and feeling wounded, there is a man slaving over his desk and feeling offended.[1]

Blessed Are the Peacemakers

Marissa didn't get hurt in order to stave off marital controversy; instead, she got busy, appeasing her spouse. Anything to avoid an argument.

"If I'd wake up and find that there was no milk for Charlie's coffee, I'd run out to the deli, even in the snow, to get it. I just didn't want him scowling at me first thing in the morning."

Marissa's efforts were not acts of generosity toward her husband; she didn't run to the deli in a blizzard to make him happy. (Remember: I warned you that suppressers can look commendable.) They were attempts to avoid the possibility of her husband's displeasure. For Marissa, it was easier to face the frigid weather outside than the frosty greeting she thought she might meet inside her own home.

Keeping the peace at all costs is often part of this lovestyle, and appeasement can take other forms. If Marissa hadn't made it back with the milk, she might have resorted, like many a suppresser, to apologizing in order to back out of controversy.

"I'm sorry" are two important words in any marriage. They provide an acknowledgment that we may have hurt the person we love. But for a suppresser, every apology is much more than a "commendable" request for forgiveness. In this angry lovestyle, an apology is really a supplication that beings (and ends) with the unspoken words: *Please don't be angry!*

Please don't be angry . . . I'm sorry, I didn't mean it.

Please don't be angry . . . I'm sorry, it was an accident.

Please don't be angry . . . I'm sorry, it won't happen again.

Please don't be angry . . . I'm sorry, I had so much to do today that I just forgot.

On one level, suppressers don't offer regrets, they appeal for mercy. If, for you, love is *always* having to say you're sorry because you always need to avoid strife, you could be a suppresser.

The supplicant suppresser is closely related to another mode of nullifying anger: assuming guilt. Suppressers all too readily declare, "It's really my fault," in order to neutralize contention. If in your marriage you continually indulge in self-condemnation rather than reproach your mate, you may be carrying the guilt in order to do away with the greater burden—rage.

Everyone Makes Mistakes

Suppressers have an exhausting array of unwitting ploys to get a spouse off the hook, and anger off their marital agenda. Rather than head to an angry showdown, they sidestep potential disputes by excusing their spouse ("He doesn't mean what he says"), by offering the apology themselves ("She doesn't come out with an apology, but I know she's sorry"), or by attributing behavior elsewhere ("It's only the whiskey talking"). To avoid angry confrontation, suppressers make their spouses "not guilty" with an explanation.

Regularly responding to annoyance with equanimity and grace, suppressers are all forgiveness and understanding in the wake of marital disappointment. They are adept at making polite excuses at all times ("None of us is perfect"; "It's not the end of the world").

Skipping anger by shifting to accommodation means suppressers don't ever get incensed or exasperated. So, if you are always courteous, quick to offer platitudes, pleasant, amiable, and congenial, instead of periodically teed off at your spouse, you are probably a suppresser.

In this "Hallmark" mode, suppressers are unperturbed, unflappable; they don't get messy. They seem to have Teflon-coated hearts—nothing sticks long enough to cause strife. As a rule, these suppressers are emotionally cool, calm, and collected, even cold. Limited in emotional range, they don't cry and they don't jump for joy either. Spontaneity is not their strong suit.[2]

Only When I Laugh

Humor can be a great gift to a marriage. We can use it to smooth out the bumps and help put things in perspective. But suppressers don't use humor that way. Rather, they use it to undo conflict.

I once sat at a dinner party where a man I know very well spoke in a most unflattering way about his wife, a speech therapist.[3] Hearing her stumble over her words, he laughingly mimicked her: "Would you go to her for your st . . . st . . . stutter?" His wife giggled—"He loves to tease." Knowing this couple quite well, I knew that in spite of her humiliation, this nervous titter would be her only response.

The speech therapist's giggle was not just a way to get through a socially awkward moment. A suppresser does not defer her angry reaction in public in order to go home and "straighten things out" in the privacy of her bedroom. No. The suppresser just giggles nervously at that dinner party and the countless others at which the scene repeats itself.

There are variants on this "misuse" of humor by suppressers. All are really an attempt to minimize the impact of objectionable behavior on the part of a spouse. They are the ways a suppresser convinces him/herself—"No, it doesn't bother me" ("Who could take that seriously"; "That's just his offbeat sense of humor"; "He loves a practical joke"; "She loves to tease"; "It's all in fun"). If you laugh when others might become livid, it's no joke: You are a suppresser!

Realigned Needs

At another of my informally chaired meetings of SA—Suppressers Anonymous—a group of men and women discussed the ways in which they had managed to keep confrontation and thus contention under wraps. Susan began by recalling a dinner planned with a small group of women friends. Initially, she was enthusiastic, but when her friends chose a restaurant that her husband, Joel, always described as overpriced, she began to have second thoughts.

"I did a complete turnaround. I said to myself, 'Why should I spend the money?' So I begged off (I don't remember what reason I gave), and I didn't go."

As is often the case with suppressers, Susan didn't simply change her mind; rather, she denied her own feelings in order to realign her views with those of her husband and so avoid conflict. Convincing themselves that they don't want or need what they want and need is often part of a suppresser's repertoire.

Suppressers may manage "a night out with the girls" (or guys) quite differently from Susan: They never even consider going out from the start. Some suppressers don't need to "talk themselves out" of their desires; they just don't allow them to exist at all! Quashing desires before they can even threaten a conflict is a most effective way to bury anger.

To Tell the Truth

We'd be lying if we said there isn't a place in marriage for the little white lie. Used sparingly, the social lie is a lubricant that keeps a marriage running along smoothly ("I told your mother we already had dinner plans for Friday night"). Show us a person who says they never lied to their spouse and we'll show you a liar.

Suppressers don't use an occasional fabrication or omission to keep their marriage putt-putting along. No. They skirt the truth (regularly or even habitually) to skirt what is for them the real danger—confrontation.

Money matters, always a potential bone of contention in marriage, are the most typical issue where suppressers color the truth so a spouse won't see red. Madge, a waitress, described her financial deception. Every week she'd "squirrel away" some of her tips, eventually spending the money on the sly.[4] Ripping up credit slips, secretly borrowing money from parents, "discounting" the price (the hundred-dollar dress that "only" cost fifty dollars) are only a few of the additional dodges on which a suppresser may rely.

Women have not cornered the market on evasion as a route to conflict avoidance. Patrick is no stranger to the "protective" lie. Since his wife, Mindy, can't stand "Thursday night poker," his brother Bob now picks Pat up for "Thursday night bowling"!

Like Pat, suppressers routinely use invention; but lies of omission are also standard fare. Robert often (if not always) forgets to tell Audrey about the parking tickets he gets so frequently. "Why burden her?" he tells himself as he "successfully" unloads any grounds for conflict.

And bear in mind that when it comes to subterfuge, children may also become a suppresser's collaborators ("We just won't tell Mommy that Daddy had a cigarette"; "If Dad calls, tell him I'm sleeping").

Suppressers who need to lie are not bad people; they are scared people. To tell the truth seems daunting. It feels as if it is throwing down the gauntlet to their spouse, and they feel unable to cope with the anticipated consequences of controversy, opposition, struggle, and so on. If you customarily substitute fiction for fact in order to avert marital friction, your lies may reveal the truth: You are a suppresser.

Tomorrow Is Another Day

Time is something suppressers use cleverly. They offset anger by putting conflict on hold. When a potential struggle rears its head, reactions get shelved ("I'll tell him how I feel tomorrow"; "I can see this isn't a good time to bring it up"; "If I give him a little time, he'll feel differently"; "I'll sleep on it"). The problem is that the time is *never* right and a suppresser swallows her ire, time and time again.

Avoidance, in the literal sense, is often a suppresser's strategy. The double feature at the Cineplex or the double bourbon at the bar may be the refuge to which the suppresser beats a retreat. Steering clear of a spouse may be a most direct way to avoid contact, and therefore friction.

But not all suppressers need to take a hike, literally, to avoid conflict. A much more common route is silence. Some suppressers play it close to the vest, offering their spouse little material for argument and contention. The premise? If we don't talk much, we don't fight much. And silence may be accomplished in a variety of ways. For instance, we hide behind the newspaper at breakfast or zone out in front of the TV at night.

Or perhaps this is less a product of a strategy and more an aspect of personality. In our marriages we may be shy and retiring, reticent and private, unopinionated and disinterested, or the strong and silent type. The point is, if you're not talkers, for whatever reasons, the real exchange left out of your marriage may be anger.

Who Said That?

Suppressers may be masterful at retraction as a technique for preventing divisiveness. At the first rumblings of confrontation, a suppressor may try to undo what she/he believes is the source of the discord ("I didn't mean that"; "You misunderstood me"; "I didn't say that"; "I don't believe that"; "No, that's not my opinion").

Disclaimers, disavowals, repudiation of their own thoughts, feelings, and/or actions may be the suppressor's desperate strategy to circumvent marital disharmony. Backing down on your own convictions may be the way you attempt to back out of marital discord. If you think Democrat but vote Republican in order not to fight with your spouse, nominate yourself a suppresser.

Forget Me Not

The capacity to forget is a healing balm. In marriage we often need to apply it liberally. A marriage can get bogged down if we keep score and remember too much. But suppressers overdo things when it comes to forgetting. They have selective memories which often completely screen out the things that might otherwise drive them to distraction ("Did my wife really say that to me? Funny, I don't remember").

Forgetting is not a gradual process; it is a complete blanking out on the offending experience. It is through lapses in memory that a suppresser can ignore, disregard, overlook, or dismiss the very things that are potentially vexing. Could this be you?

Certain suppressers, particularly men, develop into marital stoics. They have such limited expectations of married life that nothing—no disappointment, no aggravation, no adversity in their lovelife—gets them peeved. Indifference to pain because they never expect marriage to be anything other than miserable and painful is their insurance policy against ever getting teed off at their spouse. (If their wife offered them a bed of nails to sleep on, they would just climb into the sack and whisper, "Goodnight, dear.") These sorts of suppressers seem to be thick-skinned and unflappable. Detached, impassive, and imperturbable, the marital stoic gets stuck but never yells, "Ouch!"

Sex and Suppressers

Suppressers run out of sexual steam. At best, sex is occasional and/or perfunctory. Emotionally, and sometimes physically, they "just can't get it up"; suppressers feel unexcited, unenergetic, and not all that interested in sex. In bed they seem to give up on each other and the possibility of mutual pleasure. Putting a damper on anger means that other passions get extinguished as well. When sparks can't fly around conflict, sexual sparks go out, too. If sexual apathy has entered your bedroom, it is probably because conflict, and the resulting expression of anger, has exited your marriage.

Paying the Price

It is not hard to see the very dear price some suppressers may pay for this style. A suppresser has the potential to suffer indignity and embarrassment (remember the speech therapist and her "funny" husband).

A suppresser may tolerate unacceptable behavior. A suppresser may walk around burdened by guilt, saddened by hurt, the apologetic supplicant or the overworked appeaser. A suppresser may become a habitual liar. Loneliness may be a suppresser's closest and only companion.

A suppresser may become one-dimensional, slick, sweet, insincere (remember our "Hallmark"-variety suppresser) without even realizing the transformation into a false self. And with all this, a suppresser's marriage may be drained and depleted of pleasure and joy. Suppressers can be dull as hell!

But the greatest price a suppresser pays is with her (or his) sense of self. The suppresser does not define herself on the basis of what she thinks and feels, wants and needs, likes and dislikes. Rather, suppressers are defined by their need to avoid conflict. Their personalities do not grow, emerge, and take shape in their marriages. Actions and reactions are shaped by the necessity to avoid discord. Who we are takes a back seat to what we feel we must be in relation to our spouse and our marriage.

Essentially, in whatever form it takes, suppressers give themselves up in order to keep the peace. Our own honest nature is lost while we create our non-angry persona. Suppressers pay the price with their own souls. *We detour around anger and on the way we lose our true self.* Anika and Stan are two suppressers whose self-sacrifice to the god of anger knows few limits.

The Actual Marriage of Two Suppressers: Anika and Stan

Anika's eyes darted around the kitchen sink, searching for the sponge. Stan was coming down the stairs to breakfast. It was bad enough she'd spilled the coffee and messed up his morning paper; he didn't have to see it splattered down the kitchen cabinets. Not finding the sponge, Anika used the flap of her terry robe to sop up the mess—it had to go into the wash today anyhow. Stan walked into the kitchen and picked up the paper.

"How did it get to be such a mess?" he asked, curling his lip in disgust.

"The cat. She jumped up on the counter when I'd just filled your mug."

Anika knew it was ridiculous to blame her orange ball of fur, Marmaduke, but it was too early in the morning for explanations and apologies about how clumsy she could be. This morning Marmaduke could be the culprit. It just made life easier.

As usual, Stan opened the paper. This morning the front-page banner headline on the bombing of a local abortion clinic had Stan talking aloud more than usual:

"Those bad apples who get into the Right to Life movement! They spoil the reputation of people trying to change the laws the legal way."

"Don't you think," offered Anika hesitantly, "that even some legal protesters go too far, like trying to keep women who've made a decision to have an abortion from doing it?"

"Anika," said Stan firmly, starting to sound like the calm, certain insurance fraud investigator that he was, "trying to talk people out of making a morally wrong decision is perfectly all right. It is not going too far if you believe, as we *both* obviously do, that abortion is wrong."

Anika knew how she personally felt about abortion; it was something she'd never consider for herself. On the other hand, she wasn't quite sure that she believed in the Right to Life movement as strongly as Stan.

215

But how she felt didn't really matter. Even if she was pro choice (which she wasn't), she'd never tell Stan, let alone do anything about it. She thought of her friend Meg, who had voted pro choice in the last election and then had lied to her husband. Anika simply couldn't imagine doing such a thing. She put the thought out of her mind.

"I guess you're right, dear."

Stan's face relaxed. He felt much more comfortable when he and Anika understood each other, when everything worked out between them. They never fought like, some people they knew.

He went back to reading the paper. An article about sex phone-lines caught his eye. He'd never resort to such a thing, no matter what. Anika hadn't been interested in sex lately, but Stan wasn't one to push.

"This is what happens after a few years of marriage," he reassured himself. "That's just the way the cookie crumbles. You can't expect your sex life to be a bed of roses forever." He found consolation in his own thoughts.

But he wondered about himself physically. Did Anika consider him adequate? It was something Stan could think, but after all these years he could never imagine asking Anika. It was too personal.

He shook off his feeling of doubt. "This is ridiculous," he chided himself. "Anika never complains. We have a good marriage."

Anika's eye also caught the article featuring the sex phone scam. She couldn't see those things for a minute. Sex was overrated; take it or leave it was her attitude. It seemed to be Stan's, too. Anyway, now that he had taken on the evening security job at the mall, Stan probably just didn't have the energy. Everything was fine. Stan was just tired.

Yes, things were just fine in Anika and Stan's marriage. Or were they?

An Actual Marriage: Are You Suppressers?

Though they are quite different in their demeanor, both Anika and Stan are suppressers. Their actual marriage, day to day, moment to moment, is filled with endless examples of this covert lovestyle. Is yours?

Theirs is a conflict-free union. They don't fight. Hardly. They don't even flare up, let alone battle. They do the anger-avoidance cha-cha. As soon as one of them goes three steps closer to conflict, they quickly shuffle three steps back.

And they do this in a variety of ways:

- She appeases . . . cleans up the coffee; apologizes.
- She tells "white lies" . . . the cat spilled the coffee.
- He uses avoidance . . . hides behind newspaper; makes small talk; doesn't talk about feelings; doesn't discuss sex, it's "too personal."
- They deny . . . they have a good marriage (they don't fight or disagree); don't complain about their sex life.
- They both realign their views . . . around the abortion issue.

Is your actual marriage anything like theirs? A dispirited, dull, and distant union, where peace reigns but deep and heartfelt connections are missing? Where who and what you truly are gets buried under an avalanche of "Yes, dear," "I'm sorry," and greeting-card sentiments? Are you the supplicant suppresser while your spouse is the stoic, the denier, or seems made out of Teflon? If your marriage is anything like this conflict-free and joy-free partnership, you are regrettably suppressers.

Decoding Complaints: Making the Invisible Marriage Visible

What unconscious forces drive this relationship? Stan is unwittingly piloted by an unconscious need *to keep a distance.* Anika is likewise propelled by her own hidden need *to be compliant*. The interplay of these concealed needs give rise to their *invisible marriage* and keeps them locked in an angry and self-defeating lovelife. Analyzing their complaints is a way to unravel the hidden agenda in their marriage and provide a looking glass into your own.

Just a word about the notion of complaints. For some suppressers, the idea that they may have marital complaints is impossible to consider. If suppression is grounded in denial, for example, a plastic smile and a "but nothing is wrong with our marriage" stance may be the order of the day (Stan is close to this model). This is not true for all suppressers. The majority are unfortunately all too aware, even if they don't feel angry, that they do feel unhappy (Anika is unaware of her rage and all too aware of her misery).

Because of this, we will use the concept of complaints with the caveat that not all suppressers are able to work themselves up to criticizing their spouse or their marriage. They may observe (remember displacers?) rather than complain.

And as we are wont to do in these pages, let's use this information to help you pinpoint this style. If you can't say what's wrong with your unhappy marriage, maybe that's what's wrong with it!

HER COMPLAINTS—HIS NEED

Anika's complaints about Stan are our way into his need—*to keep a distance*. Anika's major objections center on Stan's failure to communicate:

"He doesn't talk to me. Really talk. I know the football scores, but I don't know what's really on his mind."

With Stan's need to keep a distance, he is reluctant to let Anika into his inner sanctum. Through intimate communication, our innermost thoughts and feelings are revealed: We let someone inside. Stan can't allow that. Small talk, or no talk, is a kind of fence he erects to keep Anika on the outside.

Of course Stan's silence does double duty. The less he communicates, the less grounds there are for conflict. The behaviors of a suppresser with a need to keep a distance fit like a hand in a glove. Just about anything Stan does to control his anger works to keep him at a distance from his wife. Two for the price of one—all the time.

This complaint of Anika's—"He doesn't talk to me"—is among the most common grievances women have about their spouses, suggesting perhaps that there may be an awful lot of men out there who are propelled by this unconscious need. Might it be your husband's?

YOUR COMPLAINT: YOUR HUSBAND'S NEED

Think about the things missing from your marriage, the things that you don't get from your husband. Run them by the thought that he might need to keep you at a distance. And understand that his need to keep you at arm's length may serve many masters.

· Your Complaint

He never tells me what bothers him. He never tells me what upsets him. He doesn't confide in me.

· His Need

Knowing his fears, worries, doubts, and insecurities means letting you into a place he doesn't want you to be. You might be disappointed in him if you knew what he knows about himself. He may keep you distant to preserve an image of himself because somewhere inside he feels, "I'm not what you think I am." He's afraid to let you in on this disappointing revelation. Keeping a distance may be his way to keep his "secret."

· Your Complaint

He doesn't seem to need me. He doesn't like me to do things for him. He doesn't ever do things for me. He's not that interested in me or my work.

· His Need

Noninvolvement is often a way to fashion distance between two people. Unwittingly, it may be your husband's strategy. After all, if he relies on you, it's risky; you could become a habit he can't do without. So, keeping a distance may be your husband's way to steer clear of dependency.

· Your Complaint

He's cold. He seems so detached. In bed, he's a cold fish. He pushes me away.

· His Need

Often men fear that if a woman gets too close, they will be swallowed up by her. They fight letting down their icy guard because they will be engulfed. If you are married to a man who gives you the "big chill," it may be his way of keeping distant in order to keep from losing himself.

· Your Complaint

He never cries. He's so unemotional.

· His Need

Another way a man may create distance is to keep you from knowing what hurts him: He keeps you outside his heart. And if you don't know his soft spots, or he doesn't appear to have any, you can't think of him as weak. This is often behind a need to keep a distance.

Or again, if you knew his weaknesses, you might take over. You could control him. You'd have the upper hand. But if he keeps you at an emotional distance, this feared domination can never be realized.

Remember, where there is contact there is friction. But with your husband's need to keep a distance this contact never occurs. So anger is banished from your home and hearth.

Perhaps this analysis gives you a chance to reconsider your husband. The man who doesn't talk, doesn't cry, doesn't seem interested or warm may actually be a man with an overriding though unconscious need to keep you at a distance.

HIS COMPLAINTS = HER NEED

Normally at this juncture we'd turn the tables and decode Stan's grievances in order to interpret Anika's need for compliance. In fact, that can't happen. After all, Anika always dutifully agrees, yields, complies, and acquiesces. Being submissive, she doesn't provide much about which Stan objects. In effect, Stan has no charges to level at his wife.

And this is what makes a woman like Anika so confusing. There is nothing objectionable about a compliant suppresser. But she still makes a lousy spouse! The only difficulty is identifying just how and why this is so.

Even though Stan is loathe to register a full-fledged complaint, he can, when prodded, make some observations about Anika that can clue us in to compliance.

Sex is a matter that comes to his mind.

"Anika never says no to sex but she never seems all that interested. She's not one to initiate it. And she's not one to go in for anything out of the ordinary."

Anika is not about to be sexually inventive because in bed—and out of it—she needs to be a follower, not a leader. Her job is to go along with her husband's desires, and she needs to know them first in order to yield to them. It can't be the other way around because then she would risk doing something "wrong." Anika isn't disinterested. She's inhibited.

While Stan doesn't "suffer" (i.e., they have sex whenever he cares to approach), what he picks up is that Anika's heart isn't in it. And it isn't. When we do things because we are unconsciously forcing ourselves to oblige, there is little room for enthusiasm. Obligatory sex is *not* about having fun in bed.

Anika's unconscious need to be compliant is her unwitting agreement to servitude. Even if her husband is a kind of beneficiary, Anika's enslavement has its downside. With "nothing" to complain about, he is sensing the damper Anika's compliance puts on their love and on their passion.

YOUR HUSBAND'S COMPLAINT: YOUR NEED

Are you ready to contemplate the driving force in your half of a suppresser marriage? Might you, through a need to be forever compliant, sacrifice your personal energy, power, and sexual vitality? If you have a hunch that this is true, an analysis of these additional complaints may confirm your suspicions.

> *· Your Husband's Complaint*

She seems scared of me; I think she hides things from me.

> *· Your Need*

If we unwittingly believe that we must be compliant, then we often feel as if we are forever on the cusp of rebuke and reproach. It might be this anxiety over the possible reprimand that dogs you and that your husband registers.

> *· Your Husband's Complaint*

It is always the movie (restaurant, friends) that *I'd* prefer. She's too nice. She doesn't have a mind of her own.

· *Your Need*

A need for compliance dictates that you relinquish your desires in favor of your husband's. Once you are cut off from your own passions, you appear boring, colorless, insipid—even dumb! You don't have a mind of your own because your primary job is to agree with your husband, not to think for yourself. Self-assertion and self-determination can't be your strong suit.

· *Your Husband's Complaint*

Sometimes I wonder if she really loves me. Our marriage doesn't seem that important to my wife.

· *Your Need*

Now here's a real kick in the head. You are so busy being compliant that you don't get really involved with your spouse. Involvement means tuning in to his complexities—and you can't. You require a fast take so you can respond. But obedience is not the same as responsiveness and tender loving care, and maybe your husband feels hurt by the difference.

And remember, compliant people never create conflict. No conflict, no friction. No friction, no anger. Two for the price of one.

OUR INVISIBLE MARRIAGE AND THE CYCLE OF SUPPRESSION

What is the cycle of this invisible marriage? The unconscious needs of Stan and Anika do not bring them into a collision course of repeated (and destructive) conflict. Their invisible marriage takes quite a different form. They spin on in a pattern of ever-increasing detachment. Theirs is a cycle of suppression where they move further and further apart. And it happens in some very startling ways.

We can begin with Stan and his need to keep a distance. With this need, Stan is a man who acts but reveals little of what is truly in his mind and heart: His need makes him hard to know. How does this affect Anika? Badly. It leaves her out on a limb. After all, how can she satisfy her need for compliance if she can't know exactly what he wants from her? Desperate to know, she tries to get a reading on him.

How does Stan respond? He can't possibly appreciate that Anika's need compels her constant attempts to "take his pulse." Rather, he can only filter this through his unconscious agenda, concluding that Anika wants more and more of him. An alarm goes off: It's dangerous, she's getting closer. What must he do in response? Thanks to his need, he must push Anika away, leaving her more anxious and confused than ever. With Stan seemingly even more remote and inscrutable, Anika becomes more nervously compliant. Unwittingly, Anika and Stan are forever at cross purposes: Anika always needs to know in order to stay compliant, and Stan always needs to remain unknown to stay distant. The cycle spins on!

The Primal Marriage: Where the Anger Began

How is it that Stan has to keep a distance and Anika must be compliant? And why do they both suppress conflict as a road to burying their anger? The answer lies in their childhood: in their respective personal histories, *the primal marriage.*

ANIKA'S PAST: HER PRIMAL MARRIAGE

Anika's most vivid memory centers on her brother Jonathan's birth. And it is a memory that echoes throughout her entire primal marriage:

"I had just started kindergarten and caught chicken pox at school. I wasn't allowed near the new baby. A few days after they were home from the hospital, my mother found me peeking in the nursery door. I was crying.

"That night at dinner she told my father what a good girl I was; crying because I couldn't make friends with my new baby brother, Jonathan. 'That's why we love you, Anika,' my father chimed in, 'because you're such a nice, sensitive little girl.' "

While anger and envy *always* play a role in the birth of a sibling, Anika came from a family that insisted on banishing all such "harmful" and "ugly" feelings. They would never acknowledge these unacceptable aspects of their child's nature, or their own, for that matter. On the contrary, they were highly dismayed by the slightest appearance of dissension or ill-will at any juncture.

Whether it was in the face of a major family event (like a new child), or an everyday occurrence around the kitchen table (everyone "loved" to eat whatever was put before them; no one was allowed to "hate" anything on their dinner plate!), their response to any sign of family hostility was to insist on harmony, even to the point where they ignored or misinterpreted behavior.

How did this affect Anika? While she was being commended by her parents, she was also being confused. The tears streaming down her face were *not* the warm tears of affection for her newborn pal; they were hot tears of hateful jealousy for her newest rival. Likewise her "maturity," so welcomed by her parents at Jonathan's birth, was an act that masked Anika's true feeling—resentment.

Anika's parents did not rely on such subtleties exclusively to convey their demand for harmony and goodwill. They could often be quite explicit on the matter. If Anika's "bad side" did emerge, she would receive a reprimand. But it was reproach with a certain devastating twist.

"Once I remember telling my mother I hated her. She looked stricken; she reacted as if I'd put a knife in her heart. I felt horrible for hurting her. For weeks she was so distant, I was convinced she'd stopped loving me. I felt so awful; I never did it again."

This reaction was typical of Anika's primal marriage. Normal rivalries, jealousies, hateful passions were not permissible. Angry conflict directed to anyone in her primal family, siblings or parents, was actively discouraged. The need to defuse conflict was so powerful it required Anika to turn anger to hurt (her "sad" tears over her new sibling), and caused her to act in complete contradiction to her true sentiments (i.e., being so "grown-up" when Jonathan arrived), or to turn her anger into guilt (i.e., her fear that she'd hurt her mother). At age four Anika, with the support of her parents, became a full-blown suppresser!

But there was another powerful message she absorbed, along with prohibitions about conflict and anger: *Parental love is conditional.* You get it only if you are good enough to deserve it.

Anika did not feel as if love was a given: You are not cherished for who and what you are. Rather, love is a prize won through merit. Love is provisional, contingent.

And for Anika, the provisions were all too clear: If you are angry, you are bad and therefore unlovable. If you are not angry, you are good and therefore lovable. Is it any wonder Anika has the need to be compliant? In her primal marriage, being loved depended on it.

Could this describe your primal marriage? And could this regrettable predicament have left you with the double burden of suppression and compliance?

Is This Your Primal Marriage?

· Was ill-will within the family considered treachery? · Did your parents always insist on harmony?

Harmony needs to be a goal, not a rule. In families with edicts about "getting along," children may feel coerced rather than understood. Coerced children often grow up to be compliant adults, cut off from their "nonharmonious" feelings. If your primal family demanded perfect compatibility, you could unwittingly be acceding to this demand in your current marriage.

· When you got angry, hateful, or jealous, did your parents react negatively—forbidding it, for example? · Were you frightened by their reactions to your reactions?

When children get out of hand, it's every parent's responsibility to set limits on acceptable behavior. Setting limits is not what we're talking about here. Rather, we are talking about emotional censorship. Perhaps you continue imposing this censorship on yourself.

· As a child, did you doubt your parents' love? · Did it seem changeable, inconstant, inconsistent? · Did you have fantasies that you'd be given away? · Could you imagine doing something that would make your parents stop loving you?

A need to be compliant may take hold in such insecurity. Perhaps as a married adult it still has you in its grasp. A climate of emotional uncertainty is also one that readily breeds suppression.

· Were you considered mature at an early age? · Were you always a very "good" girl? · Were you a model big sister?

Children who grow up to be compliant adults often get a very early start. A small child who is uncannily mature, exceedingly polite, a model sibling, is a child who is trying too hard to be good. This is a sort of pseudo-maturity that is not developmentally appropriate but is forced instead. Is this you then and now?

STAN'S PAST: HIS PRIMAL MARRIAGE

If Anika's primal marriage has led you closer to understanding your own personal history, perhaps Stan's childhood may bring insight into your husband's unconscious need to keep a distance.

Siblings also figure prominently in Stan's recollections of his primal marriage.

"I'm a twin. The 'younger one' by six and a half minutes. This is a figure I'd never forget, or more accurately I'm not allowed to forget, thanks to my 'older' brother Victor.

"According to Victor, he isn't just older—he's better. When we were kids he even had a biological explanation for it: 'I'm the egg and you're the mistake in the egg. And the proof is I came out first,' he'd tell me.

"As it happened, Victor was always bigger, more athletic. Everything came easy to him. I had a harder time of it."

Stan recalled his parents' reactions to this relationship with his twin.

"My father got a real kick out of us going at it. He always pushed us to do things together. He loved competitive sports and at an early age Victor and I would play tennis together. When we got home, my father was anxious to see us. He would never ever ask us if we had fun. Not him. His first question (and the only thing that ever really interested him): 'Who won?' "

Victor's mother kept things up.

"My mother was always talking about who walked first, who talked first, who biked first, who got better grades. And of course it was always my 'big' brother.

"To this day she still does it. I've told her I hate it, but it doesn't make a dent. She thinks she's being cute."

Stan also recalls his reaction to defeats at his brother's hands.

"Victor loved to wrestle with me. He'd pin me down. Then he'd make me promise to do something, like be his slave for the day. I wasn't a match for him, but believe me, I never let him get my goat. That's all I'd need to do, cry in front of Victor or my father. They'd have had a field day with me."

Stan's parents gained a perverse satisfaction from pitting their children against one another. His father in particular encouraged an unhealthy (even at times sadistic) competition where the goal was not just winning but domination. With such encouragement, his brother Victor took full advantage of Stan at every opportunity.

This had a profound effect: Stan learned to fear and loathe familiarity. Intimacy did not hold the promise of camaraderie, affection, and tenderness; only domination, subjugation, and humiliation. His primal marriage taught Stan an object lesson—the closer you are to someone, the more you are likely to lose at that person's hands. Is it any wonder Stan is a man who needs to keep a distance? Putting space between himself and another is his way to keep these ugly anticipated consequences from taking place.

But why is Stan a suppresser? Stan was enraged at Victor and his parents. Every victim is enraged at his victimizers! But early on, Stan discovered that anger was useless. His father ignored his complaints, and Victor, with parental support, stayed the bully with no incentive to respond to his brother's ire. His protests did not stop his mother, either (even as an adult he can't get his mother to let up).

Not only was anger ineffective, it could make things worse—for example, angry tears would invariably bring ridicule. Stoicism and avoidance, not overt anger, was the route to survival, the route Stan took then in his primal marriage, and the route he still follows in his suppresser marriage to Anika.

Your husband need not be a twin to have suffered the effects of unhealthy competition in his primal family. Could he have been in a primal marriage where closeness (whether with siblings or parents) heralded abuse instead of comfort? Regrettably, this may be his legacy that so affects your married life together.

IS THIS YOUR HUSBAND'S PRIMAL MARRIAGE?

· Did he have the sort of father who had to beat him when they played sports? · Were siblings encouraged to compete and allowed to lord it over one another if they won?

Competition in a family can be very energizing. But handled poorly, it can be devastating. A father can use competition to humiliate and belittle a child. Parents may also encourage this among their children as well. When it happens, it makes contact an uninviting and even disagreeable prospect.

· Was there a lot of teasing in his family? · Was he made fun of? · Was he mocked? · Did he have an embarrassing nickname? · Did his family tell humiliating stories about him ("Remember the time he . . .")?

Humiliation is a devastating blow for a child. It can have a crippling effect on a child's ability to reach out; there is always the risk of hurt. If he has had his share of humiliation, keeping distant may be a way of avoiding such jeopardy.

· Was he ever profoundly disappointed by his parents? · Did they ever lie to him where he later discovered the truth? · Was he ever betrayed by family members, friends?

In life we connect with others because we have a basic sense of trust in our world. If, early on, that sense of trust is shattered, the result may be a child who can no longer reach out. Instead, he finds a safe haven from the possibility of profound disappointment by keeping a distance. Could a breach of trust be the source of your husband's need?

· Did he come from a very cold, unaffectionate family?

Sometimes children learn to keep a distance through force of habit. They grow up with unresponsive parents and believe that all people, even those with whom they end up falling in love, will offer them more of the same—nothing! Perhaps your husband has grown into that sort of emotional pessimist.

· Did he have very demanding parents? · Did he have parents who were very intrusive? · Did he have an overanxious, domineering, or manipulative caretaker?

There is more than one reason to keep a distance. And parents who don't give us any room at all can be a good one! If we had parents who were suffocating, we may feel as if we are always in need of a little breathing room. Could your husband carry the fear that intimacy is stifling and smothering into your relationship?

Taking Hold of the Problem: Getting Ready for an Adult Marriage

Anika and Stan must now seem like two very different people. Can you dismiss Anika as some washed-out housewife? Is Stan just another of those men who grunt from behind the morning paper? No. They are people who have been coerced out of their anger—and their vitality.

Ironically, though their primal families were so different in style (Anika's family so very harmonious and Stan's family so very contentious), both were emotionally oppressive. Both primal families, one with sweetness and the other with pugnacity, wrested the possibility of self-assertion from their children—Anika because her parents made the stakes unbearably high (your anger vs. our love), and Stan because his family were mean-spirited bullies.

Before Anika and Stan can forge a truly *adult marriage*, they must reckon with the emotional oppression that forced them to suppress their anger. For both, it means recognizing that they are not powerless children.

Anika is *no longer a helpless child* unable to risk testing her primal hypothesis: Where there is anger, there is no love. She must see this hypothesis for what it was, a family's way of unwittingly manipulating and controlling its members.

She must throw off the shackles of this control and finally test this hypothesis. As a child, she could not dare to take such a risk; as an adult, it is her only way out.

And she will discover something simple, extraordinary, and powerfully liberating: *There is love after anger!* Love is not fragile and vulnerable. Feelings—even very angry feelings—cannot annihilate love.

For Stan, it is also *time to reject his helplessness.* It is an artifact, a leftover of his primal marriage. Bullies rely on an imbalance of strength. As a child, Stan was indeed weaker. His anger was ineffective because it wasn't a fair deal; he was not equally matched with his tormenters. As an adult, this is no longer true.

Stan and his adult anger are a match for anyone. He cannot be bullied. If Stan takes this leap and lays claim to his own power, he will discover the remarkable effectiveness of his own anger. He will find that anger can be a way to set limits, to say clearly and unequivocally: "You may not do this to me." He will find that outrage may be a clarion call for justice and fairness ("I will not stand for this unacceptable behavior toward me, this inappropriate treatment of others"). Stan, together with all of us, will discover that tyranny (within a family or in the world at large) cannot stand in the face of those who stand up and angrily declare, *"No."* And in the end both Stan and Anika must discover that *there can be no real intimacy without anger.* If they are to have genuine contact there will, and must be, friction.

When Anika and Stan can lay claim to their anger, the result will profoundly affect them and their marriage. It will allow them to seize hold of themselves and their vitality. They will feel their own richness, range, and complexity. They will have a better marriage. And we will have a better world.

Love After Anger: Another Word

Of all the many encumbrances of primal anger, this sense that there will be no room for love after anger, that anger can do irreversible damage to attachments, is, sadly, a burden many, many people bear. In my work I have seen untold marital misery that can be attributed to this fear.

The legacy of an oppressive primal marriage in which anger was impermissible can make us believe that our anger will shatter those to whom we would direct it. It deprives us, as well, of an opportunity to develop an extraordinarily important capacity, an internal emotional shock absorber, a cushion that can help us absorb uncomfortable feelings of anger rather than be shattered by them. Far too many people lack this internal shock absorber that can offer them resilience in the wake of anger.

Far too many of us end up feeling that anger and love are incompatible, contradictory, a lesson learned from parents who sent the message, "I will not love you if you dare get angry!" As a result, we bear an unfortunate legacy: anger and love can't reside within us; if one takes up residence, the other must go. Anger cannot simply be another feeling as legitimate and permissible as, for example, joy, hurt, excitement, or disappointment.

Fortunately, as we learn to express anger effectively—to find the words—we also find room inside ourselves for *both* love and anger. And we work toward developing this all-important emotional resilience, discovering, with relief, that there is indeed life and love after anger!

Where do we go from here? First, let's look back for a moment. We've explored six very different angry marital styles: The "angry-and-know-it" crowd—*venters and provokers*—and the "angry-and-don't-know-it" crowd—*enactors, displacers, symbolizers,* and *suppressers.* We've met six very different couples and analyzed their *actual, invisible,* and *primal marriages.* By *decoding complaints,* we've arrived at an understanding of their various *hidden needs:*

VENTERS: Frieda . . . to keep men at bay
David . . . to find approval

PROVOKERS: Dora . . . to prevent abandonment
Teddy . . . to prevent abandonment

ENACTORS: Laura . . . to fill the emptiness
Jason . . . to fight the sadness

DISPLACERS: Catherine . . . to remake a man
Andrew . . . to find an ideal protector

SYMBOLIZERS: Maxine . . . to maintain control
Jim . . . to rescue

SUPPRESSERS: Anika . . . to be compliant
Stan . . . to keep a distance

Ideally, each has been a springboard from which you have developed personal insights into your own marriage. This process of self-discovery can itself be transforming. But having insight is not quite the same thing as using insight. Psychological understanding once acquired has then to be applied. Our task, in the closing chapter of this book, is to do just that. It is time now to offer the specific skills and techniques that can put insight into action and make your marriage work.

An Adult Marriage: Putting Insight to Work

Remember David and Frieda, our two venters? They are finally beginning to have—and to use—insight with remarkable results. Here is how Frieda's "miracle" began: "Last night David was really irritated with me because I was out with my best friend Fran, whom he can't stand. He started raising his voice, 'She's always butting into our business and she's trying to ruin our marriage.' Usually this is the point where I'd lash out at him and we'd go on to have one of our famous bedtime battles.

"But I noticed how frightened I was. And I realized it was that same quaky feeling I'd get when my mother was having one of her fits, the kind she'd have when my father would have too much to drink.

"So, instead of shouting back, I said, in a very determined way, 'David, if you're angry, you can tell me, but please don't yell. Every shout goes directly to my stomach. It makes me feel like the helpless little girl I was when my mother was on a rampage.'

"David didn't back off instantly, but I hung in. I finally realize why I freak out when he shouts, so I just insisted, repeatedly, I don't want to be yelled at. Talk!"

Much to Frieda's amazement, her clarity, determination, and insistence eventually had their effect.

"After a while David lowered his voice and proceeded to tell me what was eating him without the usual shouting. Then I could actually listen because I wasn't busy attacking him back. And it was so different for us."

What Frieda and David experienced is no miracle. Frieda put insight to work. She employed psychological self-awareness to stop old emotional habits from kicking in. Converting destructive anger into a constructive form of communication, Frieda began to transform her relationship with David from an angry marriage into an adult marriage. And so can you!

What is an adult marriage? It is a marriage where the split between an actual and an invisible marriage is eliminated; in other words, it is a partnership in which hidden needs and their primal sources are made conscious and become a discernible and active part of a relationship. By making hidden needs conscious, the power of these secret forces is destroyed and couples are able to stop acting out the predictable and destructive patterns that define an angry marriage. And of greatest significance, in an adult marriage it becomes possible to return anger to its original use as a signal, a form of communication where couples express frustration *through words* and thus, finally, stand a chance of getting what they truly need from each other.

Ultimately, insight offers couples effective and constructive ways to manage marital anger. Through insight, we can make anger speak of our needs. We can fill in the "missing piece." With assistance, this is the discovery that all unhappy couples can make: *Forging an adult marriage is the real cure for an angry marriage.*

How to Be Your Own Marital Therapist—Before You Need One!

This book can be a useful first step in the process of developing insight-based communication, a new language of love. Ideally, both spouses need to read and review the different types of angry couples that have been described in order to help them define and delineate their own angry union. But then there is a good deal more to be done.

Working together in an attempt to understand your angry marriage is vital. In order to create an adult marriage, angry spouses need to share their developing insights with each other, just as David and Frieda did in the example above. You need to analyze and explore your *own* relationship, independently, and also—ideally—jointly. Use this book as a handbook, a guide. Take notes. Reread a chapter that strikes a particular chord of recognition. Analyze your marriage. Become your own marital counselor before you really need one.

It takes time and work. There's no way around it. The promise of a quick fix is enticing, but it's also a sham. To break the back of an angry marriage, you have to put in *time and work,* together.

But time and work are not the only considerations. Just sitting down to talk about all these issues is not enough. Angry couples need ground rules. Why is this so? Because couples can only begin to lay open their hidden emotional life when they feel safe. Rules help to establish this sense of security and reliability.

Actually, this understanding lies at the heart of all good psychotherapy (and any civilized society). No one can unravel themselves psychologically unless and until they feel secure and protected. Creating this climate of trust is essential—in order to heal we must first feel safe. The new language of love is inextricably tied to these ground rules. No couple can work on developing and eventually applying insight until this safe and secure atmosphere for change has been created.

Creating the Atmosphere for Change

Creating this atmosphere is not that complicated. But, as has been suggested earlier, it does take ground rules. Indeed, we can borrow some of the practices and guidelines that marital counselors employ in creating a healing environment.[1] Outlined below are nine ground rules:

1. Set aside special times to meet
2. Meet regularly
3. Set time limits on your talks
4. Maintain confidentiality
5. Hear each other out
6. Prohibit emotional blackmail
7. Outlaw abusive behavior
8. Change accusation to reflection
9. Mirror your partner's thoughts and feelings

1. Set aside special times to meet: The buzzer on the washing machine has just gone off. Your husband's got fifteen minutes until he picks your son up from Boy Scouts. And your daughter needs help with her science project that's due tomorrow. Can you start talking insight? The notion is ridiculous.

To work on your marriage, you need quiet, calm, privacy, uninterrupted time, a minimum of distractions. Try to create that time and space. Your undivided attention is needed to make things different and better.

2. Meet regularly: It would be great if one good talk between the two of you would do the trick. But unfortunately, insight doesn't strike as a bolt of lightning. While flashes of insight do hit on occasion, personal wisdom generally comes after a slow build-up of self-awareness. The more you delve, the more you discover. A much-needed psychological momentum is gained only if you keep analyzing your marriage routinely.

There is another reason for scheduling regular talks. Knowing you have a usual, customary time to talk makes it considerably less likely that you'll fall back into your old self-defeating patterns. Just think about it. The more routinely you look at your unconscious issues, the less likely they are to recede out of your awareness where they end up doing you and your relationship the most harm.

And there is something else. No matter how trying it may be to uncover the psychology of your angry marriage, your efforts are a statement of hope and commitment. By meeting regularly, as difficult as that may be, you are confirming your optimism about the possibility of change. Sticking with it is a statement of confidence: "I love you and I know we can make things better."

3. Set limits on your talks: Often in an angry marriage a wife feels as if there is never enough discussion ("Getting him to talk is like pulling teeth") while a husband feels there is all too much talk ("All she wants to do is talk, talk, talk!"). Setting limits to your exchange can help eliminate this sense of imbalance. If both of you agree on a period of time, there is less likelihood that each of you will bog down in your respective frustrations over how little or how much is getting aired.

Limits on your time also enable you to focus your efforts. Dora and Teddy, a pair of provokers, made that discovery for themselves, as Teddy relates.

"When we knew that it was going to be this time and only this time, no more or no less than the hour we set aside, it helped us get down to the brass tacks of our relationship. In a way it helped us zero in on things."

Limits are particularly helpful for men who, more typically than women, may feel as if marriage can become an endless discussion of "what's wrong between us" and get turned off as a result. Additionally, limits—deciding when to talk—may help couples feel as if they've taken charge of the problem rather than been taken over by it.

4. Maintain confidentiality. Don't involve third parties. Misery, and most certainly marital misery, loves company. Often when people are in an angry marriage, they look to others to bolster support for aggrieved feelings ("All my friends think I'm crazy to take this from her"; "My mother said I should think of speaking to a divorce lawyer").

When you begin to take on the work of insight, it's crucial that you don't allow this to happen. Confidants often become witnesses for the prosecution, taking sides, offering opinions and advice, making one of you the good guy, the other the bad guy. If you are an angry couple, you need dialogue, not vindication.

Confidentiality, the assurance that what you offer each other is private, just between the two of you, is an essential element to creating trust and making things better between you.

5. Hear each other out: Probably the most difficult task a couple can face when they work on developing insight and creating an adult marriage is to suspend criticism, to listen openly, without drawing conclusions, making judgments or blaming.

Realistically, you can hardly expect yourself to be very good at being nonjudgmental. After all, an angry marriage is, practically by definition, brimming over with gripes and grievances. Nonetheless, you need to hear each other out, and there are some guidelines that can help you do just that.

When you begin to discuss your angry marriage, each partner needs to speak without interruption, interference, commentary. Simply stated, when one of you speaks, the other has to listen, *silently.*

6. Prohibit emotional blackmail: Psychological exposure involves risk: We can only do it if we trust that our vulnerabilities will be safe with each other. The danger comes if you use what you know to attack. Trust may be shattered, sometimes beyond repair. Don't fall into this trap of using newly acquired intimate knowledge of each other as a weapon.

For example, if a wife admits she can't tolerate criticism because she had a disapproving father who resented her, it must be completely off limits for a husband to lash out with, "I can see why your father hated you!"

There can be no room in marital negotiations for personal assault in which intimate information becomes ammunition. When you talk insight, when you make the move to open up, when you risk psychological disclosure, such emotional cruelty must be absolutely and unequivocally prohibited.

7. Outlaw abusive behavior: Discussions about an angry marriage can become heated. This is certainly true for venters and provokers. But, as we've just seen, at some point even couples in covertly angry marriages will start to feel the full force of their ire. Eventually, even in the most therapeutic environment, no couple is immune from feeling rage.

But never, never under any circumstances is anger an excuse for abuse. Anger confers no right to hurt others. Abuse, physical or verbal, is not an acceptable part of the work of insight. In fact, where there is abuse, there can be no work on an angry marriage.

Can anyone be thoughtful, contemplative, reflective, while under siege? Of course not. When we are threatened we close down, retreat, move to protect ourself from assault; our energies are focused in one and only one direction: survival.

And if you are not the victim but the victimizer, what happens? You become someone you don't really want to be. After all is said and done, no abusive partner is proud of himself. While the order of suffering is not the same, the victimizer is also compromised. He loses something of his humanity.

No responsible therapist of good conscience would ever permit a couple to sit in her (or his) office abusing each other. The safety needed for healing cannot exist when one person is allowed to violate another's security or compromise another's well-being. Abuse and insight can't exist in the same room! Abuse must be prohibited. You *must* adopt this principle as your own when you are trying to break the cycle of your angry union.

(The next two guidelines are less about the structure of your encounters and more closely linked to developing communication skills in your "sessions"—skills that will eventually become integrated into your newly emerging adult union, skills that will enable you to use anger as a constructive force in your partnership.)

8. *Change accusation to self-reflection:* In an angry marriage, discussions meant to promote insight can all too easily deteriorate into a series of charges and countercharges. How can this be averted? Begin by omitting the word "You" from the start of your sentences. Why? Comments that begin, "You are . . . (boring, mean, selfish, frigid, stubborn)" carry the sting of accusation and invariably create defensiveness. What's more, "You are" labels a partner and implies the problems are his or her fault, hardly an attitude that creates an atmosphere for open dialogue.

How then can you discuss the complaints and grievances of your angry union? Talk in terms of how your spouse makes you feel. Substitute self-reflection for accusation. This is a crucial step in helping anger become a potent source of information about you rather than a potent weapon you hurl at each other or a deep dark secret that you keep buried. Begin your sentences with the word "I" rather than "You."

For example, instead of saying, as David might to Frieda:

"You don't have a mind of your own. *You* never give a damn about my opinions but you always listen to everything your friend says like it was the gospel!"

You can express feelings self-reflectively (as David eventually did):

'I feel very angry when you seem to respect everything your friend says. I feel as if my opinions don't count as much as hers do. *I* guess I resent feeling as if your friend is more important than I am."

Putting "I" in these statements is not merely a grammatical switch. This style of communicating enables you to convert accusations toward your spouse into clear explanations *and* expectations about your inner self: accusations can be denied or rejected, but efforts to describe what you are feeling, what you are all about emotionally, and what your needs are, are likely to be heard. (And remember, your accusations can always be denied as unfounded and undeserved, while your feelings are *always* legitimate, authentic, and valid because they belong only to you!)

"I" statements are extremely powerful tools for promoting empathy. These are declarations about your own feelings, your own inner life. They are statements through which you define yourself and ask your partner to respect that emerging self-assertion. They are requests for understanding rather than efforts to find fault. Through self-reflection, you offer your partner a chance to look inside and see what you are all about. When there is love between two people, it is an offer that cannot be refused. People who love each other, even when they are in the throes of an angry marriage, *want* to understand.

This self-reflective mode is crucial for snapping the cycle of an angry union (and as we will see continually throughout this chapter, self-reflection is a fundamental element of the new language of love). It shows your willingness to take responsibility for your marital problems. It allows partners to respond sensitively to each other's emotions instead of recoiling at each other's recriminations. It generates empathy and mutual understanding. And, above all, it allows partners to hear out one another's anger. Said with conviction and accompanied by insight, the words "I feel very angry" can actually become a message one partner transmits and the other partner listens to, finally. Said with clarity and self-knowledge, the words "I feel very angry" can actually bring lovers closer to each other. "You are . . ." builds walls. "I am . . ." builds bridges.

9. Mirror your partner's thoughts and feelings: If listening is to be therapeutic and healing, it has to be quite different from what generally goes on in your angry partnership. Stop talking *at* each other and start talking *with* each other. There is a very simple technique that can aid this transformation—*mirror listening.* You must listen until what you hear and what your partner is saying are the very same thing.

For example, when Frieda spoke about her reactions to shouting, David tried to mirror them back in his own words until they truly reflected Frieda's feelings:

FRIEDA: David, your yelling drives me up the wall. I can't stand it! It takes me back to my parents' screaming matches when my father was on a drunk.

DAVID: What you are saying is that I yell all the time.

FRIEDA: No. I'm saying that your yelling scares me and that it reminds me of my mother.

DAVID: So. You're trying to say that I'm just like your mother.

FRIEDA: No. I'm not accusing you of being like her. That's not it. It's that when you shout, I have a very strong reaction. And I realize that I feel frightened, the way I used to feel when my mother would yell.

DAVID: So you're saying that when I raise my voice, it upsets you because it makes you feel frightened—the way it did when you were a kid and your mother would get out of control.

FRIEDA: Yes. Whenever I hear a shout I'm as scared as I was all those many years ago.

The idea behind mirror listening is to arrive at a consensus of understanding, a sort of mutual or reciprocal empathy. Once you *both* agree on what one of you is trying to communicate, it's time to move on to the next issue. This technique slows down our discussions, but it speeds up our healing (it was just this sort of groundwork that made David's and Frieda's "miracle" possible). It helps angry couples develop greater sensitivity and understanding. And that makes all the difference.

You might want to take note of something else here. In an angry marriage, old habits die hard. While Frieda is trying earnestly to be self-reflective and engage her husband in mirror listening, David is trying doggedly to change their exchange back to the usual accusations ("You're trying to say that I'm just like your mother"). Only Frieda's persistence and insistence ("No. I'm not accusing you of being like her") keeps them on track.

This attempt to retain the status quo is inevitable. Both partners will attempt, at one time or another, to hang on to the old cycle of accusations and recriminations (or in the case of some couples, such as suppressers, to retreat into silence). Don't be put off—don't give in! Maintain your self-reflective stance. It will take hold. And it *will* make a difference.

As difficult as it may be for overtly angry couples to carry out mirror listening, it is particularly trying for those couples who have buried their anger. As insight enters the room, so does the ire that couples have long held in check, and anger that has been disguised is unmasked.

Our two enactors, Laura and Jason, long accustomed to burying their anger through activity, faced this challenge. They used this communication strategy of mirror listening with great difficulty.

> LAURA: I think I flirt when you aren't around because it feels like a rush of good feelings and then I can get away from the emptiness for a while.
>
> JASON: So I'm not around enough? Do you want me on a leash? Should I be on call? Maybe I could carry a beeper?
>
> LAURA: No. I'm not accusing you. I'm trying to tell you that I realize that I'm fighting a big problem, an empty, lonely feeling, and my reaction is to try and fill it up. And I use attention from other men to do it.

JASON: So I don't give you enough attention. That's your excuse for making a fool of yourself (and me) with this muscle-bound gigolo.

LAURA: First, Jason, that crack hurt my feelings. I feel as if you're using what I'm revealing to get back at me. And that makes me want to get back at you, not be more open. Don't do it; it hurts me and it pushes us apart. We can't allow that.

I know facing this isn't easy. Until now, we've pretended these problems didn't exist. In that way, if I ignored your drinking and you ignored my flirtations, we'd never have to feel angry disappointment with each other. We're going to start feeling angry, but I think it means that we might take better care of ourselves and our marriage.

JASON: I'm sorry. I'll try to listen. But you should know it's not easy for me to hear about you and other men. Among other things, I feel very humiliated and that makes me feel very angry.

LAURA: I know it's difficult for both of us. But for the moment, it's my turn to talk and yours to listen. Hear me out and I'll do the same for you.

JASON: I'll try.

LAURA: I'm not talking about what you do and don't give me. I'm only talking about the way I feel when I'm by myself. I feel very lonely, the way I did when I was a child. My parents had no interest in me; they were very self-involved and their only concern was themselves. It's that feeling of being a sad, lonely child that gets stirred up whenever I'm on my own. It's such a deep, sad, empty feeling, I'll grab at anyone to relieve it.

JASON: So, you're saying that when you're alone you feel so awful, so dejected that you need to end the feeling right away, and that a man's attention wipes it out?

LAURA: Yes.

JASON: So, a guy isn't a guy. He's just a way you calm yourself down.

LAURA: Yes. That's it. I have a lonely ache inside of me and I've tried to soothe it, all these years, by filling it up with any rush of good feeling I could grab—like a pint of Häagen-Dazs ice cream, a new dress, or even attention from a young man.

As covertly angry couples (enactors, displacers, symbolizers, suppressers) work on developing insight, they often discover, to their chagrin, that they *feel* their anger. For covertly angry couples, the truth might eventually make them free. But first it makes them mad! The goal of mirror listening is not to be derailed by anger whenever or wherever it shows up. In an attempt to forge an adult marriage, room exists for anger as long as you can "give it the words."

Doing It

Do these suggestions sound impossible, if not ridiculous? Is it unfeasible for the two of you to find a quiet place to talk? Is it completely out of the question to discuss your marriage regularly, let's say once a week for an hour? Could you not even consider keeping your mother from knowing what you and your spouse are going through?

These recommendations are bound to be challenging. They fly in the face of our usual way of going about our married life. They are a demand: Take time out, try something different. And that's not easy. So, if the thought of working toward an adult marriage seems a pretty formidable task, that's a common and understandable response.

But a word of caution: If these reactions become the reasons that keep you from working on your angry marriage, be on notice—you are resistant to change. You may not like to hear it, but if you can't find the time or make the effort to work on creating an adult marriage, you still need to hang on to your angry marriage. *You are afraid to change!*

If this is indeed your predicament, what are you being offered? Encouragement, optimism. Yes, it can be intimidating to plumb your psychological depths, to discover your hidden emotional life. But the reward for taking on this challenge is enormous. The truth, the psychological truth, can make us free. Freedom awaits you. You can do it. And most important: You deserve it.

The intent of these recommendations is to create the atmosphere for communication. This structure enables you to set the stage for real exchange. It may help make the two of you into your own marital therapists by creating an optimal atmosphere for real and intimate exchange. Ideally, once you establish psychological mind-edness as routine in your planned discussions ("sessions"), it will take hold and become a vital part of your marriage at all times.[2] Over the long term the aim is to make communication based on insight your new *everyday* language of love.

Now, the question remains—once we've created the climate for communication, just what do we say to each other?

LEARNING THE NEW LANGUAGE OF LOVE

The point of the new language of love is to create an adult marriage, to express through words what has been discovered through insight—to give words to hidden needs so that they are visible, evident, conscious, and therefore lose their power to dictate behavior. The new language of love is a way to make anger "speak," to civilize anger so that it is not a weapon, a wail, or a silent monster, but simply a signal—one we use to close the frustration gap and find the "missing piece."

When this transformation happens, couples take charge of their feelings and reactions rather than permitting primal feelings to hold an invisible but powerful sway over them. Rather than being trapped in the emotional time warp of their respective primal marriages, people in an adult marriage *live in the present.*

The new language of love means expressing your insights (you've already gotten a glimpse of how this is done in Frieda and David's "miracle" at the start of this chapter). Initially, this novel way of communicating may feel odd, stilted, artificial. And it is. Speaking a new language requires couples to do and say things quite differently from how they normally do and say them in the throes of their angry marriage. Conversing in an intimate, personal, psychological way is not what most couples are inclined to do. As a result, it will feel exceedingly unnatural.

For example, venters are so used to slinging insults at one another rather than talking about their needs that they often feel ridiculous—as if they've suddenly turned from Piranha to Pollyanna.

Suppressers find it unsettling, too, although for different reasons. Entirely unused to expressing any feelings whatsoever, suppressers often start off denying that these sentiments even exist, and then have to grapple with feeling very strange as long-ignored or overlooked thoughts and emotions emerge. Typically, suppressers encounter a "this can't be me" reaction.

Invariably, awkwardness and self-consciousness are part of the process. But bear in mind, as with any foreign tongue, practice brings fluency and comfort. When we make the new language of love our own, it ceases to feel awkward or alien. But the real beauty and power of this new form of communication lies in the fact that it can become a vital part of your relationship forever—and that can make all the difference!

Lesson 1: Talking to Yourself

We need to backtrack at this point. Before any of the exchange that's been suggested can happen, each partner in an angry marriage has to be completely cognizant of his or her own need: the primal pain that created it and the angry style to which it gave rise. Each partner must have an active personal awareness of the unconscious forces he or she drags like so much old excess baggage into a current marriage. In other words, before we can talk to each other with an informed psychological perspective, we need to talk to ourselves that way. Before we can be emotionally truthful with the person we love, we must be emotionally honest with ourself. Before we can ask our partner's help in fulfilling our needs, in supplying the "missing piece," we must identify it on our own.

For instance, one symbolizer (remember Maxine and her bad back?) may first need to own up to her need to control and to how her ailments then become her efforts to "take charge" of her marriage, as well as to express her anger symbolically.

Another symbolizer may have a different task. He may need to be clear about his need to rescue (recall the sordid, unwholesome childhood of Jim, Maxine's husband). Perhaps his task is to talk to himself about how overidentified he can get when someone seems helpless. Perhaps he, too, will have to grapple with the painful but necessary realization of how very overwhelmed he felt when his own mother was his sexual abuser, and the rage he still feels at this betrayal.

Displacers, tightly bound into their marriage, most particularly need this work. For instance, if a mother-in-law is the selected diversionary target, a displacer may need to say to herself: "When I find myself wanting to be critical of my mother-in-law, I have to stop and tell myself that I'm pushing the anger onto a safe target and away from my marriage. Not surprising since I had a mother who acted like a ferocious beast and threw me out of the house when she got mad. No wonder I see anger as such a destructive force."

Or perhaps another displacer needs to wonder out loud to himself: "Is it a legitimate gripe I have with my boss, or am I resuscitating my style, making him the enemy?"

To take another example, a woman suppresser may need practice in recognizing and admitting to herself that she often has the urge to lie to her husband even about little things, "because I can't bear the idea of him being displeased with me."

All insight-based communication in a marriage requires this sort of personal emotional candor. Once you know your need, your primal history and the way it affects your style of anger, you must continue to acknowledge this *and* its impact on your marriage. Whether you are a suppresser or a displacer, a symbolizer or an enactor, learn to talk to yourself about your insights. Try to become sensitized to your reactions. Pay attention to the signposts and signals of your angry lovestyle.

When are you most vulnerable? What circumstances might mobilize your need? Tune in to the things that set you off. Catch yourself in the act of responding to your needs and carrying out your angry lovestyle. Now that you know your heart beats, take your pulse. When you begin to speak the new language of love, have the first conversations with yourself!

Lesson 2: Revealing Insights

Whereas the first order of business is developing an inner dialogue with yourself, the next step is talking aloud and revealing insights about yourself to your spouse. This frankness, which you may find difficult initially, can alert a partner to the impact he has on you and, most important, alter his response. For example, Frieda's revelations went a long way toward getting David to lower his voice. (Bear in mind that this brings us back to the importance of starting every statement with "I." Insights always need to be framed as self-reflective statements. Frieda wouldn't have been revealing any insight if she had just declared, "You're always shouting and you're as beastly as my mother!")

While the result of exchanging insights can be profound, its power rests on the simple principle of sharing information. Sharing insight about your emotional needs supplies the person you love with as much information as you yourself possess and allows your spouse to see the complete picture of just who you are. Regrettably in an angry marriage we are, all too often, in the dark about ourselves and therefore about each other. Is it any wonder things go wrong?

But insight changes this. Every time an insight is shared, you supply each other with more details about your inner emotional landscape.[3] Invariably, the more information you acquire (especially about anger and frustration), the more appropriately and effectively you are able to respond. Remarkably, the information needn't be so elaborate. Sometimes a few words can be all it takes ("I feel frightened when you shout"; "I feel rejected when you're critical"; "I feel belittled when you don't want to have sex"). But these few words may transform a relationship from a well-worn cycle of anger into a more caring and responsive union. It can make all the difference.

Perhaps you can now reveal to your spouse why you are so disturbed by such seemingly "minor" events, as when he doesn't call home each day:

"When I don't hear from you, I feel anxious. I guess ever since my father's accident I've always walked around expecting the worst."

It is an insight that is likely to make him call more often, and changes you from the caricature of a demanding wife—someone to be easily dismissed—into a woman who has an anxiety that she wants her husband to address.

And if you want him to stop his putdowns (for instance, about your "weight problem"), revealing that you eat to fill yourself up and that sometimes food feels like your only friend may actually get him off your back. This openness may enable him to be more supportive when it comes to your dieting efforts. Instead of criticizing you for your failure, he might empathetically offer: "No wonder it's so hard for you to cut back on the Häagen-Dazs."

Insights can help alter the balance of power in an angry marriage and end the resentment inevitably created when one spouse feels victimized by the other. For example, instead of railing at a husband who "always takes over," a volatile venter might share: "I think I'm afraid to take charge. So I let you tell me what to do, and then I resent it and explode at you."

Or a displacer might admit: "I do everything you suggest because I want to believe that you're perfect. I think I make you right so that we never have to get angry at each other." Or a suppresser might acknowledge: "When you tell me what to do, I feel as if I'm being called 'stupid' and then I just swallow all the anger that gets stirred up inside me."

Sharing a revealing insight can even pave the way for better sex. The generic "I'm not in the mood" may become the revelation:

"I'm afraid to let go—I think excitement scares me"

or

"I know I'm really angry at women because of my mother's betrayal. I have a hard time letting go of that feeling and trusting that it's not going to happen again"

or

"I think it's hard for me to let down my guard and be that close to you"

or

"I feel really angry when you don't thank me for the things I do for this marriage; but I don't make a peep of protest. Instead of telling you that I'm pissed, I lose interest in having sex."

There is no assurance that a couple's lovelife will snap back into action in the aftermath of such revelations. But it can certainly help break the sexual stalemate that is so very often characteristic of an angry marriage.

These are only a few of the myriad revelations to be made. As you get to know yourself and your marriage better, you will undoubtedly find no shortage of things to say. Just think about the exchanges that currently characterize your marriage; all the usual responses that keep the angry cycle locked in place. How very different things would be if you shared your insights as you discovered them. You would be a different person in your marriage, and as a result you would find that you were married to a different spouse.

This forces us to say a word about the conventional wisdom, "You can never change a person once you are married to him—*it's wrong!*" Of course you can change someone you love: Insight transforms the person who loves us.[4] It offers the possibility for compassion. And with compassion, your partner (just like you) will be different as you finally head out of the anger trap and into an adult union.[5]

Lesson 3: Insisting on Empathy

Much of what has been described depends on empathy, the willingness of a lover to be compassionate toward us and we toward them. But empathy isn't automatic, or reflexive. Simply spilling your emotional guts to a spouse isn't going to kick empathy into high gear. Part of this new language of love will very much rest on whether both partners insist on empathy.

For example, if a venter merely says, with no clear sense of conviction, "I get a stomachache when you yell and I need you to get angry without exploding," empathy will be in short supply. Empathy as a result of shared insight only accrues if and when you truly believe in what you say.

Remember Frieda? Her words ultimately garnered a reaction from her husband because she was clear, determined, and persistent about her psychological assertions. Her insight had the full force of her belief behind it. This conviction kept her on track; in effect, it allowed her to insist on David's empathy rather than the usual knee-jerk venter response. It also kept her from being pulled back into their usual venter style, a pattern of behavior that all angry couples must struggle against. Only the persistent and consistent demand—"You and I *must* be compassionate"—will make change possible. This certainty is key.to breaking the habitual deadlock of an angry union.

Lesson 4: Acknowledging Your Partner

Once you've established a level of personal awareness and moved on to exchanging insights with one another (while insisting on empathy), the next step to an adult marriage is being able to acknowledge your spouse's need and style of anger. When we become emotionally and psychologically enlightened about each other, it is crucial that we act in a way that indicates *we listened, we understand, and we care.* If each of us has risked revealing our innermost selves, our vulnerabilities and sensitivities, we must both, in turn, act as trustees of this information. Once we discover each other's needs, we must learn to be good enough spouses for one another.

Stan, aware in his suppresser marriage of Anika's need for compliance and her insecurity, tries to be sensitive to these vulnerabilities when they talk.

"If I notice that Anika looks tense, before I ask her what's wrong I might say something like, 'Anika, even if you tell me something I don't want to hear, I'm not going to hate you.'"

This response offers a reassuring acknowledgment.

"I understand the feelings you are grappling with."

"I know what you are going through emotionally."

"I care."

Remarkably, even the most difficult problems between you can be handled if they are managed in this way. The thorniest issues can be tackled if you understand each other's struggles and acknowledge them. Everything can be said if we say it with empathy and concern. Even enactors who are engaged in self-defeating or self-destructive behavior can have an adult marriage. For example, knowing of his wife's struggle with emptiness, a husband may forewarn her about an upcoming business trip:

"I know it's not easy for you to be by yourself. I'm going to be away for three days next week. I hope it won't feel too lonely. I'm going because I really have to be there, not because I want to make you suffer."

Or ask her about her flirtations with the new aerobics instructor:

"I know that you need a lot of attention because you need people to fill up the loneliness, but I think this guy is unscrupulous; he's going to take advantage of you because he senses how needy you are."

Or a woman enactor, understanding her husband's need to fight his inner sadness, might address his drinking problem:

"I think when you drink, you try and chase away the down feelings, but I get worried that it is really making things harder on you. I heard a doctor today on TV explain that alcohol is really a depressant."

The acknowledgments you offer exert a corrective force on your marriage. How? Remember, the cycle of an angry marriage is perpetuated because people are constantly—albeit unwittingly—interpreting and reacting to each other through the prism of their unconscious needs.

Every time you acknowledge one another's personal psychology, you are actively preventing these emotional misunderstandings from taking hold. Stan, for example, is not giving Anika the chance to misconstrue him. Her unconscious need to be compliant would force Anika to see Stan's displeasure as hate. Through his empathetic acknowledgment, Stan will not permit Anika that emotional error.

Stan won't allow Anika to read him as if nothing has changed from her primal marriage to her current partnership. Stan won't permit that old emotional baggage to encumber their marriage. He separates the primal past from the present. "Anika, I might hate what you say but I don't hate you!"

In effect, Stan is demanding that Anika respond to him as he is, not as who she thinks he is because of her primal marriage. Insight used in this way permits us to say no to the past and yes to the present.

ADULTS AT LAST

Before you and your spouse can have an adult marriage, you need to learn to talk like grown-ups. The key elements to fostering adult exchange are:

Being emotionally candid with yourself.

Revealing insights to one another.

Insisting on empathy.

Acknowledging each other's psychological vulnerabilities.

The result of integrating these elements into your marriage is striking, a communication that has no hidden agendas. Everything—needs, primal past, angry style—is part and parcel of the interchange. As a result, this kind of communication is infinitely more complex and far longer than the actual conversations of most angry marriages. But it yields significant results: two people succeed in breaking the deadlock of their angry marriage and start living a happier adult partnership.[6]

While there is no question that adult exchange takes work, the payoff for this substantially more complicated approach to a marriage is considerable. Your personal psychology, emotional makeup, your sensitivities and vulnerabilities, and, of course, your anger will no longer drive you apart, as they did when you were trapped in an angry cycle (when your relationship was fragmented into actual, invisible, and primal marriages). Instead, through insight, your deepest and most painful truths bring you into an adult union where, remarkably, you will feel closer to your spouse and like each other better!

When we master the new language of love, we offer ourselves a new way to connect. Mutual understanding ensures intimacy instead of alienation and it makes the just resolution of potential conflicts possible. It makes anger work *for* us rather than against us. It maintains compassion, solace, and comfort as an active part of a marriage.

The greatest gift of insight is its reenforcement of our sense of alliance with the most important person in our life, our husband/our wife. It brings us closer to the person we love. Remarkably and happily, with the new language of love and a communication based on insight and empathy, two people who love each other find they still like each other.

As we break the cycle of anger, we are all affected very differently. Because struggles with anger are so very different, the solutions vary. Venters David and Frieda found themselves in a calmer, more tranquil marriage, as Frieda explained:

"I find myself exerting a lot more control. I talk to myself. I say, 'Hold on to the anger, don't lash out.' And I don't. I'm more restrained. We're both less likely to flare up. Not being so impulsive gives me a chance to think. Then, after I think, I talk. That's very different for us. We have a peaceful existence."

Provokers Dora and Teddy were respectively aggravated and put upon, but that's changed. Teddy describes the difference:

"We have a more balanced relationship. Now we share our anger. I say no and it doesn't feel as if it's an angry weapon I'm wielding. Dora used to be forced into using anger like a hammer over my head, which never worked. Now we jointly use anger to hammer things out between us. There is much more give and take between us. It's like we're finally in this together."

Enactors Laura and Jason find themselves angrier but closer, as Laura describes her current adult marriage:

"When we stopped doing things to chase away the bad feelings, we got angry over the way we had neglected ourselves, our marriage and each other. But when we gave up those enactments and let ourselves experience our angry feelings, we didn't self-destruct. Instead, we looked to each other for help in place of sex and food and work. Now we use anger to demand more for and from our marriage."

Displacers Catherine and Andrew find themselves in a very different sort of marriage, as Andrew depicts it:

"When we finally realized anger was no monster that could

destroy us, we could get cross at each other, disagree and not always dovetail on our thoughts, ideas, feelings.

"We don't have 'enemies' anymore. When we agreed to disagree with each other, we stopped deflecting our anger onto outsiders. We've become closer with my family."

Symbolizers Maxine and Jim have a very, very different marriage, as Jim says:

"We don't have big doctor bills anymore but we do have fights. Max is always trying to run the show, but at least now she says so rather than using her body to do it. Personally, I went through a very hard time where I was really enraged at my mother for her sexual abuse. I went into a therapy group. Now I'm coming to the point where I can use the rage productively by helping to start an abuse hot line through my church." (Jim's unleashed anger not only makes for a better marriage, it makes for a better community!)

Suppressers Anika and Stan also have a different sort of marriage, as Stan reflects:

"We were in a marriage that was DOA because we couldn't bear the possibility of conflict. Anika and I are much better now about knowing what we feel and speaking up. We find ourselves in the strange position of not liking everything we hear out of each other's mouth but liking each other much better. It's so odd that the very thing we were so scared of—anger—has brought us closer. We do have more conflict, but we have much more fun, especially in bed."

If we are venters, we learn to restrain angry impulses. If we are provokers, we learn to share anger. If we are enactors, we learn to sit still long enough to feel the anger. If we are displacers, we learn that we can be safe with anger inside the sanctuary of a marriage. If we are symbolizers, we trade in physical ailments for anger. If we are suppressers, we learn to express anger and regain our selfhood. And in doing so we are, each in our own way, forever transformed.

Once you break the cycle of anger, your marriage can and will be different. The arid sameness of your relationship will be gone. You will be two adults in a dynamic, ever-changing relationship. Staleness and predictability will give way to joy and warmth, vitality and intimacy. And you might even find you like, *really* like, the person you love!

A Final Word on Anger

An adult marriage does not mean that two people live happily ever after in a blissful and anger-free union. Hardly. Anger—constructive anger—deserves its rightful place in marriage. Constructive anger is a signal to those we love most. Constructive anger delivers a clear message: "This is the way I insist on being treated." It is a declaration of our selfhood as we finally understand it through the wisdom of insight. But constructive anger is not the insistent demand of a self-absorbed child. Rather, it is the strong, clear, determined request of an adult who also realizes that her needs, desires, requirements are balanced against those of others in her immediate and extended universe. Constructive anger is the demand that the world acknowledge us balanced against the recognition that others have their need for self-determination as well.

Constructive anger gives us our shape, enabling us to draw a line around ourselves, a boundary that asserts our self-definition: *This is me!* A boundary, not an impenetrable wall. One that encloses us in the sanctuary of our selfhood but at the same time leaves openings through which we can let others enter in and through which we can reach out. In this way, anger marks our separateness but seals our union. Ideally, when used this way, anger draws our beloved to us and makes love possible. That is our challenge—and that is our goal.

$$\boxed{\text{N o t e s}}$$

CHAPTER ONE

1. Actually, it is more accurate to say that we know how to get angry from our very first moment. After all, most of us enter this world kicking and screaming. For those of us who don't make such a fuss on first entry we get turned upside down and slapped on the bottom. It's enough to make anybody angry!

2. This phrase is the title of a very fine book on anger by Harriet Goldhor Lerner (New York: Harper & Row, 1989). The notion of being locked in a "dance" is one which developed in two of my earlier books, *Loving Men for All the Right Reasons* (New York: Dial, 1983), and *Not Quite Paradise: Making Marriage Work* (New York: Doubleday, 1987).

3. It can be useful to visualize this gap between needing and getting as a sort of "missing piece." Under most circumstances we can manage the frustrations of our missing piece, provided it is not "too large."

However, problems arise when this gap, this missing piece, is allowed to grow too big. When the space between the two feels like an unbearable void, it fills with frustration and anger. A happy (nonangry) marriage does not require a perfect fit between what we need and what we get. Happy marriages only require a reasonable relationship between the two.

In many spheres we human beings are endowed with a capacity to function well under a range of conditions; we do not need perfection, but rather we need things to fall within an adequate and reliable range. For example, we are warm-blooded creatures. This means that as the temperature rises and falls around us, our bodies are capable of tolerating the changes . . . up to a point. If it's too hot or too cold we reach a level beyond which we cannot adapt, and we cease to function normally. Similarly, we can "take" being angry . . . up to a point.

4. If they were we would, for example, read the warning labels on cigarette packages and never take that first puff.

CHAPTER TWO

1. My thoughts on good will are inspired by the ideas of Themis Dimon on this subject.

2. G. R. Birchler, R. L. Weiss, and J. P. Vincent, "Multimethod Analysis of Social Reinforcement Exchange Between Maritally Distressed and Nondistressed Spouse and Stranger Dyads," *Journal of Personality and Social Psychology* 31 (1975): 349–60.

CHAPTER THREE

1. I found an allusion to this purported statement of Freud's in Irving Singer's *The Nature of Love,* Vol. 3, *The Modern World* (Chicago: University of Chicago Press, 1987), p. 378.

2. Ibid., Chapter 10, "Toward a Modern Theory of Love," pp. 369–437.

3. See Robert Stoller, *Sexual Excitement: Dynamics of Erotic Life* (New York: American Psychiatric Press, 1979), pp. 1–35.

4. We women can have intercourse under any circumstance— whether we have our heart and soul in it or not. We can split ourselves into mind and body; sexually, we can act one way while feeling quite another way. In the extreme, we can even "fake" orgasm since our body does not offer conspicuous markers of level of sexual arousal or involvement.

5. David Cole Gordon, *Self Love* (out of print).

6. Quacks advertised mechanical devices designed to be worn on errant genitals in order to keep the male organ under control (masturbation was originally regarded as a singularly male predicament). See Louis Kaplan, *Adolescence: The Farewell to Childhood* (New York: Simon & Schuster, 1984), pp. 190–206.

7. My thoughts here are an extrapolation of the ideas of Dr. Kaplan. Ibid., pp. 201–7.

CHAPTER FOUR

1. In fact, to get the most out of this book, you might want to compile a detailed list of your mutual complaints about one another at this point.

2. While the therapeutic process always depends on analysis—a decoding of what we are ostensibly saying in order to discover what we are actually feeling—the specific concept of decoding complaints is a construct originating with my work. First attempts at writing about this can be found in an earlier book, *Not Quite Paradise: Making Marriage Work.*

3. This is not an excerpt from an actual session with any of my patients. Rather, it is a re-creation of a typical encounter between two venters as I have witnessed it in my office, and is in effect a composite couple based on my clinical experience. All couples in this book are composites.

4. When this sense of identification happens in treatment, therapists need to be extremely careful that they do not let their own "take" on a situation intrude on the patient. Because a therapist uses herself as an instrument she must always be on guard, separating her issues from those of her patients. When properly understood, a therapist's own experience creates the opportunity for empathy.

5. The fact that Brian "joined us" after a time is not, in my experience, unusual. Often one spouse starts treatment and somewhere along the way even the most reluctant partner becomes involved in the therapeutic process, either on their own or in couples treatment.

6. I'm reminded of a discussion I once had with a beloved and esteemed Israeli colleague, Dr. Hillel Klein. In talking about Oedipal feelings, he happily reminded me that "Oedipus isn't all bad, after all." If your father had good qualities, you will seek those out in the man you love too! The point is that your primal marriage sets the stage for your adult love, and no doubt the goodness, not just the frustration or disappointment, of your first love shows itself in your adult passionate attachments. Not all our attractions are neurotic.

7. This human tendency toward consistency carries into all aspects of human functioning. For example, a recent survey on food preferences showed that in spite of the vast array of foods available in this country, most people eat the same thing for lunch every single day. Check it out—you probably eat tuna most every day of the week!

Still not convinced? Try this experiment. Clasp your hands together in front of you. Which thumb is on top, your right or left? Unless you deliberately force yourself to do otherwise, you will *always clasp with this thumb on top*. Try changing it. Clasp your hands with the opposite thumb on top. Feels weird? It feels odd because you are human and that is an inconsistent behavior for you.

8. Categorizing angry lovestyles is an attempt to help you organize your thinking, to offer you new ways to consider your anger and your marriage. The intent isn't to pigeonhole you and your relationship into one type or another. Frankly, most marriages don't fall strictly into one style; in life and love, things are never that neat. So, don't try to squeeze your marriage into a type. Instead, try to see whether each type can help you become more informed about your own relationship and the role anger plays in it.

CHAPTER SIX

1. It should be stressed that the "sessions" created in this book are a distillation of the real therapeutic experience. I have attempted to extract from my clinical work aspects of therapy I think may be useful to the reader. Sessions with my patients are never as neat or structured as they appear here. The course of the type of treatment I conduct in my office is far more free-ranging than is suggested by the interactions described in these pages. Many, many things go on in the sessions, and I am not as directive nor didactic as it might seem. In my office, I am a therapist; in my books, I see myself as a psychological educator. This book is not therapy; it isn't meant to be. My effort is to offer the reader an opportunity to develop insight, rather than offering the complicated and long-term process of therapy in theory. That would make this ersatz therapy, and I'd rather write a real book.

CHAPTER SEVEN

1. My favorite "enactor" is Norm, one of the regulars at "Cheers." For countless years the barflies at this tavern have provided Norm with a flock, so he never has to go home and get mad at his much-maligned but unseen wife, Vera.

CHAPTER NINE

1. Anyone doubting the power of the mind to rule our bodies need only look at documented cases of hysterical pregnancy. Women have been known to cease menstruation, develop distended abdomens, go into "labor" after nine months, and even begin producing breast milk—never having been pregnant! By comparison, converting anger into a backache seems plausible and easy.

2. The famous case illustrating this error is that of the gifted songwriter George Gershwin, who was in analysis discussing his headaches while he was dying of an undiagnosed brain tumor.

3. Modern technology has made it easier for a physician to unwittingly collude with her patient's symbolizing. With the growing number of noninvasive methods for medical diagnosis such as CAT scans, MRI, sonograms, it is easy to keep on testing a patient when no immediate cause for a physical complaint is determined. Noninvasive testing is virtually medically risk-free for a patient. Unfortunately, noninvasive tests still create significant problems for the symbolizer. First, it can become enormously costly since these procedures are among the most expensive diagnostic tools. And second, once a symbolizer starts looking, she may indeed end up finding something to fuel her symbolizing fires (and help further extinguish her angry fires).

One woman with a long history of symbolizing developed spots before her eyes. A complete ophthalmic exam followed by an extensive neurological exam found nothing; she was then referred for a CAT scan of her brain. When the brain scan results were reviewed, the physician informed the patient that the test results were negative. However, he added, "I have noticed a 'tortured' blood vessel." The doctor went on to explain that this meant the scan had revealed a twisted blood vessel; it was described as not medically significant and there was nothing to be done about it. When the patient asked why she was being informed, the doctor was quick to reply: "Well, if five years from now someone had found it and I hadn't told you, you might want to sue."

Needless to say, this woman went home more tortured than ever—and it wasn't about her anger!

4. Dr. Asch is not the real name of this physician.

5. In some ways Maxine bears a psychological resemblance to the passive partner in a provoker marriage. In that relationship, a person "takes over" by his inaction (he doesn't want to do something, and it doesn't get accomplished by virtue of his inactivity). Perhaps you remember back to provokers Dora and Teddy and the unfinished basement that

stayed unfinished. Ironically, by "doing nothing" the passive spouse exerts a good deal of power. So does Maxine. Lying on the floor inert is the way she unconsciously seizes control of her marriage.

6. You may not be exactly like Maxine. For one, you may be much more up to date, unwittingly choosing "the disease of the week" rather than a mundane fourth lumbar vertebra. At the time of writing, cases of Yuppie flu and Chronic Fatigue Syndrome were gaining among symbolizers.

7. Our language helps with this confusion: "mad," of course, has two meanings, "angry" and "crazy."

8. Sometimes we may have the memory of watching ourselves (not someone else) in an insignificant scene, but remember it often enough to suggest there is another, more potent memory behind our original seemingly innocuous recollection.

Getting behind these "screen memories" help the development of our insight. In using a case in which inappropriate sexual behavior on the part of a parent was involved I want to issue a special caution: This in *no* way is meant to suggest that the origin of *all* symbolizer behavior has this aberrant behavior at its foundation. This would be a misguided conclusion. What's more the "sudden" discovery of repressed sexual memories by reading a list of indicators in a book is to my mind highly suspect. It is not my intention to promote such discoveries. (Regrettably, the betrayal of a parent by sexually inappropriate or abusive behavior is often an indelible memory which cannot be repressed.) Rather, if you think you may symbolize your anger, use the couple offered to reflect on your own life and consider how it may have developed in the complicated arena of your primal marriage.

9. Prozac, the well-known antidepressant drug, is also used for anxiety, as are other medications such as Zooloft, Buspar, Xanex. As these are psychotropic medications—that is, drugs that affect the mind and emotions—they should be administered by a psychiatrist or a psychopharmacologist.

CHAPTER TEN

1. Ironically, with more women taking on the role of breadwinner and more men assuming "Mr. Mom" status, I've begun to see and hear about men "slaving over a hot stove" and feeling hurt by their wives' apathetic or critical reaction!

2. Suppressers tend to meet the disappointments of marriage hair in place, devoid of rancor, and well armed with excuses and full of forgive-

ness. Could you survive your marriage without an antiperspirant? Could you be nominated for sainthood? Yes? Then you might elect to think of yourself as a party to this lovestyle.

3. While this episode is unfortunately true, I have disguised the couple.

4. Many a mother has advised a married daughter to have a little secret cache of pin money—one generation of suppressers offering advice to the next.

CHAPTER ELEVEN

1. People often balk at the fact that therapists set guidelines and maintain boundaries. I cannot emphasize strongly enough my commitment to this approach that, to me, sets the therapeutic process apart from any other sort of relationship. Boundaries (i.e., confidentiality, the adherence to words as the only suitable form of therapeutic exchange) are absolutely critical to the creation of the safe haven that is essential to a truly therapeutic process. Couples who can establish ground rules for themselves—most difficult for those who are most angry—have the greatest possibility for change.

2. Actually, the real marker of successful therapy occurs when two people find themselves talking to each other in the kitchen the way they talk to each other in their therapist's office. The work of therapy is accomplished when there is no difference between the way a couple interacts with or without a therapist on hand. When I hear a couple remark, "Gosh, we're sounding just like a couple of shrinks," I know we're home free!

3. Without sharing insight, you are asking your partner to navigate your inner psychological terrain without a road map.

4. Often a woman comes into therapy to give me the task of "fixing" her husband. I refer to this as the chiropractic view of psychotherapy. "Doctor, straighten my husband out" is the tacit request. This sort of treatment is doomed to failure. The husband invariably drops out because he feels that he's been corralled into treatment to get "fixed" rather than to be understood.

5. Perhaps a very different sort of example will help make this point: A friend you barely know invites you to dinner and serves lobster. You don't touch it. She notices, is more than a bit miffed (lobster is her best dish and it cost her a bundle), but says nothing. Neither do you. But the next time she invites you, you mention that "I'm highly allergic and I might get quite sick if I eat shellfish." What is bound to happen? You're

friends, so invariably she'll say, "If I'd only known!" And rest assured, even if it's the only dish she knows how to cook, she won't serve you lobster again. Conclusion: Personal revelations provide information about your sensitivities, and people's behavior changes as a consequence of knowing this about you.

6. But let's not minimize the effort and attention to detail this requires. Running through an adult interchange of our two provokers, Teddy and Dora, will give us a realistic picture of just what it takes to talk this new language of love.

If provokers Dora and Teddy had been able to converse as adults, their battle over the finished basement (the one that never actually got finished) might have taken a completely different course.

Dora, cognizant of her own fear and anxiety (and expressing these insights through self-reflective "I" statements), but also aware of her husband's sensitivity to domination might say:

"Teddy, I've been asking you to finish the basement because it disturbs me to have the twins running around the living room. I'm afraid they'll get hurt. I also get anxious about the mess. I know I seem pushy when I get anxious.

"But I'm not your father. He was a tyrant who had to have everything his own way. I'm not like that. I do want you to do things for me but I'm not interested in only having it my way and only my way."

Perhaps she might introduce into their interchange another facet of her psychological wisdom—her fear of abandonment.

"When you don't help me, my need kicks in—I get spooked. Teddy doesn't love me . . . He won't help me . . . He won't take care of me . . . are the sorts of scary thoughts that seem to rush through me. I'm finally realizing that I'm still so very affected by my parents' divorce and I'm always waiting for you to abandon me!"

Perhaps she'll even reassure her husband, who struggles, albeit in a very different way (he can't risk saying no), with the very same fear of abandonment.

"But I'm not going to freak if you tell me what you're really feeling. You can say what you really feel. Your saying, 'No, I don't want to finish the basement,' might make me antsy, but it won't make me rant and rave. I won't withdraw from you because I'm frustrated. That's your family's way of reacting to what they don't like, not mine! But I do want you to understand that it is really important to me to get this done—some way."

And certainly Teddy, psychologically informed about himself and Dora, could make his own attempts at reciprocal empathy. Knowing that his need makes him angry about perceived oppression but that his wife is, at the same time, highly anxious, he might express his insights to Dora:

"Having a messy house doesn't feel crucial to me. In fact, since my parents were so strict and demanding, asking kids to be careful and neat can feel oppressive, as if I'm saying to them what my parents said to me—'You can't be yourself.' On some level I feel angry—'Let the kids be themselves' is what I feel like shouting.

"But I think the kids need to be safe—that's important for them. And I think you're entitled to have the house look a certain way because it's important for you—it reassures you."

Perhaps he'll acknowledge his unwitting susceptibility to saying yes when he really means no, and the passive/aggressive behavior to which it can give rise.

"But I don't want to spend my free time doing it. I think it would make me feel very resentful and then my tendency (when I force myself to do something against my will) is to sabotage—and get back at you in some indirect way. I could imagine that I'd leave the job half done for a month. And I don't want that to happen. That keeps you after me and it makes me feel harassed. And it's just more of the same old thing."

Having laid out their real psychological conflict, perhaps Teddy might also offer a possible resolution:

"Maybe we could afford to have someone come in and do the dirty work and the trim. I wouldn't mind doing the painting. Then I wouldn't feel as if I'm doing something against my will and you'd feel more relaxed because the basement would actually get done pretty quickly. Could that be a solution to our potential conflict?"

This is an adult exchange. It is infinitely more complex and considerably longer than the "actual" conversation that Teddy and Dora had over the unfinished basement ("Damn it, Teddy, why don't you get off your duff and finish the basement," was probably the extent of their original "discussion" on the matter). But it frees them from the self-defeating cycle of their provoker marriage, and it actually might result in a finished basement that makes them both happy rather than miserable.

Index

adult marriage *(cont.)*
  and empathy, 101–2, 251–52,
    254–56
  of enactors, 153–54, 255
  as formidable task, 245
  and insight, 60, 74, 153, 234–35
  key elements in, 254–56
  and new language of love, 74–75,
    246–57
  of provokers, 126–29, 255
  and revealing insights, 249–51,
    254–56
  of suppressers, 230–31, 256
  of symbolizers, 203–4, 256
  of venters, 101–3, 234–35, 255
affairs, extramarital, 48–49, 134
affection, physical, 24–25
aggression, passive, 107
alcohol, as escape, 136, 142
alliance, marriage as, 31–32, 255
anger:
  constructive vs. destructive,
    32–37, 257
  as corrosive force, 4–5
  covert, *see* covert anger
  cycle, 12–14, 73, 119
  destructive, 32–37
  dissipation of, 81–82
  expression of, 232
  facts about, 178
  as gift, 3–4, 18
  as hurt, 207
  as illness, 180–81, 185
  at illness, 184, 187
  as internal shock absorber, 231
  and intimacy, 231
  joint ownership of, 127
  legitimacy of, 147–49
  and love, 230–33
  as odd emotion, 6–7
  overt, 8, 14, 36, 128–29
  primal marriage as origin of, 3,
    70
  as signal, 18, 246

  as tool, 3–4
  toxic, 10–12
  unconscious, *see* unconscious
    anger
  Vesuvian, 33
  as weapon, 32–36, 177–78
antagonism, escalation of, 33–34, 79
anxiety:
  of children, 122
  and compliance, 222
  and need to rescue, 190
  of parents, 122
  about sexuality, 38–39
anxiety attacks, 193, 197, 203
apologies, 25–26
  of suppressers, 208
appearance, neglect of, 50–52
arguments, like broken record, 35
attraction, and unconscious needs,
    72
autoerotic urges, 54
avoidance, as strategy, 212

beauty and beast (provokers), 107–8
behavior:
  and need, 94
  options, 102
benefits, from marriage, 29–31
betrayal, by parents, 229
blackmail, emotional, 237, 239
blame, 34–35
  of provokers, 106–7
boredom, sexual, 56–57

candor, emotional, 247–48, 254
Carson, Johnny, 35
change:
  commitment for, 238
  creating atmosphere for, 237–45
  fear of, 245
  possibility for, 75
  resistance to, 245
  and silence, 102
  of spouse, 251

love *(cont.)*
  conditional, 225–26
  gestures of, 22
  and goodwill, 19–21
  new language of, 16, 69, 74–75,
    236, 246–57
Love Story (Segal), 25
lovestyles, 8–10, 14, 17, 76–77
  and actual marriage, 15, 61–64
  and covert anger, 129
  driving forces of, 14–16
  and invisible marriage, 15
  and overt anger, 128–29
  and primal marriage, 15
  see also specific styles

marriage:
  actual, *see* actual marriage
  adult, *see* adult marriage
  as alliance, 31–32, 255
  anger's place in, 257
  benefits from, 29–31
  friction in, 20
  improvement of, 17–18
  invisible, *see* invisible marriage
  as one-way street, 29–31
  paradox of, 72
  primal, *see* primal marriage
  sex affected by, 39–40
  structure of, 59–61
  styles of, *see* lovestyles
  as war, 96
masturbation, 115–16
  and orgasms, 54–56
meetings, ground rules about,
  237–38
memory:
  repression of, 195, 199
  selective, 213
mirror listening, 237, 242–45
money:
  deception about, 211
  meaning of, 116
mother:
  as ball-buster, 150–51

helplessness of, 175–76
mental illness of, 196–98
relationship with, 96, 98–99,
  147–48
see also parents
mutuality, lack of, 41
myths and lies, in families, 195–99

needs:
  and behavior, 94
  and complaints, 66, 67, 232
  in cycle of anger, 12–13
  learning about, 14–18
  unmet, 147
  vs. wants, 191–92
  see also specific needs; unconscious
    needs
noninvolvement, and distance,
  219–20, 223

object, lover as, 40–41
one-upmanship, 34
one-way street, marriage as, 29–31
option, to act differently, 102
orgasms:
  from masturbation, 54–56
  mutual satisfaction from, 46
  of women, 43–44
outbursts, of provokers, 108
overt anger, 8, 14, 36, 128–29

panic attacks, 193, 197, 203
paradox:
  of marriage, 72
  of unconscious needs, 12–13
parents:
  anxious, 122
  betrayal by, 229
  children abused by, 200–202
  conditional love from, 225–26
  control by, 121, 125–26
  depression of, 100–101, 151–52
  divorce or separation of, 120–21,
    175–77
  harsh, 172–73

inability to cope, 175–77
lack of involvement of, 147–49
loss of, 101, 122
as models, *see* primal marriage
rigid, 124, 126
unaffectionate, 229
see also father; mother
partner:
  acknowledgment of, 252–56
  changing, 251
  excused by suppressors, 208–9
  remake of, 164, 167–70, 171, 173
partnership:
  good guy/bad guy, 107–8
  parents in, 70
  safe haven of, 31–32
  through insight, 13–14
passion, and friendship, 20
passive aggression, 107, 111
past, power of, 73
peacemakers, suppressers as, 207–8
perfectionism, 117, 128
personal neglect, 50–52
politics, and displacers, 155–56
primal marriage:
  and current courtship, 72–73
  defined, 15, 60
  of displacers, 172–77
  of enactors, 147–52
  as origin of anger, 3, 70
  parents in, 70–74
  vs. present life, 246
  and present relationship, 72–73
  of provokers, 120–26
  of suppressers, 224–30
  of symbolizers, 195–202
  of venters, 94–101
procrastination, and suppressers, 211–12
protector, idealized, 164, 166, 171
provokers, 8, 9, 104–29
  actual marriage of, 62, 109–11
  adult marriage of, 126–29, 255
  and blame, 106–7
  and cycle of anger, 119

decoding complaints of, 111–19
good guy/bad guy, 107–8
as growing apart, 109
invisible marriage of, 111–19
as opposites, 106
outbursts of, 108
primal marriage of, 120–26
separateness of, 109
psychologists, and symbolizers, 183, 193, 204
punishment, sex as, 40–41
putdowns, sexual, 45–46

reaction:
  and need, 94
  and venters, 102
recognition, need for, 100
reflection, accusation into, 237, 240–42
relationship, as target of anger, 127
relationships, replacement, 133–34
reliability, through rules, 236
remake of spouse, as need, 164, 167–70, 171, 173
replacement relationships, 133–34
repression, of memories, 195, 199
rescue, need to, 188–91, 194
restraint, for venters, 102–3
retraction, by suppressers, 212
revelation, of insights, 249–51, 254–56
revenge, 36
rules, ground, 236–45
  abusive behavior, 237, 239–40
  accusation to reflection, 237, 240–42
  confidentiality, 237, 238–39
  emotional blackmail, 237, 239
  listening, 237, 239, 242–45
  meetings, 237–38
  time limits, 237, 238

safe haven, marriage as, 31–32
security, from rules, 236
Segal, Erich, 25